DATE DUE

	November 28, 2011
FEB 2 1 2007	DEC 0 5 2012
MAR 2 1 2007 APR 1 8 2007	JUN 1 2 2013
APR 2 4 2007	
JAN 1 4 2008	MAY 1 2 2015
SEP 0 9 2008	SEP 1 1 2017
NOV 2 5 2008	
JUL 0 7 2009	
NOV 1 9 2009	
APR 1 5 2010	
FEB 2 1 2011	
OCT 0 5 2011	

D1087599

Inside the Minds
of Serial Killers

Inside the Minds
of Serial Killers

Why They Kill

KATHERINE RAMSLAND

Westport, Connecticut
London

Library of Congress Cataloging-in-Publication Data

Ramsland, Katherine M., 1953-
    Inside the minds of serial killers : why they kill / Katherine Ramsland.
        p.   cm.
    Includes bibliographical references and index.
    ISBN 0–275–99099–0 (alk. paper)
    1. Serial murderers—Case studies.   2. Serial murderers—Psychology.   3. Criminal
    psychology. I. Title.
    HV6515.R252   2006
    364.152′3–dc22   2006015429

British Library Cataloguing in Publication Data is available

Library of Congress Catalog Card Number: 2006015429
ISBN: 0–275–99099–0

First published in 2006

Praeger Publishers, 88 Post Road West, Westport, CT 06881
An imprint of Greenwood Publishing Group, Inc.
www.praeger.com

Printed in the United States of America

The paper used in this book complies with the
Permanent Paper Standard issued by the National
Information Standards Organization (Z39.48–1984).

10 9 8 7 6 5 4 3 2 1

Contents

Acknowledgments   vii

Introduction   ix

1 Jack the Ripper and the History of Serial Murder   1

2 Lust   9

3 Omnipotence   21

4 Intellectual Exercise   33

5 Glory   43

6 Delusions   53

7 Rage   65

8 Profit   77

9 Blood and Bodies   85

10 Living with Death   97

11 No Particular Purpose   109

12 Early Aspirations   119

13 Related by Blood   133

14 Matches Made in Hell   143

15 "Care" takers   153

16 Close to a Killer   163

17 Behind the Eyes   177

Appendix: How They're Caught   185

Bibliography   187

Index   195

Acknowledgments

In many ways, this book is the result of years of interaction with many people, as well as opportunities to research and write about individual cases of serial killers. Therefore, I'm sure I can't name everyone who should be acknowledged, but among those with whom I discussed portions of this book and received significant feedback are

- Marilyn Bardsley, my editor and friend at Crime Library, and my most encouraging friends, Ruth Osborne and John Timpane
- The FBI profilers, who have told me a great deal about serial killer investigations: Gregg McCrary, Robert Ressler, Roy Hazelwood, and John Douglas
- Robert Hare, whose work I deeply respect and who provided me with great resources for understanding psychopaths
- Gary Craig of the Rochester *Democrat and Chronicle*, who alerted me to an unusual case of twins
- My student intern, Karen Pepper, who proofread some of the manuscript and provided research support
- The serial killer, who will remain unnamed, who first inspired me to become interested in this field of research
- Suzanne Staszak-Silva, my editor, for her enthusiasm for this book and her clear-eyed guidance
- John Silbersack, my agent and trusted friend, whose vision and encouragement have kept me going over many years

Introduction

In 2005 in Rochester, New York, Robert Spahalski turned himself in to the police, claiming he had committed four murders. They charged him initially in two while they investigated the other two, and eventually Spahalski was indicted for all four. Reporters covering the case were confused as to whether, if convicted, Spahalski would qualify as a serial killer. He had allegedly committed four murders, to be sure, but he had different motives for each and three had happened in 1990 and 1991, while the fourth had occurred fifteen years later. Three victims were female and one was male; he had known them all and one was a friend whom he had supposedly killed unintentionally while hallucinating on cocaine.

Spahalski's behavior does not fit what has been claimed about serial killers: supposedly they have a "victim type" and they're compulsive, predatory, cannot stop, and suffer no remorse. Spahalski felt badly enough to turn himself in, went for a long period of time between murders, and none seemed either compulsive or particularly predatory. The confusion over Spahalski is understandable, but in fact, when analyzed case by case, serial killers often do not fit into neat categories.[1] The more details we know about each one, the more evident this truth is.

Serial killers fascinate us. We want to know what makes them tick, in part because their antisocial behaviors are so extreme but also because we hope we'll find a collection of causal factors that clearly set them apart from the rest of humanity. Yet unless one singles out a subcategory of serial murderers, such as healthcare serial killers or sadistic lust killers, the lack of uniformity from one case to the next makes a definitive analysis unlikely. Thus, the goal for the current study is not so much to offer an explanation as to show the various motives attributed to serial murder in their respective manifestations. This provides a basis for taking an approach that will acknowledge the many differences and deflect simplistic generalizations. It's not intended as an exhaustive study, but merely a demonstrative one.

Little previous effort has been made to look at the diverse psychological manifestations of serial killers in the context of comparative cases. As a result, information from outdated studies has been perpetuated, such as the idea that most serial killers have above-average intelligence, that they're only sexually motivated (some even say that only men can be serial killers), that they have a clear victim type, and that they've all been abused as children. While those early studies had their merits for the time, they're not representative of serial killers as a whole. In fact, these ideas were largely derived from studying articulate, imprisoned, white, male American serial killers—and in limited numbers at that. From what I have seen as a researcher, there really is no "profile" of a serial killer, no set of characteristics or causes that provides us with a way to set them apart, and people whose work involves the investigation of serial murder concur.

Former FBI profiler Robert K. Ressler told Sue Russell when she was writing a biography of Aileen Wuornos that there were no hard and fast rules. Too many people, he said, try to oversimplify the psychology of these killers, but for every attempt to state a "truth," one can find counterexamples that undermine it. Some killers have a victim preference, for example, but many do not. While a lot of killers grew up in abusive homes, some enjoyed plenty of privilege and experienced no abuse whatsoever. Generalizations, Ressler indicated, do a disservice to the subject.[2]

The current study is not intended as a way to categorize serial killers for investigative purposes, such as behaviorally organized or disorganized, or for statistical purposes, like figuring out the percentage of sexually motivated vs. profit-oriented killers. Instead, it is intended as an exploration of the development of different serial killers toward their specific goals. Most of the chapters offer cases that illustrate particular motives, but I also approach the subject in terms of whether working with a partner affects the dynamic, what we know about killers who started young, what killers are like in a contained context such as a healthcare community, and what people who have been close to them say about them. I have examined more than a thousand cases of serial murder, looking at several hundred in detail via court transcripts, correspondences, newspaper archives, and true-crime biographies. In the process I have found that there are many motives that drive these offenders, they come from diverse backgrounds, and for almost every claim that has been made about them there are exceptions that weaken or undermine it.

Even the definition of serial murder can be confusing, so let me address it. While it was once the case that any type of incident that involved a number of murders was called "multiple murder" or "mass murder," eventually it became clear that some distinctions were needed. The phrase "serial killer" was first used in *The Complete Detective* in 1950, but it's generally believed that in 1976 with the Son of Sam case, Special Agent Robert Ressler initiated its use for cases on which he and his colleagues were consulting in the FBI's Behavioral Science Unit (now the Behavioral Analysis Unit). Thus, it became common parlance for a specific type of multiple murder incident, as opposed to denoting a spree or mass murder.

The FBI's official manual indicates that to be a serial killer, there must be at least three different murder events at three different locations, with a cooling off period between events, but the National Institute of Justice (NIJ) and some criminologists allow for only two. In addition, some killers bring their victims to the same location at different times. Some experts reserve the notion of serial murder exclusively for sexually compelled offenders, while others also include nonsexual goals. And then there's the confusion over how to differentiate serial murder from incidents involving spree or mass murder. Thus, to achieve clarity for my purpose, I have defined the various terms thus:

1. Mass murder is a concentrated response to a single event or idea, occurring in one basic locale, even if the killer travels to several loosely related spots in that general area, and there are at least four fatalities.
2. A spree is a string of at least three murders arising from a key precipitating incident occurring close in time to the murders, but the spate of killings is fueled by continuing and associated stress, taking place in several locales and across a relatively short period of time, no longer than a few months; there is no psychological cooling off.
3. A serial killer murders at least two people in separate incidents, with the mental disposition or propensity to kill again. There is a psychological rest period between incidents, which could be considered a time of predatory preparation. He, she, or they also choose the modus operandi and may either move around or lure successive victims to a single locale. They view victims as objects needed for the satisfaction of their goals, and manifest an addictive quality to their behavior, such that choosing murder is a satisfying act.[3]

Serial killers are not all alike. They're not all male. Some are younger than twelve or older than fifty. They're not all driven by sexual compulsion. They're not all intelligent or even clever. A single killer may choose different weapons or methods of operation. I could go on, but the point of this book is to examine specific details involved in how and why some people kill again and again. They might be profit-driven, in search of thrill or self-gratification, or compelled by some other deep-seated desire, fear, or need. Occasionally, serial murder is about revenge or inspired by a delusion. In many cases, the killer is relieving pressure and does not wish to be stopped or caught. Yet a few do intentionally stop of their own accord or undermine themselves. Some have even professed remorse or killed themselves. While several motives may be present in any given killer, and the categories I've chosen certainly overlap, I have selected cases that clearly exemplify a specific driving ambition (or lack of). Thus a woman who kills for financial gain may also enjoy the act of murder, and conversely, a man for whom murder is sexually gratifying may also rob his victims. Yet I present the former as motivated by profit and the latter as a lust killer.

Since the cases speak for themselves, let's begin.

NOTES

1. Jane Flasch, "Serial Killer Faces New Murder Charges," www.13WHAM.com, January 3, 2006.
2. Sue Russell, *Lethal Intent* (New York: Kensington, 2002), pp. 379–381.
3. Katherine Ramsland, *The Human Predator* (New York: Berkley, 2005), p. xi.

CHAPTER 1

Jack the Ripper and the History of Serial Murder

EARLY PREDATORS

Many people believe that London's Jack the Ripper was the world's first serial killer, but this misconception derives from the extensive exposure the case received at the time. The five murders attributed to "Saucy Jack" during his six weeks of terror in the Whitechapel area of London was the first series of linked murders to occur in a major city in such a way that it gained international media coverage. But let's place it in its proper context, so we can see how diverse the methods and motives of serial killers have been throughout the ages. There is little doubt that cultural factors affect the manifestations of serial murder, so it's important to examine the conditions in which these acts have occurred.[1]

One of the earliest documented serial killers was Locusta, a female poisoner, who put Nero on the throne in ancient Rome. In A.D. 54, Nero's mother employed her to poison Emperor Claudius, and Nero then became emperor. He allowed Locusta to continue, so she refined her trade and became a predator for her own purposes until, after Nero's demise, she was eventually executed. As the Roman emperors declined in power, Christianity took hold and spread throughout medieval Europe, with extensive missions launched by Rome and Constantinople to fend off Muslim attacks around the Mediterranean. Bloodthirsty aristocrats took advantage of the lack of criminal accountability for people of their status to feed their gruesome appetites. The feudal lord ruled and no one dared question his actions.

Gilles de Rais was among the wealthiest men in France during the early-to mid-fifteenth century. He was an ardent supporter of Joan of Arc, her military mentor and personal confidante, and he firmly believed in her apparent miracles. After she was burned to death in 1431, Gilles de Rais' mystical fanaticism took a new turn: He engaged in the practice of magic rituals that included the sacrifice of children. He apparently enjoyed it, and he had his servants gather up children from peasant families for him to rape and murder—often at his dinner parties. When he was tried under torture and threat of excommunication, he admitted to over one hundred victims. Though torture-inspired confessions are suspect, it is a fact that bones were found in several of his castles.

De Rais had a female counterpart just over a century later in the Hungarian Countess Erzebet Báthory, born in 1560. She, too, was accorded a certain amount of latitude as a result of her aristocratic status. When she was fifteen, she married the sadistic Count Nadasdy, the "Black Hero." He taught her how to beat the servants to the edge of their lives. After Nadasdy died in 1604, Erzebet stepped up her cruel and arbitrary beatings and was soon torturing and butchering the girls. She sent her maids to lure children and young women to her quarters, so she could satisfy her lust. She would stick pins into sensitive body parts, cut off someone's fingers, slit her skin with knives, or break her face. In a dungeon, girls were chained to the walls, fattened up, and "milked" for their blood.

When Erzebet turned her sadism toward young noblewomen, she was stopped. After a murder in 1609 that Erzebet tried to stage as a suicide, the authorities investigated. On finding corpses in her castle, they arrested Erzebet. She went through two separate trials, and during the second one, a register was discovered in her home that included in her own handwriting the names of over 650 victims. Accounts of her tortures by witnesses made even the judges blanch, and they could not imagine how a single person had devised so many different types of tortures. Erzebet was imprisoned for life in a small room in her own castle, where she died in 1614.

Legend has it that Báthory once got blood on her hand after slapping a servant girl and believed that it made her skin look younger. To restore her beauty, she made a practice of bathing in the blood of virgins. Whether or not this folklore is based on fact, the countess is credited as the first person on record to be murderously motivated by blood. If the interpretation of the records is to be believed, she is also the most prolific.

Even as the wealthy enjoyed the privileges of their rank, among peasants across Europe certain superstitions spawned delusions that also inspired acts of brutality. The Catholic Church ruled Europe for centuries, despite the fact that science was discovering how the earth revolved around the sun, how the body functioned, and how gravity behaved; philosophers were issuing in the Enlightenment; and Luther was birthing a Protestant revolt. During such religious times, between 1573 and 1600 several men were prosecuted for "lycanthropy"—killing as a werewolf. During one period some 30,000 such cases were reported to authorities. Some people even viewed themselves as being cursed with an animal compulsion, and it was not uncommon to have cases that involved cannibalism or necrophilia, or both. Among the prominent "werewolves" was Gilles Garnier, who claimed at his trial that after he had received an ointment to change his shape into that of a wolf, he felt compelled to stalk and kill children. He tore at them with his teeth and took pieces home for his wife to cook. In 1573, he was burned alive.

Germany had a similar problem with Peter Stubbe, who terrorized the countryside for twenty-five years. According to pamphlets, he claimed that he had an enchanted belt that assisted his "change," and he too went after children, including his own son. He was tried with his wife and daughter as a "pack," and all three were convicted of murder.

A century later, during a ten-year span, Marie de Brinvilliers in Paris poisoned more than fifty people, and in 1680 Catherine La Voison, the mistress of King Louis XIV of France, was caught with a priest in scandalous rituals involving infant sacrifice and blood drinking. Their victims were said to number into the hundreds, perhaps more than one thousand.

Poisoning was in vogue during medieval times, and in Italy in 1719, La Tofania was implicated in the deaths of over 600 victims. Germany had Gessina Gottfried, who poisoned people unchecked for thirteen years. There were probably many more serial poisoners who were never caught or documented, because some people turned it into an art and hired themselves out to wealthy people looking to dispatch someone who stood in the way of their inheritance. It was not until the nineteenth century that forensic toxicology was able to definitively determine that arsenic had been used on someone, so poisoning was an easy way to commit murder. Even when arsenic became detectable, there were other poisons. So serial murder and toxicology developed a complex relationship.

Serial killing came to America in the form of a team of cousins—Micajah and Wiley Harpe—who murdered relatives and strangers at whim in the Kentucky and Tennessee territories. They racked up anywhere between twenty and forty victims, including their own children, killed quickly after birth, before they were finally caught and executed.

MODERN CONDITIONS FOR MURDER

Back in Europe, with the growing sophistication of scientific inventions, industrial technology, and medical discoveries occurring parallel to the waning of religion's dominance, a certain practice arose in the medical community that inspired a new type of serial killing. Physicians needed cadavers to dissect to advance their knowledge about disease and to teach human anatomy to medical students. So they encouraged the act of grave robbing. The "resurrectionists" grew adept at spiriting a body from its grave, but a few decided to forego the effort. In Scotland, William Burke and William Hare figured out a way to deliver a body in prime condition, unmarked. They ran a boarding house and they would get their victims drunk and grab them in an arm-lock around the throat or sit on their chests while holding their noses closed. In nine months, they killed sixteen people, selling them to a physician before they were caught in 1828.

Throughout that time, many more poisoners surfaced: Helene Jegado killed twenty-three in France, while across the Channel, Britain's Dr. William Palmer poisoned fourteen, and in Germany Anna Maria Zwanzinger dispatched eight. Pretty Mary Cotton used arsenic to kill her children, several stepchildren, husbands, and mother. It was a time when many people died of a vague malady known as gastric fever, and when one could collect on insurance policies. So Mary Cotton progressively improved her social status by trading in one family for another.

Even children were becoming cold-blooded killers, and America was shocked by the case of Jesse Pomeroy, 14, arrested in 1874 and dubbed the "Boston Boy Fiend." His rampage of assault included torture, mutilation, and murder of other children. Also in Boston, in 1876, church sexton Thomas Piper was convicted as "the Boston Belfry Murderer." He confessed to four brutal sex murders, including that of a five-year-old child, which he claimed he had done under the influence of that era's pervasive hallucinogenic drug, opium. His excuse proved insufficient to mitigate the crimes, and Piper was hanged.

At the same time, the "Nebraska Fiend" claimed nine lives before he was unmasked as Stephen Richards and arrested in 1879, while in Austin, Texas, five years later, seven women were murdered over the course of a year. The killings ended on Christmas Eve, 1885. While the murders were never solved, evidence in retrospect points to a wealthy politician as "the Servant Girl Annihilator." An association was also made to a more infamous person three years later when the next set of murders came to light: those of Jack the Ripper.

"JACK"

Clearly, then, Red Jack was not the first serial killer. However, according to "Ripperologists," the spate of killings attributed to Jack the Ripper was the first to occur in a major city in such a way as to garner considerable police attention and media coverage. More than three hundred newspapers around the world reported on it. He may also have been the first serial killer to communicate about his crimes with investigators (if he did indeed author any of the letters, which no one knows). Since this spate of killings stands as the epitome of repetitive and compulsive lust murder, which we will examine in chapters that follow, let's look at the details.

In the Whitechapel area of London's East End, it started on Friday, August 31, 1888, just after 1:00 AM, when Polly Nichols, 42, went out to earn four pence. She was found with her throat cut, her skirt pulled up, her legs parted, and severe cuts into her abdomen. There were also two small wounds to her genitals. Despite the brutality, as she was a prostitute, the killing did not inspire much attention.

The next victim was Annie Chapman, 45, discovered about a week later on the morning of September 8. Her dress, too, had been pulled up over her head, her stomach ripped open, and her intestines draped over her left shoulder. Her legs were drawn up, knees bent and spread outward. The killer had used a sharp implement, like a surgical knife, to slit her throat, nearly to the point of decapitation. Coins and an envelope had been arranged around her and the bladder, half of the vagina, and the uterus had been removed and taken away.

Then several notes arrived between September 17 and 29 at the Central News Office, signed, "Jack the Ripper." One author claimed that he was "down on whores" and would continue to kill them. These notes may have come from journalists seeking to inspire more incidents to report, although some experts claim they are genuine links to the killer, but the moniker was published and it stuck, especially when there were more deaths.

By the end of that month, on September 30, two victims were attacked on the same night. The Ripper slashed the throat of Elizabeth Stride, 45, only a few minutes before she was found, and less than an hour later slashed and disemboweled Catherine Eddowes, 43, who was also quickly found (she was a five-minute walk away from Stride's body). It was clear from this night's work that the killer was growing bolder and more expressive of his mental pathology. With Eddowes, the intestines had been pulled out and placed over the right shoulder, the uterus and one kidney had been cut out and taken, and the face was mutilated with triangles cut into the cheeks. Her eyelids were nicked and the tip of her nose was cut off.

Then came a letter "from Hell" to the head of the Whitechapel vigilante organization, with a grisly trophy: half of a kidney that turned out to be afflicted with Bright's disease—a disorder from which Eddowes had suffered. The note's author indicated that he'd fried and eaten the other half. It was believed that this note was definitely from the killer and he even offered to send "the bloody knife" in due time. He closed with the taunt, "Catch me if you can."

The police realized they had a killer driven by rage, and they were stymied. Expecting something to happen on both October 8 and 30, since those had been the dates in September when the killer had struck, they stepped up patrols; but there were no more murders that month. Still, their instincts about the dates were not wrong; they were just early.

It was the last and youngest victim, Mary Kelly, 24, who took the brunt of this offender's disorganized frenzy. On November 8, she apparently invited a man into her room. She closed the curtains in preparation, and at some point he pulled the sheet over her head and stabbed her through it. He slashed open her throat and then ripped through her lower torso, pulled out her intestines, and skinned her chest and legs. Blood was splattered all over the room. When police arrived, they found a severed breast on the table next to her, along with the tips of her nose and ears. Her abdomen had been emptied and its contents spread all over the bed and thrown against the walls. Her heart, too, had been removed and was missing, and flesh had been cut from her legs and buttocks clear to the bone. Doctors estimated that the frenzy had gone on for around two hours.

The police investigated many suspects, but in the end, no one was convicted of these murders. Some experts believe that there were at least two more, one before the Nichols murder and one after Mary Kelly. Regardless of the final count, the Ripper's brutality marked him as a demented and dangerous man not likely to stop, short of imprisonment or suicide (and some suspects did commit suicide or were committed). Yet the murders did appear to end, even if not with Mary Kelly's death. Whoever the Ripper was, he seems to have gotten away, and his lack of identity has contributed to his fame for over a century.[2]

Red Jack also inspired copycat killings in other places, such as Moscow, Nicaragua, and Vienna. At least one true-crime author believes that he came to America and was instrumental in San Francisco's two "Monster of the Belfry" murders, for which medical student Theodore Durrant was tried and convicted.

Yet even as the Ripper murder frenzy died down, H. H. Holmes was arrested for a murder he committed in Philadelphia and an entirely new serial killer was unmasked. Herman Webster Mudgett, a.k.a., H. H. Holmes, had built a "castle" in Chicago during the development of the 1893 World's Fair. He let rooms to young ladies, locking them in and gassing them to death while he watched. He would then slide them down specially built chutes to the cellar where he had installed a massive furnace, and either burn them to ash, dissolve them in a vat of acid, or strip the flesh from their bones so he could sell their skeletons to medical schools. He confessed to as many as twenty-seven murders, although he later recanted, but some experts believe his victim toll is well over one hundred.

The story was this "castle" he had built, for inside investigators found sleeping chambers with peepholes, asbestos-padded walls, gas pipes, sliding walls, and vents that Holmes controlled from his bedroom. The building had secret passages, hallways that went in circles, false floors, rooms with torture equipment, and a specially equipped surgery. Tourists bought tickets to see it, but the building was burned to the ground. Holmes was executed.[3]

The list of serial killers in the twentieth century and beyond is quite long. There's no room in this book to discuss them all, but we'll look at representatives of the various motives attributed to them. Red Jack was among the category that we understand now as the lust murderer—those killers who apparently are aroused by murder. We turn first to them.

NOTES

1. Katherine Ramsland, *The Human Predator: A Historical Chronicle of Serial Murder and Forensic Investigation* (New York: Berkley, 2005), pp. 1–105.

2. Donald Rumbelow, *Jack the Ripper: The Complete Casebook* (New York: Contemporary Books, 1988), pp. 37–124; Dirk C. Gibson, *Clues from Killers: Serial Murder and Crime Scene Messages* (Westport, CT: Praeger, 2004), pp. 147–172.

3. Frank Geyer, *The Holmes-Pitezel Case: A History of the Greatest Crime of the Century* (Salem, MA: Publisher's Union, 1896); H. H. Holmes, *Holmes' Own Story* (Philadelphia, PA: Burk & McFetridge, 1895); "The Confession of H. H. Holmes," *Philadelphia Inquirer*, April 12, 1896.

CHAPTER 2

Lust

Lust killers are aroused by the act and fact of murder; some criminologists call them thrill killers. Their motive generally forms from fantasies associated during puberty with anything from underwear to dead animals to body parts. Jerome Brudos in Oregon, for example, was attracted to women's feet, high-heeled shoes, and female undergarments. For a while, he contented himself with stealing shoes, bras, and panties from neighborhood homes, but eventually he spotted an opportunity to engage his fantasies more fully—with murder and the possession of a corpse that yielded a foot. One of the strangest lust killers was Sylvestre Matushka, who engineered a series of train crashes in Hungary during the 1930s, claiming it was the only way he could achieve sexual release. He had eroticized the image of bodies ripped up by machines, but he was caught before he could finish his apparent agenda of one wreck per month.

We've just seen how Jack the Ripper seemed to find pleasure in stabbing and mutilation. Let's look at some of the cases that involved eroticized harm of others, along with theories about how people can act this way.

SEX SLAVES

Elizabeth Kenyon, a teacher in Miami, Florida, disappeared on March 4, 1984. She was not the irresponsible type and if she had planned to go somewhere, she would have informed someone. Her parents filed a missing persons report, but their suspicions were on a former boyfriend whom Elizabeth had declined to marry—Christopher Wilder, an entrepreneur with a construction business and a photographer. He'd been seen with her at a gas station. He also had a record of sexual deviance. Indeed, he was associated with another missing woman, Rosario Gonzales, as well from the same area. She had disappeared on February 26 and was seen in his company at a race track.

Wilder, 39, realized he was being investigated. He withdrew money, got into his 1973 Chrysler New Yorker sedan, stole his partner's credit card, and left. But he didn't just flee. Along the way, he murdered pretty young women.

Wilder's childhood in Australia was fairly stable, but he did some window-peeking in early adolescence and was arrested with a group of teenage friends for the gang-rape of a girl on the beach of Sydney. That experience apparently provided some fuel for his fantasies, for unlike before this event, he now imagined shocking girls with electricity while having sex with them. Therapists noted his need to dominate women and his desire to turn them into slaves for his pleasure.

In 1969, Wilder moved to Florida, where he did very well for himself during a building boom in the electrical and construction business. He got into trouble forcing oral sex on a girl and went to court, where a doctor who examined him said that he was not safe in an unstructured environment. Psychiatrists recommended supervised treatment, but then the jury acquitted him. Three years later he raped a girl. She turned him in, but his attorney plea-bargained the charges down to probation with therapy.

On the run, Wilder stopped long enough to pick up a girl from a shopping mall by luring her with the promise of a modeling career. She ended up dead. By the time they found her body, Wilder had grabbed and imprisoned another girl in a hotel room. There he tortured her by shocking her with electricity and gluing her eyes shut. He made her exercise naked in front of him and when she did not do it right, she later reported, he shocked her feet. The girl managed to lock herself into a bathroom and make enough noise that Wilder fled.

But he was on his way across the country, using his partner's credit card to book rooms and sometimes killing women just to steal their cars. He also continued to find attractive young girls to be his victims. In one incident, he attended a fashion show, selected a girl, posed as a photographer, and abducted her. On April 3, 1984, the FBI placed Wilder on its "Ten Most Wanted" list and issued a nationwide alert.

Wilder was compulsive about killing. It was a sexual addiction. He was a charming white male in his thirties, spurred by sexual fantasies and excited by a certain type of victim—in this case, beautiful young women who could be models. Hence, he was dubbed "The Beauty Queen Killer." Someone brought forward photographs that Wilder had left for developing, which included women he did not know and prepubescent children.

He had told his girlfriend that his photography hobby was a sickness, but he had to do it.

Oddly, Wilder picked up one sixteen-year-old girl, Tina Marie, from a store and forced her to help him to lure others. They grabbed a girl in Indiana and took her to New York, where he attempted to murder her and left her for dead, but she survived. He killed another woman for her car. Then he took Tina Marie to the airport and drove off alone. Shortly, he was recognized by a New Hampshire state trooper, and in a struggle over his gun, Wilder was killed. Another girl he'd grabbed had just managed to escape by jumping from his car.

Found in his possession were handcuffs, rolls of duct tape, rope, a sleeping bag, the specially designed electrical cord, and a novel by British author John Fowles called *The Collector*. Published in 1963, this story features a lonely entomologist who collects butterflies and who also captures and imprisons a pretty art student named Miranda. He keeps her in his basement. Seeing nothing wrong with what he has done, he treats her well, expecting that this will eventually win her love, and willingly gives her anything she wants, except her freedom. While she grows to need his attention, since he's the only person she ever sees, she also views him as evil for his imprisonment of her. Nevertheless, she belongs to him, and this fantasy of ownership is not uncommon among sadists. Therapists who had treated Wilder over a period of time knew that he loved this book and had practically memorized it.

Besides the victims he killed on his spree, Wilder was associated with several more rapes and murders, including ones committed in Australia. While he's credited with eight victims, he's tentatively linked to so many others that it's impossible to know the final count.

He demonstrates the fact that some serial killers use different methods to kill. He used suffocation, stabbing, and shooting. Many were tortured, but some were killed quickly so he could steal their cars.[1]

Not unlike Wilder, but perhaps more imaginative was Robert Hansen in Alaska. In June 1983, a prostitute in Anchorage went to the police to claim that a redheaded john had tortured and raped her, and had been planning to fly her to a remote cabin, but she had escaped. She identified the home of local baker Robert Hansen, but he insisted she was lying. Yet the remains of several women had turned up in the wilderness, shot or stabbed, and most had been prostitutes. The police got a warrant, which turned up a weapon that ballistics matched to bullets removed from the murdered women, as well as their missing jewelry and IDs. Hansen confessed and admitted using his victims as "game." For a sexual thrill, he would drop them off, naked, in the wilderness and hunt them down. Although he confessed to seventeen murders, he only pleaded to four.[2]

How do killers develop the ideas for such hideous acts of violence?

THE INFINITY OF DARKNESS

In *Dark Dreams*, former FBI profiler Roy Hazelwood, who specialized during his stint with the Behavioral Science Unit on sex crimes, discusses the formation of violent fantasies. He believes it's important to appreciate that there are no limits to human imagination, which means that things offenders can dream up are unlimited. Thus, says Hazelwood, there is an indefinite number of combinations of sexual crimes. Some offenders are attracted to prepubescent children, some to teenagers, some to the aged, and some have no particular preference. Some want a dead victim to work on, some like them unconscious, some conscious and struggling or afraid. There are no absolutes. Hazelwood finds that sexual crimes originate in the mind, and once the consequences of acting out the fantasies are considered, the offenders make the decision to proceed when an opportunity is at hand. Or they may look for or create the opportunity. After the crime is accomplished, the offender generally rationalizes why the behavior was acceptable.

Sexual assault is generally motivated by aggression, sex, or power, and the fantasies through which these urges are expressed develop around puberty, acquiring force from the developing sex drive. They influence the type of victim the offender selects, and his approach, preferred sexual activities, rituals, and decision to complete the act (or not) with murder.

Hazelwood views sex offenders as either impulsive or ritualistic. Impulsive offenders are opportunistic and generally of lower intelligence and economic means, and their sexual behavior often serves power or anger needs. Ritualistic offenders, on the other hand, indulge in paraphilias (abnormal sexual behavior) and compulsive behaviors that satisfy some psychological need. They have specific sexual preferences and are willing to commit time, money, and energy to pursuing their sexual interests. As they center their lives around this activity, they learn to lie and manipulate in order to keep it secretly active and hidden from others. These type of people tend to record their fantasies and/or activities in order to relive them. They may also have very rich, complex, and interactive fantasies.[3]

Deviant sexual desires have been organized into psychiatric categories known as paraphilias, which are recurrent, intense urges or behaviors that involve unusual objects, situations, or activities. The *Diagnostic and Statistical Manual*, or *DSM-IV-TR*, lists them and describes their manifestations. Among them are exhibitionism (exposure of genitalia), fetishism (sexual arousal from an object, such as a doll), causing or craving suffering or humiliation, and pedophilia (sexual arousal from a child). Although these are psychosexual disorders, not sex crimes, they are often linked with sex crimes, particularly when they involve non-consenting people. We'll examine these in detail in Chapter 9, but for a general application to the way fantasy can inspire murder, let's look at a case of ritualistic serial murder.

In 1995, a young woman in Douglas County, Washington State, was unable to get her mother or fourteen-year-old sister to answer the phone. She checked and found them both murdered. Amanda, the sister, had been stabbed and bludgeoned in the head, then raped, after which the killer had shoved a baseball bat deep into her vagina. He'd also eviscerated her, placing skin from her genitals onto her face. The mother, Rita, had been stabbed thirty-one times and viciously mutilated, her breasts removed and placed near the daughter in another room. Her genital area was excised and stuffed into her mouth. Both victims had been provocatively posed.

When investigators checked incident reports for the night, they learned that a man named Jack Owen Spillman III had been arrested that morning not far from the crime scene, on the suspicion of burglary. His rap sheet indicated a record of rape and burglary. While under surveillance, Spillman tossed out an item that, when retrieved, turned out to be a blood-soaked ski mask. The blood was matched to one of the victims. There was blood near the mouth area, as if he'd put his mouth to a wound. More questioning turned up evidence that Spillman had been watching Amanda for weeks. He was arrested, and more evidence turned up to implicate him. A butcher by trade, Spillman had no alibi. He apparently had a history of the torture and mutilation of animals.

Spillman confessed to the double homicide and added a third—a missing girl. When she was exhumed, it appeared that she had been buried in the same position as Spillman had left Amanda on the bed. Spillman had studied other killers to learn how to avoid being caught, such as shaving his body hair. He fantasized about torturing girls and he wanted to cut out the heart of a victim to eat it. He had thought of himself as a werewolf, so he had stalked "prey" the way a ravenous beast might do. He said to a cellmate that he had exhumed the body of his first victim several times to have sex with it. Spillman pled guilty to three counts of aggravated murder and received life in prison.[4]

Spillman is not altogether unique. He's like some killers who were documented during the nineteenth century by Richard von Krafft-Ebing—a German neurologist, and an alienist at the Feldhof Asylum and professor of psychiatry in Strasbourg. He published cases of sexual deviance in *Psychopathia Sexualis with Especial Reference to the Antipathic Sexual Instinct: A Medico-Forensic Study.*

One featured twenty-two-year-old Vincenz Verzeni, accused in 1872 of several murders and attempted murders. His case began with the mutilation of a fourteen-year-old girl along a village path. Her intestines had been torn out and tossed some distance, a piece had been torn from her leg, and her mouth was stuffed with dirt. Another woman in the area was likewise violated, and a third nearly met the same fate but survived to finger Verzeni. He admitted his guilt, saying that the murders and mutilations sexually aroused him. He enjoyed putting his hands around someone's neck. If he climaxed before they died, he admitted, they were allowed to live. Otherwise, they died. From one corpse, he claimed he had sucked blood and from other bodies he had ripped out and carried off pieces because, as he put it, he derived a powerful sensation from them.[5]

Sexual fantasies take many forms, and the most intense and extreme involve murder. When attached to a psychological drive, the need to satisfy it becomes repetitive, producing one type of motivation for compulsive serial murder.

NEED TO HARM

Psychiatrist Ethel Person says that we rely on fantasies to create our lives. Fantasies are instrumental in how we choose to behave, view ourselves and our world, test possibilities, and sooth ourselves when necessary. We even use them to "change" our past and recreate our frame of identity. Our fantasies are drawn from early life experiences, including both our experiences within our families and the influences from our specific culture. They provide a "language of desire" via images, actions, and aspirations. Some are "organizing fantasies," which resolve conflicts and map out our identities. Murder fantasies, it turns out, are common when people are in conflict with someone, but for some people, murder can become a central way to resolve all problems. When combined with erotic associations, a lust murderer is born.[6]

The first victim of this particular killer was discovered on May 13, 1984, southeast of Tampa, Florida. The nude female victim lay facedown, her wrists tied behind her and a noose draped three times around her neck. Beaten about the face before she died, her hips had been broken to position her legs at right angles to her body, which indicated that the killer had been with her for a while after she died. When she was identified as Ngeun Thi Long, investigators learned she had been a dancer in Tampa, with a drug habit.

Two weeks later, Michelle Simms, a drug-addicted prostitute, was found on her back, clad only in a green T-shirt that had been ripped and pulled back, leaving her arms in the sleeves to bind them. Her wrists had been tied and secured behind her, and a rope was wound three times around her neck. She had been stabbed, strangled, raped, and beaten to death.

Both scenes yielded tire tread impressions and red trilobal carpet fibers, which linked them to the same offender. Semen samples indicated his blood type and hairs found on the second victim were Caucasian.

By June 8, there was another murder with similar features, another in September, four in October, and one in November. Several victims eventually linked to this series were found too long after they were killed to determine a cause of death, but they had the red carpet fibers and/or the same method of binding, posing, or strangling. Most were prostitutes or dancers.

It appeared that the leash-like rope around the neck had been placed there while the victims were alive, and that fact, along with the brutal antemortem beatings that exceeded what was necessary to kill them, showed a particular type of sexual deviance. This offender was believed to have fantasies of dominating women. He seemed to be a power-assertive rapist who needed to reassure himself. His apparent comfort with corpses, based on how he posed them and broke bones postmortem, indicated a long history of antisocial behavior. He was expected to continue to kill, but he made the mistake of allowing one victim of rape to live, and she gave the police a description sufficient to make an arrest.

Robert "Bobby" Joe Long, 31 and Caucasian, learned about the evidence against him, so he readily confessed to ten murders, giving the police the location of a victim not yet discovered. Prior to committing murder, he said, he used to answer classified ads to find women or girls alone in their homes to rape them. He appeared to have raped at least fifty women. He knew how to charm women, although he liked dominating them. He was found to have survived numerous blows to the skull, and he had an extra X chromosome that had produced abnormal amounts of estrogen during puberty. He suffered from blinding headaches and driving obsessions with sex.

By the time the state of Florida had finished prosecuting Bobby Joe Long, he had received two death sentences and thirty-four life sentences, plus an additional 693 years. Had he not been stopped, he would likely have continued to rape, torture, and kill.[7]

THE "WEAKER" SEX

Although a number of criminologists have stated that females do not kill for sexual pleasure and thus there are no female lust murderers, there are in fact a number of them. Nannie Doss, the "Giggling Grandma," murdered four husbands between 1929 and 1953, as well as two children, two sisters, a grandchild, and her mother. She said she had enjoyed it. Karla Homolka and Rosemary West participated in murder with their husbands, and from records of the crimes both appeared to have found the experience erotic. Let's look at some representatives of female lust murderers in more detail.

On the afternoon of April 5, 1905, a woman entered a Paris hospital with a baby that appeared to have been choked. The child had been left in the care of her relative, Jeanne Weber. In fact, four babies had died from apparent suffocation among relatives in this family, and all of them had red marks on their throats. Not only that, but Weber's own three children were also dead, and two children had actually died while in her care. Thus, she was charged with murder. Yet there was no evidence of wrongdoing, so she was freed. Not long afterward, another child died of "convulsions" in her care. Again, Weber was arrested, and again acquitted. However, she could not keep her hands to herself. In 1908, she was caught actually attacking the son of an innkeeper. The doctors had her committed to an insane asylum, noting that her motive for killing appeared to be the sexual ecstasy she derived from it. Oddly enough, Weber died trying to strangle herself.[8]

She might perhaps be viewed as psychotic, but another killer, Jane Toppan, clearly enjoyed the deaths of her victims. As a child, she was a liar and troublemaker, quick to blame others, and full of envy. She became a nurse and used the position to experiment on patients. Using morphine to slow the breathing and contract the pupils, she would then apply atropine to produce the opposite effect, including convulsions.

In 1891, when Toppan was thirty-four, she became a private nurse, much in demand, but one patient recalled an odd experience. Amelia Phinney had been medicated and had gone into a near-unconscious stupor. Nurse Toppan had then crawled into bed with her and held her as she slipped in and out of consciousness. Toppan tried to give Phinney more medicine, but she refused. Then something caused Nurse Toppan to leave in a hurry. It came out later that this was Toppan's *modus operandi*. She achieved a sexual thrill from experiencing her victims dying as she medicated and then held them.

By 1899, Toppan had grown careless. She poisoned her sister, her brother-in-law, a good friend, and the entire Alden Davis family. However, with the last of the four victims, she did one thing differently. Instead of lying in bed holding the woman, Toppan woke the woman's ten-year-old son and held him in her arms while his mother slowly expired. These deaths were eventually investigated, with Jane showing up as the common denominator. During the interim, she poisoned two more people and attempted to poison a third. On October 29, 1901, Jane was arrested, on the verge of poisoning two more people.

Bodies were exhumed, toxicity tests done, and murder charges brought against Toppan, but she denied any involvement. A panel of psychiatric experts examined her, at which time she confessed. She said that she killed because of an "irresistible sexual impulse" and claimed that dying people excited her. The doctors decided that Toppan suffered from a mental disease of a moral type: she was a psychopath who killed without motive or remorse. She was sentenced to life in Taunton Insane Hospital. Eventually Toppan confessed to her attorney that she could recall at least thirty-one victims, and it has been alleged that she actually murdered more than a hundred.[9]

Female sexual predators represent about 10 percent of sexual offenses and their abuse often involves their own children, or at least someone in a vulnerable position. Psychologist A. J. Cooper points out that the reasons why women become offenders is incompletely understood but believes it may result from a combination of hypersexuality and early sexual experiences—usually abuse perpetrated on them. Most are immature, dependent, and sensitive to rejection, so they tend to gravitate toward those they believe they can control.[10]

A series of murders that clearly excited the female team that committed them occurred at the Alpine Manor Nursing Home in Michigan in 1987. In fact, it was during a sexual liaison that the perpetrators dreamed up the evil scheme, and it was largely the erotic high they achieved from their fatal activities that kept them going. Nursing home employees Gwendolyn Gail Graham, 23, and Catherine May Wood, 24, were lovers and in the midst of their secret fun, which included sexual asphyxia for greater intensity, they discussed the subject of murder. Then they decided to carry it out, finding patients whose initials would help them to spell out M-U-R-D-E-R. They killed five elderly women in a period of about three months.

Placing a washcloth over the patient's face, Graham would smother the victim while Wood kept vigil. At times, the act of killing so excited them that they went to an unoccupied room for a quick sexual encounter. Graham even took items such as jewelry or dentures from the victims to help relive the act and she reportedly found enormous emotional release in killing. Sometimes they washed the bodies down as part of the post-mortem routine, and handling them added another layer of erotic fun to their game.

However, when Graham pressured Wood to take a more active role to prove her love, Wood transferred to another shift. Graham quit and moved to Texas. A terrified Wood confessed everything to her former husband, who called the police. After an investigation, both women were arrested. Wood turned state's witness against her former lover for a sentence of twenty to forty years. Graham was convicted on five counts of first-degree murder and one count of conspiracy to commit murder. She got six life sentences, with no possibility of parole.[11]

ADDICTION AND SERIAL MURDER

Some people seek out intense experiences just to stimulate themselves, and certain offenders may be born with a need for greater stimulation than the average person, if only to get past an emotional deadness. Antisocial activities that escalate, says psychiatrist Robert Simon, indicate that they fulfill a need for stimulation. In fact, some killers report that they feel normal only after killing. Thus, they become addicted to their compulsive patterns, similar to other types of addictions.[12]

Psychologist Stephen Giannangelo agrees, noting that the excitement of an assault or rape can propel someone over the line to commit a murder. Killers will often say they can't remember the details of their first kill. They may understand the crime's seriousness but will nevertheless experience a rush from discovering "what they truly need." If they get away with it, they may experience confidence, which inspires them to seek the same excitement again. "These killers seem to evidence a pervasive lost sense of self," Giannangelo points out, "an inadequacy of identity, a feeling of no control. These could all be factors in a pathology that manifests itself in the ultimate act of control—the murder ... of other human beings."[13]

Giannangelo is describing the mechanisms of addiction, a complex process involving the brain's neurochemistry. The brain choreographs the body's information processing system, directing the behavior of the neurotransmitters. Serotonin is implicated in moods, for example. When we find ourselves in a novel situation, dopamine and norepinephrine levels surge, triggering the brain's reward system. Thus, we approach with anticipation those behaviors and situations that may feel good, and pending a continued pleasurable experience, dopamine in particular provides an edgy high that spurs us to seek it again. To ensure it, we start to notice particular stimuli more than we used to. Thanks to this neurotransmitter, we have a biological investment in life's unpredictable twists.

The salience theory about dopamine's function indicates that it's quite involved in helping us to focus, especially in unusual situations. That is, when something important happens, the release of dopamine assists us in being alert to new material, so we can process it. So novelty stimulates the brain into action and dopamine fuels the thrill of being alive and may be a significant contributor to activities that make us learn, grow, and feel in control.

Yet the brain also adapts. Dopamine keeps track of whether we actually get what we anticipate getting, and its levels increase or decrease accordingly. When dopamine levels diminish, the person seeks more stimulation and new avenues of reward. In addition, research indicates that those people with fewer dopamine receptors in the brain seek even more stimulation and may thus be vulnerable to addiction or compulsive pleasure seeking. In other words, if we get a lot, we anticipate a lot and thus want a lot.[14]

If the prefrontal cortex fails to function as an inhibitory agent, as seems to be the case in certain people who've been prone to violence, increased desire and reduced control may facilitate seeking what the neurons reward—that which interests us. For those who grow fascinated with certain types of violence—and experience that fascination repeatedly rewarded in fantasies and activities—it feels better to act out than to inhibit the impulse. The person grows bolder in pursuit of it. If they succeed at getting it, they anticipate having the same pleasurable experience again.

Yet it's not quite that straightforward. Other bodily processes affect the dopamine surge as well. Oxytocin may diminish dopamine's effect such that new stimuli are required to reproduce the high. Elevated testosterone levels also increase dopamine production, and adrenaline can kick in during risky situations.

So to make this specific to the development of a predatory serial killer, in other research I have proposed an environmental/physiological feedback, the spiral of erotic enthrallment. An individual finds something stimulating, such as women's shoes, red hair, or dead animals. The brain responds with pleasure, rewarding an approach to the exciting object. Afterward, the person eventually grows bored and seeks more such stimulation. In addition, his or her fantasy life would fill with these images and repeat them in some titillating scenario. The more of the object the person gets, the more excited he or she will be. But eventually the dopamine level will diminish, making him or her feel empty and bored again. So the cycle would repeat, further strengthening the erotic charge. Enthrallment with harm to others for one's own gratification starts with environmental opportunities and associations and becomes stronger via acts that stimulate the brain's reward mechanisms. The neural reward system processes these behaviors in a way that ensures repetition.[15]

Because these behaviors involve crimes, the person would also shroud them in secrecy and develop a fantasy life that would encourage them to withdraw from normal life and seek greater stimulation and pleasure from their private thoughts. They would live doubled lives, going through the motions of normalcy as much as possible to prevent others from detecting their darker activities, but also seeking opportunities to engage in that which has become most pleasurable to them. And that pleasure can take many different forms, so let's turn now to specifics. We'll start with killers who view themselves as gods. As we move along, we'll see how this theory plays out in other cases, despite a multiplicity of fantasies and motives.

NOTES

1. Bruce Gibney, *The Beauty Queen Killer* (New York: Pinnacle, 1984).

2. John Douglas, *Mindhunters: Inside the FBI's Elite Serial Crime Unit* (New York: Scribner, 1995), pp. 239–248.

3. Robert R. Hazelwood and Stephen G. Michaud, *Dark Dreams: Sexual Violence, Homicide, and the Criminal Mind* (New York: St. Martin's Press, 2001), pp. 15–38.

4. Vernon Geberth, *Sex-Related Homicides and Death Investigation* (Boca Raton, Florida: CRC Press, 2005), pp. 434–457.

5. Richard von Krafft-Ebing, *Psychopathia Sexualis with Especial Reference to the Antipathic Sexual Instinct: A Medico-Forensic*, rev. edn. (Philadelphia, PA: Physicians and Surgeons, 1928 [1886]), pp. 91–93.

6. Ethel Person, *By Force of Fantasy: How We Make Our Lives* (New York: Basic, 1995), pp. 10–11.

7. Anna Flowers, *Bound to Die: The Shocking True Story of Bobby Joe Long, America's Most Savage Serial Killer* (New York: Pinnacle, 1995).

8. Jurgen Thorwald, *The Century of the Detective* (New York: Harcourt, Brace & World, 1964), pp. 156–175.

9. Harold Schechter, *Fatal: The Poisonous Life of a Female Serial Killer* (New York: Pocket, 2003).

10. A. J. Cooper, "Female Serial Offenders," in *Serial Offenders: Current Thought, Recent Findings*, Louis B. Schlesinger, ed. (Boca Raton, FL: CRC Press, 2000), pp. 263–288.

11. Lowell Cauffiel, *Forever and Five Days* (New York: Zebra, 1992).

12. Robert Simon, *Bad Men Do What Good Men Dream: A Forensic Psychiatrist Illuminates the Darker Side of Human Behavior* (Washington, D.C.: American Psychiatric Press, 1996), pp. 308–309.

13. Stephen Giannangelo, *The Psychopathology of Murder: A Theory of Violence* (Westport, CT: Praeger, 1996), p. 39.

14. Steven Johnson, *Mind Wide Open: Your Brain and the Neuroscience of Everyday Life* (New York: Scribner, 2004), pp. 135–157.

15. Katherine Ramsland, *The Human Predator: A Historical Chronicle of Serial Murder and Forensic Investigation* (New York: Berkley, 2005), pp. 282–283.

CHAPTER 3

Omnipotence

"For you, Mr. Police, Call me God."

So began a letter to the authorities who were tracking the "Beltway Snipers" in 2002. It was the second communication that had requested recognition of their omnipotence during a three-week killing spree from Rockville, Maryland, to Washington, DC, and beyond. Thirteen people were shot at random with a Bushmaster .223-caliber semi-automatic rifle, and ten of them died, while a boy in a schoolyard was critically wounded. The snipers had demanded $10 million to stop shooting before being discovered asleep in a Chevy Caprice along I-95 on October 24. Ballistics linked them to all thirteen attacks, as well as to six other shootings, three of them fatal, in other states.

After a seven-hour interrogation, Lee Boyd Malvo, 17, admitted to being the triggerman in several of the shootings, so he was tried as an adult. He said the plan had been well organized, with forty-five-year-old John Allen Muhammad teaching him and serving as a lookout. They had rigged the car so they could shoot undetected from inside, used two-way radios to communicate, and listened to news coverage that allowed them to create maximum fear and confusion.

Muhammad, a former military sharpshooter, had issues with an ex-wife in the area and had manipulated the boy to act on his plan. In Virginia, he was tried, convicted, and sentenced to death, while Malvo received life in prison. For a time, they felt invincible, but in the end, their mundane mistakes revealed their limited intellect. They were not God.[1]

THE ULTIMATE RUSH

Some killers have said that to take a human life makes them feel like God, with power over life and death, while the occasional offender has identified himself with Christ. In some cases, a killer simply bears disdain for a specific type of person and believes that it is his religious duty to rid the world of them. The driving force behind such murders is the need for outright control, and it's girded with the killer's belief that he is special in some superior way. Generally, these killers are narcissists or psychopaths.

The Diagnostic and Statistical Manual of Mental Disorders (DSM-IV-TR), 4th edition, includes narcissistic personality disorder (NPD) in Cluster B on Axis II, with three other disorders that can manifest in extreme forms of egocentric behavior. A personality disorder is a persistent pattern of maladaptive behavior that causes dysfunction in relationships or at work. While not all people with NPD are criminals, NPD is the disorder most commonly found among sex offenders. They feel entitled to their victims, and their self-involved arrogance contributes to their sense of personal importance. Serial killers John Wayne Gacy and Ted Bundy, for example, seemed to truly believe that although they were in custody with numerous murder charges and substantial evidence against them, they'd neverthe-less beat the rap. "That's all you'll get on me," Bundy said upon being told of the indictment, while in court Gacy assured an investigator that he expected to keep a dinner date.[2]

The DSM-IV lists a number of characteristics of NPD, most noticeably a pattern of grandiosity and excessive need for admiration. People with NPD must be the center of attention and will sacrifice "being liked" for "being admired." Such people possess a high level of self-regard, but they treat others as inferior beings. People diagnosable as having NPD may show a long-standing pattern of any five of the following behavioral man-ifestations:

- Believe without merit that they're important
- Obsess over power and success
- Associate only with those considered "worthy"
- Demand admiration
- Believe they are entitled to immediate compliance with their wishes
- Exploit others to advance their own ambitions
- Exhibit little sense of what others feel or need
- Believe others envy them
- Exhibit arrogant behaviors or attitudes

While it's not appropriate to diagnose anyone without having gone through extensive assessment procedures, it's also not difficult to see in detailed stories about offenders that they do exhibit many of these traits. They are self-centered, insecure, incapable of learning from helpful comments, and they know how to find the "heat"—the means of recognition for anything they've done. Narcissistic criminals, when captured, will attempt to draw the limelight to turn themselves into the most superior criminal ever beheld. Often, they will defend themselves because no one else is deemed sufficiently competent to do the job. Or they will choose whatever role in court will best put them on display.

In *Dark Dreams*, Robert R. Hazelwood discusses how narcissistic criminals often keep records of their crimes as a way to relive them, reminding themselves of what they have done and how they have overpowered another person. "The crime scene," writes Hazelwood, "is a central feature of a sexual criminal's work product, his canvas, if you will. For many offenders, the work is so valuable that they devise elaborate and occasionally ingenious ways to preserve it for later delectation."[3] Despite the risk this can pose of letting obvious evidence get into police hands, these offenders are so certain they won't be apprehended that they keep these records. Their belief in their superiority is particularly strong in relation to law enforcement. As part of this grandiose invincibility, some killers even exaggerate their victim count in order to make themselves seem more powerful, but we'll deal with that behavior more specifically in Chapter 5. Among those who thought so highly of himself that he believed someone ought to write a book about him was Paul John Knowles, dubbed the "Cassanova Killer."

CASSANOVA

In 1974, the FBI hunted for a man who appeared to be committing a string of murders across the southeast United States. The suspect was Paul John Knowles, released from prison in Florida thanks to the attorney of one of Knowles's female correspondents—now his fiancé. Soon after he came to see her in San Francisco, she felt skittish and broke off the engagement. This so enraged Knowles that he went out, he later said, selected three people at random, and slaughtered them. He then left California and went roaming across the country.

During the next month in Florida, three more people died, and in quick succession Knowles murdered five, sometimes individuals, sometimes couples. He selected children, older women, younger men, or older men ... the victim type did not seem to matter to him. From Connecticut to Georgia, he continued to kill and rob, stabbing one man with scissors and stealing his clothing and car. Then in Atlanta, he met a British journalist, Sandy Fawkes. Since she was a writer, he mentioned that he might be an interesting subject for a book. Over the course of several days with her, he hinted at what he had done that made him stand out, but did not actually admit to murder. Knowles told Fawkes that he wanted to leave a mark on life so he could be remembered for something.

The idea of devoting a book to this strange man seemed absurd to Fawkes, but she humored him to try to learn why he was so self-flattering. He told her he would soon be killed for something he had done. He believed in fate and said there were marks on his body that affirmed that he would die young. He referred to astrology and tarot, and said that his favorite book was *Jonathan Livingston Seagull*, about a mystical seagull that becomes a Christ figure, both revered and reviled. The central character gives his message about living fully to a young disciple before he shimmers into nothingness.

Knowles identified himself with this bird, along with other significant transcendent figures, and believed that he ought to be as famous as they were. Then he and Fawkes parted and it wasn't long before she learned the source of his certainty about his fate. There was nothing mystical about it. In fact, Knowles was a suspect in several murders and after he was captured, Fawkes discovered that he had lied to her about several things, notably his age. He was twenty-eight, although he had told her he was thirty-three—the age at which Jesus Christ had been crucified. Apparently he identified himself with Christ, and in fact, Knowles's father was a carpenter, as Jesus's father was.

For posterity, as if he was certain that people would care, Knowles had entrusted his attorney with taped confession of his crimes. As the court attempted to confiscate them from this man, during a prison transfer the "Casanova Killer" grabbed for a gun and was shot dead by law enforcement officers. Finally, the tapes were reviewed and it turned out that Knowles claimed to have killed thirty-five people, but only eighteen murders across a number of states over a period of four months are officially attributed to him.

Knowles is among those killers who have used the act of murder to try to transcend their status as nonentities. Without that, they've done nothing and might be considered losers, but once they've made headlines, they believe they're now "somebody"—a person worthy of a book or film. Knowles had urged Fawkes to get the tapes he'd made, assuring her it would be the most important book she would ever write. Thus, a woman he might ordinarily have killed as part of his spree became for him the means for immortality. In fact, Fawkes' 1977 book, *Killing Time*, was revived in 2005 and reprinted as *Natural Born Killer*. Her description of the six days she spent with Knowles affirms how special he thought he was, despite all evidence to the contrary. It's not hard to view him as someone with NPD.[4]

Yet NPD often seems too trifling a label to attach to these killers. Given their general lack of remorse and their outright predatory behavior, they're closer to the condition of psychopathy, a more extreme and dangerous character disorder. For that we turn to the groundbreaking work of Robert Hare, among others.

SOMETHING MISSING

Dr. Robert Hare has spent nearly four decades engaged in research on the nature and implications of psychopathy. He developed the Psychopathy Checklist (PCL) and its revised version, the Psychopathy Checklist-Revised (PCL-R), for the reliable and valid assessment of the disorder of psychopathy. The PCL-R and its derivatives have been affirmed as among the most accurate instruments for assessing the risk for offenders to repeat their crimes. Hare is professor emeritus at the University of British Columbia and sits on the Research Board of the FBI's Child Abduction and Serial Murder Investigative Resources Center (CASMIRC), which consults in the disappearances of children, child homicide, kidnapping, and serial murder investigations. He has published and co-published numerous articles on psychopathy, as well as book chapters and two groundbreaking books—*Psychopathy: Theory and Research* and *Without Conscience: The Disturbing World of the Psychopaths among Us.*

Hare came into contact with psychopaths as the prison psychologist for the British Columbia Penitentiary, a maximum-security prison near Vancouver. The first inmate to visit him was "Ray," who pulled out a knife and said he was going to use it on another inmate (but did not). That act placed Hare in an awkward position: he could report it or keep quiet and thus violate the rules. He elected not to report it, which gave Ray the leverage he was looking for. During the remainder of Hare's stint at the prison, Ray plagued him with requests for favors, often lying about why he needed them and showing no shame when caught in a lie. In fact, he was usually ready to cover himself with yet another lie. Hare found Ray to be infinitely frustrating and yet he became interested in the kind of person who charms, lies easily, bears no responsibility, and likes to manipulate others.[5]

He read the work done on psychopathy, particularly that of Hervey Cleckley, whose 1941 book, *The Mask of Sanity*, had crystallized sixteen traits of the type of person that Ray had been. Hare was impressed, so he used Cleckley's ideas as a foundation for his own projects, and during the 1970s and 1980s he became a central figure for researchers attempting to codify research on the psychopath. Hare and his colleagues offered the initial version of the PCL in 1980.

"Psychopathy," he writes in *Without Conscience*, "is a personality disorder, defined by a distinctive cluster of behaviors and inferred personality traits, most of which society views as pejorative."[6] Along with other researchers, Hare points out that among the most devastating features of psychopathy are a callous disregard for the rights of others and a propensity for predatory and violent behaviors. Without remorse, psychopaths charm and exploit others for their own gain. They lack empathy or a sense of responsibility, and they manipulate, lie, and con others with no regard for anyone's feelings. They're predators and parasites, quick to blame and exploit.

Swiss psychiatrist Adolf Guggenbühl-Craig adds his own understanding of psychopathy in *The Emptied Soul*. To him, these people are "psychic invalids." That is, they lack the ability to love, to nurture life and community, and to form lasting bonds with others. They can carry on conversations but quickly forget the subject and person. Relationships are strictly in the present moment, with no demands. In addition, these people lack any sense of shame, even when they have hurt someone. They have no concept of telling the truth, keeping a promise, extending themselves altruistically, or repaying debts. Yet they have the ability to persuade others that they are moral people because they know how to adopt appropriate behaviors when needed. Instead of love, they are intrigued with power, domination, manipulation, and control.[7]

To add one more interpretation, Dr. Robert Rieber wrote in *Psychopaths in Everyday Life* that people with this disorder experience a profound dissociation that affects how they process language, behave, and form goals. It also saves them from becoming psychotic. He notes that all people possess some ability to ignore moral or social requirements, but psychopaths take this ability to an extreme. They lose control over their conscience and thus fail to develop any depth of human concern. They can fool others with a public persona until they have a serious run-in with the law. Rieber also indicates that psychopaths sometimes create situations of danger in order to feel alive.[8]

Researchers Yaling Yang, Adriane Raine, and their cohorts used functional magnetic resonance imaging to study the prefrontal cortex in the brains of twelve men known for their ability to lie, cheat, and manipulate to an extent considered pathological—a trait of psychopaths. When compared against normal individuals and even other antisocial types, he and his colleagues found that liars showed a 22–26 percent increase in prefrontal white matter and a 36–42 percent reduction in prefrontal gray/white matter ratio. Since autistic children, who have difficulty lying, show a converse pattern, the researchers suggested that liars have a structural brain deficit that allows them (1) an increased cognitive capacity to devise complex narratives and (2) a decreased inhibition against antisocial tendencies.[9]

Among the most psychopathic of the serial killers, who exhibited all of the aforementioned behaviors, was the notorious and charismatic Ted Bundy.

CROSS-COUNTRY RAMPAGE

Although Theodore Robert Bundy stated in a famous confession that his first murder occurred in 1973, it was not until the following year that his handiwork was noticed. A number of young women disappeared in Oregon and Washington State, but only when two women went missing on the same day in July from Lake Sammamish in Washington did witnesses offer some leads. They described a slender man named "Ted" who had driven a tan or gold Volkswagen Beetle. Unfortunately, during that time, there were many cars by that description, and running down a name as common as Ted turned out to be a major undertaking. But several months later, a mile from the lake, the remains of both women were found, and the Washington authorities realized they had a predator in the area.

What they did not know was that he had already moved on to Utah and Colorado, where more corpses of young women were found. But then the killer picked up a woman in Colorado, Carol Da Ronch, who managed to fight back and escape. She assisted the police to make an arrest as she identified Ted Bundy, a law student from Washington who drove a tan Volkswagen. That alerted officials in the Pacific Northwest.

But Colorado already had him. As they processed him for trial in the murder of Caryn Cambell, he escaped. Caught again, he manipulated another official and escaped again by pretending he needed legal research for his case, going into the library, and jumping out a second-story window. He crossed the country, checking out several locations and ended up in Tallahassee, Florida. Yet it was clear by January 15, 1978, that Bundy was "decompensating." In short order, he made several key mistakes that were uncharacteristic of his generally controlled manner.

First, he entered the Chi Omega sorority house at Florida State University, raping and clubbing four girls in their beds. Lisa Levy and Martha Bowman died, but the other two survived. Another girl in the house had seen him. On the same night, Bundy also attacked a girl in another sorority house. In his murderous frenzy, Bundy had also bitten one of his victims, leaving a firm bite mark bruise and skin impression. Although he got away that night, and even managed to grab a twelve-year-old girl in broad daylight a month later, he finally drew police attention with a traffic violation. Once in custody, he told them who he was. He then used the opportunity to get as much attention as possible. As cameras played on him, he assured reporters that he would beat this rap and be free again. He was clearly full of himself and probably believed that he could escape once again. But this time he was wrong.

As Bundy's trial approached, he decided to represent himself. Thus, he could show the world his amazing skill as well as control the proceedings—or so he thought. In courts, he preened, flirted with girls who flocked to see him, and winked at people he knew, as if to say, "I'll show them." However, he took such delight in milking police officers on the stand for details about his crimes that he angered the jury. He also mistakenly identified himself as the offender while questioning a witness.

It did not take the jury long to convict Bundy for three murders (including the twelve-year-old girl, whose body was found raped and strangled in the woods). Still, he figured that he could at least beat the death penalty, and again he was wrong. He was sentenced to death three times. Yet he had more cards to play.

Not only did he appeal his cases on various grounds to the U.S. Supreme Court, he also tried to interest scientists in the idea that he was so unique, he ought to be kept alive and studied. To add to his notoriety, he revealed more of his crimes, eventually confessing to thirty murders in six separate states. He discussed his compulsions as a predator to investigators who came to interview him, describing his need to totally possess his victim. Often he strangled them, he said, but sometimes he bludgeoned them. They were merely objects to him, to gratify his desires, and afterward, he felt no remorse. Why would he? They had belonged to him. He could not understand why their families were so grief-stricken over it.

In addition, while a task force investigated the forty-plus murders attributed to the Green River Killer in Washington State during the 1980s, Bundy wrote from Florida's Death Row to offer the officers in Washington an "understanding" of the "Riverman's" mind. He knew the area intimately, he said, and he proposed to "figure out" how this new predator operated. A team came to question him, which appealed to his vanity, but they soon realized that as Bundy talked with them, he was merely describing his own *modus operandi*. They accepted his "help" and kept in touch, allowing Bundy to believe in his superiority as America's premier serial killer. In other words, they manipulated him by playing to his arrogance, and with the information they extracted they managed to close a few cases in the Seattle area.

Officials spotted how Bundy was attempting to delay his execution, but in the end his assistance failed to help anyone, including himself. Just before Bundy was to die in Florida, he hinted at more undiscovered victims, and then attempted to say that there was still a fruitful area to explore: the influence of pornography on his behavior. He invited a prominent minister to talk about how his reading of sexualized violence had caused him to go astray, but only the most naïve people bought into this new ploy. On February 24, 1989, Ted Bundy was finally executed.[10]

Even without Bundy's help, investigators finally learned the identity of the Green River Killer, another man who had decided to act as God, but in a different manifestation. This man decided that he should improve the world by killing prostitutes: even as the act thrilled him on a personal level, he also infused it when he talked about it with a sense of purpose that gave his compulsive killing the aura of a divine mission. Ultimately, murder was his way of gaining total control.

ON A MISSION

Over a period of two years, from 1982 to 1984, numerous female victims were found strangled or stabbed and discarded around the Green River area in Washington State. In 1983 alone, twenty-seven women had disappeared and nine were found dead. Many of the victims had been prostitutes or runaways, and witnesses had described seeing a white male with a few of them. They were generally left in one of four dump site areas, and sometimes more than one was found in a single day. A few had stones pushed into their vaginas and one victim was left posed with a wine bottle and a dead fish, as if her murder was a joke or a bizarre message. A local paper, the *Seattle Post Intelligencer*, received a letter in 1984 with the heading, "whatyouneedtoknowaboutthegreenriverman," and the author claimed to be the killer ("callmefred"). An FBI profiler evaluated it as being unconnected to the murders, although it cited facts not released to the press. Since the man was having sexual contact with victims after they were dead, investigators knew he was returning to crime scenes. Yet still they could not catch him.

The computerized investigation cost more than $15 million, having at its height as many as fifty-five officers involved on the task force. While DNA samples were taken from many suspects in the local area, a few were eliminated via lie detector tests and others failed to pan out with evidence. The task force eventually was disbanded but several persistent detectives kept the case alive. Finally in 2001, the thrice-married Gary Leon Ridgway was linked via DNA analysis to several victims and as the trial approached in 2003, he pled guilty, showing authorities more graves until his toll reached forty-eight. (Some people believe it is probably higher, and Ridgway himself estimated the number to be around sixty, although he could not recall some of the victims' names.)

Ridgway said that he had indeed tried to communicate with the press, but his letter had been ignored. Nevertheless, he'd become a suspect several times. He had been cleared with a polygraph, and in 1987 (before DNA analysis was widely used) a lack of evidence linking him to any victim had gotten him off the hook. While he would not say when he last had killed, he hinted that it might have been in 1998. In any event, when he had been investigated during the 1980s, he had decreased his attacks. Many of the victims, he said, had been killed in his home. Changing the rugs had eliminated the evidence.

In his confession, which consisted of a series of interviews over five months, Ridgway told the police that he'd picked prostitutes and runaways because they would not be quickly missed. (To an earlier investigator, he had said that prostitutes to him were like booze to an alcoholic.) No one would file a missing persons report on such women, at any rate. Ridgway often watched for these victims, sometimes sleeping only a few hours so he could use the night hours to troll for them. He liked younger women, he said, because they talked more when they were dying. He thought of the ones he killed as his possessions, to do with as he pleased, and he enjoyed the feeling of control he had over them. He even once killed a woman as his own son waited for him in his truck, and thought nothing of it. In fact, if the boy had observed anything, Ridgway said, he would have eliminated the witness. He did what he needed to in order to continue his perverted acts.

Ridgway did not like it when victims were found, because he then "lost" them. He often referred to a victim as "it" rather than "her." He told the police that he saw himself as helping them to rid the world of prostitutes. He could control them by killing them, one after another. When the police asked him to rate himself on a scale from one to five, with five being the worst kind of evil person, he gave himself only a three.[11]

It turned out that much of the detail that Ted Bundy had provided about the way the Riverman operated was accurate, which probably meant that they had a similar deviance and similar MO. Bundy's descriptions would not have assisted in a capture, but they showed a remarkable parallel between two killers who liked to view themselves as God. Both were organized, generally careful, loved the act of killing, and needed to dominate and feel in charge.

The same is true of those killers who used their depravity to seek glory, and some of them offered claims more grandiose than even Bundy had considered.

NOTES

1. Dirk C. Gibson, *Clues from Killers: Serial Murder and Crime Scene Messages.* (Westport, CT: Praeger, 2004), pp. 29–44.

2. "Ted Bundy," Mugshots, Courtroom Television, 1995; Terry Sullivan, *Killer Clown* (New York: Grosset & Dunlap, 1983), p. 139.

3. Robert R. Hazelwood and Stephen G. Michaud, *Dark Dreams: Sexual Violence, Homicide, and the Criminal Mind* (New York: St. Martin's Press, 2001), p. 70.

4. Sandy Fawkes, *Killing Time* (New York: Taplinger, 1977).

5. Robert Hare, *Without Conscience: The Frightening World of the Psychopaths among Us* (New York: Simon & Schuster, 1999), pp. 9–12.

6. Ibid., p. 6.

7. Adolf Guggenbühl-Craig, *The Emptied Soul: On the Nature of the Psychopath* (Woodstock, CT: Spring, 1980), pp. 29–48.

8. Robert Rieber, *Psychopaths in Everyday Life* (New York: Psyche-Logo Press, 2004), pp. 82–90.

9. Yaling Yang, Adrian Raine, Todd Lencz, et al., "Prefrontal White Matter in Pathological Liars," *British Journal of Psychiatry*, 2005, 187, 320–325.

10. Ann Rule, *The Stranger beside Me* (New York: W. W. Norton, 1980); Stephen Michaud and Hugh Aynesworth, *The Only Living Witness: A True Account of Homicidal Insanity* (New York: New American Library, 1983).

11. Staff of the King County Journal, *Gary Ridgway: The Green River Killer* (Bellevue, WA: King County Journal, 2003); Ann Rule, *Green River, Running Red* (New York: Free Press, 2004); Tomás Guillén, *Serial Killers: Issues Explored through the Green River Murders* (Englewood Cliffs, NJ: Prentice Hall, 2006).

CHAPTER 4

Intellectual Exercise

THE WILL TO POWER

In 1924, Nathan Leopold and Richard Loeb had an idea; they wanted to commit "the perfect murder." They became famous not only for the crime but also for their rationale. Leopold was an avid reader of the nineteenth-century German philosopher, Friedrich Nietzsche, and was especially enthralled with Nietzsche's description of superior men unhindered by anyone's moral codes but their own. As a genius, Leopold considered himself similarly superior and he found a rationale for his arrogance in Nietzsche's discussion of the *übermensch* ("overman" or superman). He persuaded his companion, Loeb, equally arrogant if not quite as bright, that they could prove their exceptional quality by committing the perfect crime.

They started with arson and burglary. When the thrill wore off, they planned a more spectacular crime: They would kidnap and murder a young boy, and they chose Bobby Franks. Killing him, they used acid to try to conceal his features before dumping him and writing a ransom note. But they got caught, were tried, and soon learned that they were not above the moral code at all: In fact, they barely escaped execution.[1]

In 1948, Alfred Hitchcock was inspired by their crime to produce *Rope*, a film about two young men who believe they have proved their superiority by killing someone, and several serial killers during the "existential decades" singled out the aspects of Nietzsche's thought that seemed to support such *hubris* by extinguishing the lives of others. It's important, then, to see the aspect of Nietzsche's philosophy that could support extreme antisocial acts.

By the mid-nineteenth century, when Nietzsche was born, many radical new philosophies, such as humanism and Darwin's theory of evolution, were having an impact on ideas about human experience. Toward the end of the century, Nietzsche proposed that people should learn about the true way to live life from the exuberance of the early Greeks, before science or Christianity had blunted man's natural instincts. Nietzsche had read about the half man/half god Dionysus and was intrigued by the frenzied cultic rituals organized in his honor. Dionysus was god of the vine, so those who sought a mystical union with him did so through drunken, ecstatic orgies. Thus, Nietzsche viewed Dionysus as the supreme union of the forces of culture and base instinct, showing how people could be at once both refined and primitive. According to the legends, Dionysus had sacrificed himself to human ecstasy and was torn to pieces, but his act made possible a recovery from the spiritual fatigue evident in late nineteenth-century culture.

Nietzsche also proclaimed the death of God, calling for people to devise life's meaning for themselves. However, since most people seemed to him no more courageous or intelligent than sheep, only the elite few could step to the plate to devise an honest moral code. Nietzsche proclaimed that a moral genius, or *übermensch*, would overturn modern values that honored Christianity and the "herd" mentality to make way for the creation of new values based on domination and superiority. Without such a person to renew our society, Nietzsche claimed, we would be doomed to go through phases of soul-deadening nihilism until we finally lost all spiritual momentum.

In 1886, Nietzsche published *Beyond Good and Evil*, in which he stated that the idea of an absolute morality based in religion is illusory. He postulated that crime might be regarded as an invigorating condition that made the human species stronger. Social exploitation is normal, he said, because life is based in overpowering the weak. In other words, life is a "will to power," his title for a more forceful book in which he described the human ideal as an intense Dionysian affirmation of human existence as it truly is, including violence and a show of strength. There existed a master morality and a slave morality, he wrote, and those people who could assimilate the will to power would survive, be honest about the aggressive instinct, become leaders, and determine what is good and what is evil for the rest of society. The greatest enjoyment, Nietzsche said, was to "live dangerously," that is, to live on one's own terms.[2]

It's no surprise that Nietzsche's passionate articulation of the rewards of domination might inspire certain intellectual criminals, especially since he emphasized the superior intellect and character of individuals who were up to the challenge, and they generally encountered his work as part of their education. Nietzsche's books became part of university curriculums, grouped with the "continental philosophers" (European-based) who espoused similar themes about life and self-identity, and were thus labeled as "existential." During the 1950s, existential philosophy became a means by which people in the European and American counterculture set themselves apart. Musicians, artists, poets, and their various groupies learned the rarified language of this school of philosophy. While existential notions were originated by Danish thinker Sören Kierkegaard, keying in on the solitary individual who shouldered the burdens of free will and who was most concerned with the state of the soul, several key European philosophers applied them to postwar anxieties over the nuclear ability of certain countries to end human existence. To them it seemed difficult to even care about meaning in the face of annihilation, but French philosophers struggled to do so. The most notable were Jean-Paul Sartre and Albert Camus, who often discussed existential ideas in cafés in Paris's Latin Quarter (although Camus rejected the label), making popular the image of the educated, cigarette-smoking, coffee-drinking *artiste*. Existential thinkers in those days were quite sexy to people who wished to buck the norms and carve out an identity for themselves as superior people.

Sartre was especially radical; he insisted that people were entirely free to choose how they lived and that their choices defined them: You are what you do. With freedom came consequences, he stated, and individuals were essentially on their own. Everyone merely used everyone else as an impenetrable "other" and Sartre wrote that true bonding was not really possible.

Not as pessimistic but nevertheless stark, Camus, a French-Algerian, published *The Stranger* and *The Myth of Sisyphus* in 1942. *The Stranger* portrayed the antihero, Meursault, a man utterly detached, showing what it was like to essentially be a stranger to oneself, one's friends, and one's own world: Meursault is indifferent to everything, including his mother's death, a random murder he commits, and his impending execution. The book was depressing but it nevertheless expressed the war-ravaged outlook of a generation of people who felt lost and out of place.[3]

All four philosophers had a significant impact on the intellectual subcultures of the 1950s and 1960s, and among them, well-read killers found macabre inspiration.

JAZZ, SEX, AND DEATH

On January 11, 1959, Carroll and Mildred Jackson, along with their two young daughters, were out for a Sunday drive, and were abducted in their car near Apple Grove, Virginia. The car was found abandoned, but the Jacksons had vanished. The police scoured the area but found no clues that provided leads for further investigation. Days became weeks, with searchers turning up nothing. The Jacksons had been decent people with no enemies, so their disappearance was a disturbing mystery.

Then a couple came forward who told the police about a suspicious incident that had happened to them on the same day. During the afternoon an older model blue Chevrolet flashing its lights had forced them to the side of the road. After they'd pulled over, the driver got out and approached them, but given his demeanor they had quickly reversed their car and escaped. They described the man as tall, threatening, with a thin face, heavy brows, dark hair, an odd gait, and unusually long arms.

Two months after the abduction, on March 4, the remains of Carroll Jackson were discovered in a ditch under some brush. He had been shot in the back of the head. As police moved him, they found the remains of his infant daughter beneath him. An autopsy revealed that she had suffocated to death. Investigators surmised that the Jacksons's abductor had run their car off the road, in the way that the other couple had described, and then forced them to get into his.

Over two weeks later, the remains of Mildred and five-year-old Susan were found deeper in the woods, buried in a shallow grave, with Susan on top. They both had been raped and Mildred had been tortured before she was bludgeoned to death. A stocking was loosely tied around her neck, as if used as a leash to force her into performing other sexual acts. Susan had simply been beaten to death with a blunt instrument, possibly a gun butt. Within a few hundred yards, the police came across a cinderblock building and found a red button inside that matched the buttons on Mildred's dress, which was missing one. That gave them some idea about where the killer had taken the two females. It seemed likely that he had abducted the family only to gain possession of the woman and girl for his own pleasure. The father and baby had been killed and dumped quickly.

The police soon received an anonymous letter from a man with suspicions about his acquaintance, Melvin David Rees, a twenty-six-year-old, self-styled existential philosopher and jazz musician. He traveled around the area a lot to play his saxophone or the piano at various clubs. Their conversations, the letter went on, had been filled with commentary on life, death, and meaning, and one evening the subject had turned to murder. Rees had insisted that it was not necessarily wrong to kill; only social standards made it so. Under the influence of Benzedrine, Rees had confided that he craved to have every possible intense experience, from love to violence to death. The day after that very conversation, the Jacksons had been abducted.

The anonymous writer indicated that Rees had been arrested in 1955 on charges of assaulting a 36-year-old woman, and he'd also tried to get her into his car. The victim would not press charges, however, so the case had been dropped. The letter writer, who suspected him in yet another murder of a woman in 1957, indicated that he had confronted Rees after news of the Jackson murders had surfaced, and Rees had seemed evasive. The things he had said, along with his earlier record, seemed too coincidental to have no connection.

Inspired by this note, the police pursued an investigation, learning that Rees had dated a coed at the University of Maryland who had been questioned during the 1957 investigation, so they reexamined the central incident. On June 26, 1957, Margaret Harold was in a car with her boyfriend, an army sergeant. A man pulled up in a green Chrysler, got out and gestured for them to roll down the window. To their shock, he then pulled out a gun and demanded money. They refused, so he shot Margaret in the face. The soldier ran for help, and when he returned, it was clear that Margaret had been sexually assaulted. The sergeant's description of this man matched that of the couple who had encountered a motorist on the Sunday the Jackson's had been abducted: tall, dark hair, clean-shaven, and thin face. The similarities among these incidents seemed more than coincidental. And there was more.

Looking for evidence in the Harold case, investigators had discovered a cinderblock building with a broken basement window. Inside, taped to the walls, was a collection of violent pornography along with what appeared to be morgue photos of women who had been murdered. With this collection was a University of Maryland yearbook photo of Wanda Tipton. But when questioned, Tipton claimed not to know anyone by the description the police had given her. Clearly, she had known Rees, since he had dated her, but she had been unwilling to admit it at the time. Still, Rees was gone from the area, with no forwarding address, so for the time being, the Jackson murder investigators came to a dead end.

But a year later, the letter-writing "friend," who turned out to be Glenn L. Moser of Norfolk, Virginia, went to the police in person. He had heard from Rees, who was now living in Hyattsville, Arkansas, and was working as a piano salesman in a music store in West Memphis. Moser provided an address. Since Rees had crossed a state line, the FBI was alerted and several agents entered the case. They went to Arkansas, arrested Rees at the store, and brought the army sergeant from Annapolis there for a line-up. He identified Rees as the man who had approached them that fateful night in 1957 and killed Margaret Harold.

The agents then searched Rees's home, and it wasn't long before they found what they were looking for: links to the murders. Inside a saxophone case Rees had secreted a .38-caliber handgun—the attacker in both cases had shot the victims with a .38—along with notes describing a number of sexually sadistic acts. One was attached to a newspaper page that featured a photo of Mildred Jackson. It described killing a man and baby on a lonely road, and included a chilling statement: "now the mother and daughter were all mine." He'd gone on to indicate that he had indeed tortured the woman, sadistically drawing out her death. He had "tied and gagged, led her to a place of execution and hung her. I was her master."

Newspapers quickly dubbed Rees the "Sex Beast." He was tried in both Virginia and Maryland, and also suspected in the unsolved murders of four adolescent girls in Maryland: Mary Shomette, 16, Ann Ryan, 14, Mary Fellers, 18, and Shelby Venable, 16. In Maryland, in February 1961, Rees was convicted of the murder of Margaret Harold and received a life sentence. Then in Virginia that September, his conviction for the four Jackson family murders got him a death sentence. That may have given him reason to consider the thoughts of Camus' character, Meursault, as he pondered his own execution after committing a murder.

But when the U.S. Supreme Court suspended all death sentences in 1972 to evaluate the constitutionality of the death penalty, Rees's case was among them. He survived for two more decades before dying in prison of natural causes.[4] He did confess to several more murders, and we can only wonder how long his existential pretense held up during his incarceration.

THE LURE

Rees wanted to kill merely for the sake of collecting experiences. There's a lining of evil around that decision, and psychoanalyst Carl Goldberg, who wrote *Speaking with the Devil* about similar senseless acts of evil, indicates that the development of this kind of aggression is inspired initially by shame. As it builds, it moves through six stages in which the person feels contempt for others (as Rees did), rationalizes and justifies his own actions (Rees used existential philosophy to accomplish this), fails to think about the consequences or his own actions (or to care enough to do so), and develops a type of thinking in which he has convinced himself (or herself) that he is perfect (the *übermensch*). Thus, he has developed what Goldberg refers to as "malevolent magical thinking," which involves obtaining power over the source of life by creating "moral and emotional distance between perpetrator and victim." This stance is a form of grandiosity in which the person believes that others have failed to recognize his unique qualities and must thus be *forced* to see. "Self examination is impossible," says Goldberg, "because it is believed to be unwarranted."[5]

His analysis certainly fits those killers who have decided they are superior to others and are therefore entitled to kill them. A similar line of thought supported the next series of murders, undertaken by a team who collectively identified with Nietzsche's morally superior being.

UNDER THE INFLUENCE

Ian Brady and Myra Hindley were Britain's notorious Moors Murderers. Called "the most evil man alive," Brady penned a book while in prison, *The Gates of Janus*, to offer his insights into other murderers. He interprets the act of killing as a creative expression of nihilism, viewing his own antisocial behavior as an extension of his intellect. Brady had been a longtime fan of Russian author Fyodor Dostoevsky, who wrote such classics as *Crime and Punishment* and *The Possessed*. Both books feature a character who plans a crime via an intellectual frame of justification. Raskolnikov in *Crime and Punishment*, in particular, is obsessed with proving that he is beyond the laws of society because he is "superior." This means to him that he could kill someone at whim, without consequences. He selects an elderly woman whom he believes would be no loss to society and carries out his plan, having to also murder another woman who happens along.

While Raskolnikov ends up disintegrating emotionally, which undermines his intellectual arrogance, Brady accepted Raskolnikov's plan, with its philosophy, as a possibility for himself. He therefore decided that crime was an acceptable way to make a living, and he wanted to experience power over others via murder.

Raised in Glasgow, Scotland, Brady developed into a loner who indulged in petty crimes that landed him in jail. His exposure at age 17 to hardened criminals apparently ignited in him a generalized rage against society. He fantasized in his cell about amassing as much money as he could as quickly as possible, and once he was released from prison, he sought such opportunities. He also continued to read, becoming a fan of Hitler and Nazism. Then he met his future accomplice.

Myra Hindley was 18 when she first encountered Brady in 1961. They worked for the same agency in Manchester, England, and she became infatuated with him. In fact, Brady later described their connection as nearly telepathic. Soon he persuaded her to accept his philosophies, including the Nietzschean notions that there was no God and that morality was relative. Brady also taught Hindley about Nazism and the violent hedonistic philosophies of the Marquis de Sade. Eventually he had changed her from a girl who loved children into a cynical young woman who despised people as much as he did. He proposed that they enrich themselves with crime, to which she acceded, but she soon found herself helping him to rape children and bury them on the moors.

Their first victim in 1963 was a sixteen-year-old girl, but the children got progressively younger. The next one was a 12-year-old boy. Brady hoped to acquire another accomplice in Myra's brother-in-law, David Smith, but when he tried to get Smith to assist him in secretly removing a body from Myra's grandmother's home, Smith went to the police. They arrested the two killers, and in 1966, both were sentenced to life in prison. Brady exonerated Hindley, but a jury considered them equally responsible. They continued to write to each other from their separate cells, but Hindley eventually converted to Catholicism. As if to redeem herself, she penned a document that detailed how Brady was entirely responsible for the murders. Upon hearing this, Brady changed his story, implicating her in everything they did, claiming that some of the torture was on her initiative.

Hindley stated that Brady had aspired to commit the perfect murder, and while she admitted to helping him to acquire victims, she denied being present to the actual killings. Yet for all her admissions, it is Brady who revealed the actual motives. In his book, he makes it clear that he thinks of crime as an exciting venture for the solitary explorer, "consciously thirsting to experience that which the majority have not and dare not."[6] When not bound by social convention, human nature, he indicates, is inclined toward "the crooked." Nevertheless, crime is not the ultimate high; in fact, the lack of satisfaction one achieves from committing a crime can be a real disappointment. As well, the offender is generally so preoccupied with the possibility of discovery that he fails to fully experience the pleasure of what he has done.

As for murder itself, "viewed scientifically, the death of a human being is of no more significance than that of any other animal on earth," says Brady. Serial killers, he adds, are people who are "unavoidably a failure in many normal walks of life." This would describe both himself and Hindley. Such a person lacks patience, he says, and eschews the kind of boredom that most other people accept. "The serial killer has chosen to live a day as a lion, rather than decades as a sheep." Once he has committed homicide, he accepts his acts as normal, and the rest of humanity as "subnormal."[7]

Myra Hindley had stated that Brady possessed a certain charm that made her believe anything and want to do anything for and with him (a sentiment often heard from partners of psychopaths, as if a temporary madness had seized them). Whether she was a dormant criminal, with Brady's nihilistic criminality as a catalyst, or whether she acted out of some other motivation, it does seem clear that Brady, with his violent fantasies and intellect, was the dominant personality.

Oddly enough, some killers who seek glory of this kind by taking credit for murder to enhance their status, sometimes decide that their actual deeds aren't quite enough. We turn now to those individuals.

NOTES

1. Hal Higdon, *Crime of the Century: The Leopold and Loeb Case* (New York: Putnam, 1975).

2. Friedrich Nietzsche, *The Portable Nietzsche*, translated by Walter Kaufman (New York: Viking, 1977).

3. William Barrett, *Irrational Man: A Study in Existential Philosophy* (New York: Doubleday, 1958), pp. 177–205.

4. Colin Wilson, *The Killers among Us: Sex, Madness, and Mass Murder* (New York: Warner, 1995), pp. 294–299.

5. Carl Goldberg, *Speaking with the Devil: A Dialogue with Evil* (New York: Viking, 1996), pp. 37–60.

6. Ian Brady, *The Gates of Janus* (Los Angeles: Feral House, 2001), p. 35.

7. Ibid., p. 52.

CHAPTER 5

Glory

Serial killers draw attention to themselves through various means. The primary one—the one in which they can revel while no one knows who they actually are—involves anonymous or pseudonymous communications to the press. Zodiac, BTK, Son of Sam, possibly Jack the Ripper, and several others have utilized this avenue to taunt and torment. They seek glory for themselves and the acts they have committed, maintaining their claim to superior intelligence by evading detection. Yet once serial killers are caught, some of them posture in other ways. During the 1980s, a few even managed to get on talk shows. Also, toward the end of that decade and into the 1990s, some claimed many more victims than they actually had.

Let's look first at the killers who communicated with the press.

SENDING CODES

Among the most notorious communicators was a man who referred to himself as Zodiac and who showed a preference for codes and cryptic references. Between December 1968 and July 1969 in Vallejo, California, he shot two couples on two separate occasions. Three victims died but one male survived. Still, this victim was unable to assist with an identification. By early August 1969, the editors of three San Francisco area newspapers each received letters and one-third of a strangely coded cipher, meant to be published by all three so the code could be put together. The author of this code claimed to be the Vallejo killer. He had used more postage than necessary, which helped to authenticate his communication, and learning his "message" involved solving the printed cryptogram. He signed each part with a crossed-circle symbol.

The papers published their pieces, hoping that someone would step forward and help to decipher the communiqué, even as the police put specialists on the project. Finally a schoolteacher, Donald Harden, and his wife did it, offering the following message, all in capital letters, and including spelling and grammatical errors:

I LIKE KILLING PEOPLE BECAUSE IT IS SO MUCH FUN. IT IS MORE FUN THAT KILLING WILD GAME IN THE FORREST BECAUSE MAN IS THE MOST DANGEROUS ANAMAL OF ALL TO KILL SOMETHING GIVES ME THE MOST THRILLING EXPERIENCE IT IS EVEN BETTER THAN GETTING YOUR ROCKS OFF WITH A GIRL THE BEST PART OF IT IS THAE WHEN I DIE I WILL BE REBORN IN PARADICE AND THEI HAVE KILLED WILL BECOME MY SLAVES I WILL NOT GIVE YOU MY NAME BECAUSE YOU WILL TRY TO SLOI DOWN OR ATOP MY COLLECTIOG OF SLAVES FOR AFTERLIFE. EBEORIETEMETHHPITI (These letters were never decoded, and the killer's identity was not revealed in his code, as he had indicated it would be.)

Detectives realized that the killer was playing a game, and believed that he had some knowledge of naval codes and mythological symbols. The police requested another letter and they got one a week later. From it, they learned that he called himself "the Zodiac," that he used a small penlight taped onto his weapon, and that he seemed to enjoy what he was doing. That suggested he would undertake another attack, and it occurred on September 27, 1969. At Lake Berryessa, Cecelia Ann Shepard and her friend, Bryan Hartnell, sat together on a blanket. A stocky man wearing a black executioner's hood approached them, revealed his weapons, and instructed Bryan to bind Cecelia Ann. Then the hooded stranger stabbed both of them, aiming most of his frenzy at the girl. She was stabbed ten times, dying at the scene, but Bryan survived to describe their attacker. He said that the man had driven down the road. In fact, it was later learned that he had stopped to call the police to report his attack and claim credit.

Two weeks later, this same person killed cab driver Paul Stine in San Francisco, leaving two bloody fingerprints in the cab. Soon after, the San Francisco *Chronicle* received a letter in an envelope (with too much postage) that contained a torn piece of Stine's shirt and issued a veiled threat against schoolchildren. It was an arrogant missive, full of bravado and criticism of the police. Yet no leads proved productive. Zodiac demanded to speak to a renowned area attorney, and a meeting by phone was set up, but while calls came in, they were not necessarily from the Zodiac. Yet he (or someone) continued to send letters, often with codes. He was also linked with an earlier murder on a college campus at Riverside,

California, where someone had apparently written a message on a table inside the library and sent letters claiming credit for the murder. (Not everyone agrees that this murder should be attributed to Zodiac.)

Until 1984, the Zodiac (or someone using his style) kept in contact with the police and the *Chronicle*, but despite claiming thirty-seven victims, his killing spree seemed to end with six or seven. His identity is still a mystery, which means he got away with murder, enjoyed the press coverage and books written about him, and slipped away. He successfully manipulated the media—newspapers and television—to respond to his demands, and he led the police on a chase that went nowhere. Even today, the Zodiac commands respect from true-crime aficionados as being the equal in nerve and savvy of Jack the Ripper.[1]

KEEPING SCORE

One of the more demanding killers who reveled in the glory of media coverage was a man who referred to himself in communications as "BTK" for "Bind them, Torture them, Kill them," but his story turned out quite differently, and it was his very need for glory that triggered his downfall. He seemed to measure his prowess by the media response, and when it was not sufficient or not correct, he felt a compulsion to set the record straight. Thus, another "superior" being proved only how desperately needy he was.

In Wichita, Kansas, early in 1974, a family of four was murdered. The victims were Joseph and Julie Otero, and their son and daughter. The killer had entered the home, bound and strangled the parents and boy, and then singled out the eleven-year-old daughter for torture and strangulation by hanging. She wore only socks when found, and BTK had left evidence that his treatment of her had sexually excited him. Six months later, a young woman was bound, strangled, and stabbed to death in her home. While arrests were made, no one was identified as the killer. Then a newspaper editor received instructions to locate a letter placed inside a book in the Wichita Public Library. The letter referred to the Otero slaughter and indicated that the killer had studied the habits of other sexual criminals and identified with them. He named himself BTK and offered a sexually graphic signature by which to authenticate his communications. He also said he had a "monster" in his brain and would continue to kill. It was a terrorizing threat.

Then in 1977, two women, Shirley Vian and Nancy Fox, were murdered by strangulation in the area, followed by a poem sent to the press referring to Vian. BTK had masturbated onto the body of the second victim. He had also called from one of his crime scenes to direct the police to her. Clearly, he wanted attention. In particular, he wanted credit for his crimes, just in case they did not notice that the murders were linked. He then asked, "How about some name for me?" and referred to himself as The B.T.K. Strangler.

FBI profilers suggested downplaying media coverage, since that was apparently this offender's ultimate aim. This seemed to anger him, because he soon sent a letter to a local television station explaining that he was among the "elite" serial killers. He included a list of others that he considered in his class and explained that serial killers were motivated by something called "Factor X," which compelled them to murder. He whined that he had not gotten the amount of media attention that others had, and said that he was already stalking victim number eight. (He did enter a home but left before the woman arrived.) "How many do I have to kill," he asked, "before I get my name in the paper or some national attention?" He was not amused, he said, that the papers were failing to provide details. He included a drawing of the seventh victim that was a perfect match to the actual crime scene.

He liked to send cryptic notes, puzzles, and leads that proved to be false. No one was quite sure which of the things that BTK said were truthful and which were lies. He continued to communicate until 1979, but he continued to kill (that we know of) until 1991, although this fact was learned only later. At one point, a panel of psychiatrists evaluated the communications and decided that BTK viewed himself rather grandiosely as part of a larger scheme. In addition, with his references to "the monster," he was possibly setting up an insanity defense, should he need it.

The residents of Wichita felt terrorized, wondering who might become this man's next victim. Profilers suggested planting a subliminal message into a news program, as well as placing a classified ad to "BTK," but neither strategy hooked a response. Then in 1986, Vicky Wegerle was killed in Wichita, but investigators did not think she was linked to the others. In any event, no one took credit and there were no communications at the time. It seemed that BTK had stopped, moved, or been arrested for something else. Nearly two decades passed before he was heard from again.

In March 2004, a reporter for the *Wichita Eagle* decided to write a thirty-year retrospective of the Otero slaughter and other murders associated with BTK. Soon the newsroom received a letter from "Bill Thomas Killman" that contained three photographs of a woman who was clearly dead. She had been posed in a variety of ways and a photocopy of her driver's license was included: it was Vicky Wegerle. Hoping to identify the killer, the police ran a DNA test on evidence from that crime, also analyzing thousands of suspects in an offender database, but they failed to link it to anyone. A geographical profile indicated that BTK probably lived or worked not far from the crime scenes, which were only four miles apart, and that he had some association with Wichita State University (a letter had been Xeroxed there and the toner had been matched to a copier).

Late in 2004, a package was found in a park that contained a partial manuscript entitled "The BTK Story," as well as the driver's license of one of the 1977 victims. BTK had reported this murder to police dispatchers. He also used the right signature, which had never been publicized. Although they could not necessarily trust his "autobiography," the task force believed they knew his age and some of his interests. Some of the language from BTK's notes indicated familiarity with law enforcement. Still, despite more than 5,000 tips, they still could not identify him. Then they got a break.

Early in 2005, BTK sent a computer disc with a single file in rich text format that directed police to read the 3 × 5 card included. The card indicated that all future communications would be assigned a number. But the disc contained hidden information from deleted files and computer-specific registration, and was traced to someone named "Dennis" and a local Lutheran church. The pastor offered the names of people who had access to the computer, including the congregation's president, Dennis Rader. He had graduated from Wichita State University and drove the kind of car caught on a surveillance tape near one of these communication drops. A DNA sample subpoenaed from Rader's daughter clinched it: Rader, a family man, security specialist, and seemingly stable citizen, was the man who had bound, tortured, and killed at least eight people. He was arrested and charged with the murders. It turned out that his occupations had included installing security systems and enforcing city ordinances. It would not have been difficult for him to get people to let him into their homes.

When he went to court to confess to his crimes as part of his plea deal, he obviously relished the attention. In retrospect, it was clear when police reexamined his communications that he had actually provided his name and home address in one of his puzzles. He did not even hesitate to confess, a good indication that he wanted complete credit for his crimes, and he added two more victims to the list, as well as identifying someone he'd targeted for the future. In court, he went meticulously over the details of his "projects," and talked about them as if they were just business as usual. He appeared to revel in the national limelight. He said he had killed to satisfy his sexual fantasies. But he also tried to mitigate his actions by saying that a demon possessed him and had driven him to engage in fantasies about torture and murder. He received ten consecutive life sentences, and the Kansas Department of Corrections has jurisdiction over the types of material that Rader will have access to. In other words, he may not get to indulge in his favorite pastime—reading about himself. That could be worse for him than being locked up.[2]

Dirk C. Gibson, journalism professor at the University of New Mexico, examined more than two hundred cases in which murderers communicated in some form during or after their crimes. He includes both

Zodiac and BTK in his case analyses. Among the forms of communication he includes are messages left at crime scenes or on bodies, notes to police, phone calls, emails, journals, logs, videotapes, notes to the media, and letters from prison. He believes that "communication is an integral part of many, if not most, serial murder cases. He also states that the motives vary from wanting to be caught to taunting the police to justifications for what they are doing, and "serves a variety of psychological and rhetorical functions." If police overlook the clues in the messages, Gibson states, their investigations are incomplete.[3]

Although communications play many different roles, it's clear that any form of recording one's crime for someone else indicates the desire to gain some degree of glory, even if the killer is the only one who ever knows who he or she is. However, in cases like BTK, communications can provide significant clues that facilitate an arrest. Killer Maury Travis, for example, anonymously sent a map to a reporter that led to one of his victims, because he wanted it to be published in the newspaper. The State Police Cyber Crime Unit recognized the map's design and used computer logs from the Web site to track him down. He committed suicide before he could be tried, but in his home police found a substantial cache of evidence that indicated that he had sadistically tortured and murdered numerous women.

CONFESSIONS

In another type of grab for glory, killers across history have confessed to high numbers of victims, most noticeably when publicity is offered. In 1892, H. H. Holmes, whom we discussed in Chapter 1, at first said that he had killed no one, but then he wrote a confession admitting to twenty-seven. It was not long before he recanted the confession, and in fact it was learned that several of his "victims" were either not dead or had died in ways unassociated with him. When told by police that his tale was untrue, he supposedly said, "Of course it is not true, but the newspapers wanted a sensation and they got it." At the gallows he claimed to have killed only two people, and he was actually convicted of only one, but authorities and many true crime aficionados believe his victim toll was over one hundred.[4]

Holmes's "fictional" confession had been motivated by a desire to seem notorious and to collect money from a newspaper, but in recent decades this type of braggadocio is more closely associated with one-upmanship and the desire for historical notoriety. During the 1980s and 1990s, a number of serial killers made claims of outrageously high victim counts, agreeing to interviews and writing books as a way to enhance their status. Larry Eyler, Donald Leroy Evans, Richard Bigenwald, Glen Rogers, Pee Wee Gaskins, and Paul John Knowles all claimed to have killed many more people than police were able to link to them, while Joseph Fischer's numbers increased with each talk show appearance. By that time, society was so fascinated with serial killers that they could say anything and be believed. Yet it turns out that in many cases, the numbers were exaggerated or entirely falsified.

Police are familiar with several types of false confessions, including those from people who confess spontaneously to something they did not do. That's usually in response to a high-profile case, in the hope of becoming famous. Sometimes confessing falsely arises from misplaced guilt, where the confessor believes he or she should be punished for something ... anything. In fact, police techniques for interrogation are often aimed toward assuming guilt and moving a person from silence or denial to admission. They may even cite nonexistent evidence or provide subtle inducements. The point is to get the person being questioned to believe that only by talking will he or she find relief. Suspects confess when motivated, especially when focusing on the immediate cost-benefits ratio of a situation.

There are also coerced confessions, usually offered when the person under interrogation is exhausted, naïve, frightened, or mentally impaired. Some people fear that the interrogation will be stressful so they capitulate quickly, but on rare occasions, a person may internalize the event and actually believe he or she did it when they did not. That occurs when an interrogator seems confident of the suspect's guilt and may even lie or use manipulative tactics. The characteristics of those most likely to falsely confess include youth, a low IQ, mental illness or confusion, a high degree of suggestibility, a trusting nature, low self-esteem, high anxiety, and possessing a poor memory.

Psychologist Saul Kassin is among the professionals who have studied the phenomenon of false confession, and he offers his own typology. Among his six categories is the "compulsive type – attention seeker," or the person who uses confessions to gain notoriety, impress others, or get attention.[5] That's the type of confession often made by serial killers seeking glory.

The most infamous of these false confessors was Henry Lee Lucas, a one-eyed drifter arrested in 1983 in Texas. Picked up on an illegal weapons charge, he shocked the courtroom by confessing to two murders and then said that he had killed more than one hundred around the country. He included Ottis Toole as his partner in crime, who was in prison in Florida, and together they confessed to numerous murders in many states. By some accounts, Lucas's figure went as high as 600, while others place it at 360. However, when an enterprising reporter caught Lucas in several lies in 1985 and some of the cases were further investigated, he recanted everything and it became clear that many law enforcement professionals had actually fed him details as a way to close open cases. Yet for a time,

Lucas had enjoyed his status as the world's worst serial killer, especially since it got him attention, better food, frequent outings, a good bed, and plenty of notoriety. He had figured out how to milk details from eager investigators and offer them back.

"I set out to break and corrupt any law enforcement officer I could get," Lucas said. "I think I did a pretty good job." In the end, he was convicted of eleven murders, although it's impossible to know if he even did those. The one for which he received the death penalty turned out to have been impossible for him to have committed, so his sentence was commuted to life.[6] He died in prison of natural causes.

ASPIRATIONS

Thanks to the powerful spotlight of the media during the 1980s and 1990s, some people added a unique new motive to commit repeat murder: to gain the identity of a serial killer. Jason Massey kept journals about how he would become the world's worst serial killer, and at the age of nineteen began his "career" with a double homicide in Texas. Quickly caught, he was convicted and executed, so he never did achieve the notoriety he craved, or even the status of serial killer. But another man with the same motive managed to succeed.

In England, Colin Ireland claimed that he wanted to become known as a serial killer. As a juvenile and young adult, Ireland committed a series of petty crimes. Once he felt bold enough for something stronger, he prepared a murder kit containing handcuffs, extra clothing, rope, gloves, and plastic bags. Then between March and June 1993, he entered several London gay clubs to select men who would willingly allow themselves to be bound for kinky sexual escapades and thus make themselves vulnerable. He considered them "easy" victims.

The first person that Ireland approached was West End theater director Peter Walker, 45. Ireland bound and tortured Walker in his South London flat, and then suffocated him with a plastic bag. Now that he'd done the deed, he spent time with the corpse, placing condoms in his mouth and nostrils, and posing two teddy bears in an obscene position against him. Clearly, he enjoyed what he was doing to another human being. He couldn't wait for the news reports, but to his surprise, nothing was printed about the murder. Determined to start the process of being noted for his brutality, Ireland anonymously telephoned a newspaper, the *Sun*, to "leak" the information. He reportedly mentioned that the murder was the result of a New Year's resolution.

Two months later, he suffocated Christopher Dunn in North London by shoving material down the man's throat. Dunn, too, was left in a sexually provocative position, handcuffed and wearing a black leather harness, with evidence of burning in his pubic area. Yet when this crime was discovered, the police failed to link it to Ireland's first murder, which frustrated him. Despite his hope for fame, Ireland found himself making yet another anonymous call. The police investigated, but Ireland had left no fingerprints and no way to trace the paraphernalia he used on the victims. He strangled yet a third man, Perry Bradley III, in Kensington in June. Then he anonymously told the police there were two important clues at the scene.

Stymied by these cryptic messages, the investigative team contacted Robert Ressler, a profiler from the FBI's Behavioral Science Unit, who agreed to examine the three crime scenes. He noted that the victims had frequented the same west London bar, the Coleherne Pub, where during the 1980s gay serial killer Michael Lupo had picked up some of his own victims. Ressler also speculated that this killer got perhaps a greater thrill from media attention than from the murders: The crimes were nearly identical, and all had been followed with phone calls. It seemed clear that this killer wanted to be identified and given credit for these murders.

Then a fourth victim turned up. Andrew Collier, 33, was found in his apartment, with his cat, its neck broken, placed beside him, its mouth on his genitals. This time, a fingerprint from an unknown source was preserved. The killer made several phone calls to police, claiming he was losing control. He warned them that he would kill one victim per week if they did not stop him, and expressed frustration over their inability to link the four murders. It seemed clear that he would eventually make a mistake.

On June 15, Ireland strangled a fifth victim, Emanuel Spiteri, 41, in southeast London. No one seemed to notice, so Ireland again called the police to send them to the crime scene. In another phone message, he admitted that he had read many books about serial killers and knew that he could now be classified as one (erroneously believing it required at least four victims), so he was going to stop. "I will probably never reoffend again." He seemed on the verge of not only *the* perfect crime but five of them.

Detectives from Scotland Yard checked surveillance cameras that recorded activity on the transit platforms at Charing Cross Station. They spotted the fifth victim on the blurred videotapes, in the company of another man. That person's image was made public and other men came forward to say they had met him. Once that occurred, on July 19, Ireland went to his solicitor to say that he was the man in the video but he was not Spiteri's killer. However, the police had his fingerprint from the Collier murder, so when they confronted him with this evidence Ireland eventually confessed in detail to the five murders. He was convicted and received five life sentences.

Ireland proved to be a loner in his thirties, twice married and twice divorced, unemployed, and with a history of mental instability and violence.

He had put a lot of thought into his targeting and murder of the victims, so Ressler was convinced that pressure from long-building fantasies had motivated the crimes. Yet Ireland blamed the bullying he had received as a child for being a "lanky little runt." He had developed several paranoid obsessions and suffered from dramatic mood swings. When he decided to become a serial killer in 1993, he said it was because he just generally disliked people and had lost control. But given the amount of effort he put into being mentioned in the papers, he clearly wanted to be "known" for his crimes.[7]

Sometimes those who act from any of the motives mentioned thus far know exactly what they're doing, but in a few cases, they're psychotic and delusional. Any account of serial murder would be remiss to characterize them all as clear-sighted predators. Some cases pose an odd assortment of reasons for why they must kill.

NOTES

1. Robert Graysmith, *Zodiac* (New York: Berkley Books, 1986).

2. Erica B. Simons, "Forensic Computer Investigation Brings Notorious Serial Killer BTK to Justice," *The Forensic Examiner*, Winter 2005, 55–57.

3. Dirk C. Gibson, *Clues from Killers: Serial Murder and Crime Scene Messages* (Westport, CT: Praeger, 2004), p. 2.

4. Frank Geyer, *The Holmes-Pitezel Case: A History of the Greatest Crime of the Century* (Salem, MA: Publisher's Union, 1896); H. H. Holmes, *Holmes' Own Story* (Philadelphia, PA: Burk & McFetridge, 1895); "Confession," *Philadelphia Inquirer*, April 12, 1896.

5. Saul Kassin, "The Psychology of Confession Evidence," *American Psychologist*, 1997, 52, 221–233; Richard Leo and Richard J. Ofshe, "The Consequence of False Confessions: Deprivations of Liberty and Miscarriages of Justice in the Age of Psychological Interrogation," *Journal of Criminal Law and Criminology*, Winter 1998, 429–496.

6. Mike Cox, *The Confessions of Henry Lee Lucas* (New York: Pocket, 1991).

7. Robert Ressler and Tom Schachtman, *I have Lived in the Monster* (New York: St. Martin's Press, 1997), pp. 161–189.

CHAPTER 6

Delusions

THE DIE SONG

From October 1972 until February 1973, a series of murders occurred around Santa Cruz, California. Among the victims were four campers (killed in a mass slaughter), a priest, a man digging in his garden, a young girl hitchhiking, an acquaintance and his wife, and a mother and her two children (also killed together). The police caught the offender minutes after he'd killed his thirteenth victim; he was Herbert Mullin (spelled Mullen in some sources), age 25.

It was soon learned that he had been institutionalized in 1969 for shaving his hair and burning himself after hearing voices but had been released. Hospitalized and released again, he became a drifter. According to his account, he had stopped taking his antipsychotic medication and had then "heard" a voice that urged him to kill. He believed that the earth "understood" when its death rate was too low and it triggered a natural disaster to rectify the situation. Thus, it became Mullin's mission to save the people of California from a super earthquake that was going to break up the state and send it into the ocean. (Sometimes he referred to it as "my continent.") He could do that by creating "small disasters." He decided that he had to "sing the die song" to persuade thirteen people to either kill themselves or allow themselves to become human sacrifices (which he said they conveyed to him telepathically). With a knife, rifle, revolver, and baseball bat, he attacked his victims at random until police picked him up. Diagnosed with paranoid schizophrenia, he pleaded not guilty by reason of insanity. Nevertheless, a jury found him to be legally sane and they convicted him on two counts of first-degree and eight counts of second-degree murder (with another one added later).[1]

A number of killers were clearly psychotic when they committed multiple murder, but rarely does a jury find such a person not guilty by reason of insanity. That can be attributed in some cases to fear that the offender might be released at some point should he or she be incarcerated in a psychiatric hospital. Yet it's also true that psychosis, a psychological condition, does not necessarily imply insanity, a legal definition. One can be delusional at the time of a crime but still appreciate that what one is doing is wrong. That's why attorneys on both sides rely on mental health experts to prove precisely what kind of mental state the offender was in at the time of the offense(s).

MENS REA

The legal system is based in the idea that people are rational agents who freely choose their actions, for the most part, and are therefore both responsible and punishable. However, mental health professionals are just as sure that a large part of human behavior is conditioned by factors beyond one's control or awareness. Therefore, culpability is mitigated to some extent, if not fully. Even though a person may have the *actus reus* (did commit the act) he or she may not possess the *mens rea* (ability to intend the act, appreciate its wrongfulness, and foresee the consequences). Both conditions are required to find a person criminally responsible.

The key finding in a criminal proceeding that involves an insanity defense refers to the defendant's state of mind at the time of the offense and the fact that whatever mental illness or disability they may suffer has a bearing on the crime committed. This idea dates back to the Greeks, but more specifically, the wording of the American insanity defense derives from a case in England in 1843. Daniel M'Naghten felt persecuted by imaginary spies and so as a preemptive strike, he shot the Prime Minister's secretary (mistaking him for the Prime Minister). He did intend to kill, but his cognitive impairment was found to be such that the court decided that he did not appreciate that what he was doing was wrong. In response to immediate public outrage, a royal commission reviewed the case and formulated a standard for a finding of insanity: "at the time of the committing of the act, the party accused was laboring under such a defect of reason, from a disease of the mind, as not to know the nature and quality of the act he was doing; or if he did know, that he did not know he was doing what was wrong." That is, the disease or defect robbed the person of the power to be able to freely choose, and he or she would not appreciate criminal sanctions sufficiently to be deterred.

In the United States, over the years there have been attempts at reform, including adding a notion that while one might appreciate the criminality of an act, one is nevertheless compelled to commit the act. In other words, a person may have impaired control over his actions, which can arise from certain psychological conditions. Some serial killers have been thus defended as being either unable to appreciate the wrongfulness of their actions or unable to control their behavior. Certain disorders are often associated with this disability. Before we describe them, let's compare a case that did manage to win an insanity finding with a few that did not.

ABBERRATIONS

When the police went to the 195-acre farm outside Plainfield, Wisconsin, in 1957 to talk to eccentric loner Edward Gein on suspicion of robbery, he was not home. They looked around and entered a summer kitchen, noting the dressed carcass hanging from the rafters. On closer inspection, they were shocked to find that it was the headless, gutted body of a woman, hung upside down. They wondered if this deceased person might be a missing storekeeper named Bernice Worden. They also thought back three years earlier to the missing Mary Hogan, who had been shot and carried away.

Then inside the house, searchers found a disgusting scene: chair seats made of human skin, a box of preserved female genitalia, another box containing four women's noses, a belt made of nipples, a heart in a bag near the stove, the crania from several skulls, intestines in the refrigerator, preserved death masks taken off nine women, a female skin vest complete with genitals, a face and scalp with black hair (later identified as Mary Hogan's), Worden's head between two mattresses, and a pair of lips hanging from a string. Once everything was collected, it appeared that Gein, the seemingly harmless recluse, had the parts of at least fifteen women in his home. He had also kept his deceased mother's bedroom as a perfectly preserved shrine to her memory.

Taken in for questioning, Gein readily admitted to stealing parts for the past ten years from freshly dead female bodies in the cemetery. He had also killed both Bernice Worden and Mary Hogan, because they seemed the right size for supplying what he needed for his skin suit (which he wore to dance in the moonlight). He seemed unaware that what he had done was wrong. The bizarre case drew international attention, especially among those who studied criminal psychology, and they made much of the fact that Gein had been raised by a puritanical, domineering mother, now dead, after his alcoholic father and brother had died years earlier. She had taught him that sex was perverse and wicked, "causing" a mental imbalance. Thus, he had become sexually confused. Gein had been an avid reader of books on human anatomy, cannibalism, and Nazi experiments, sending away for shrunken heads to decorate his home (which he even showed to children).

At a hearing in 1958, Gein was declared mentally ill and committed for an indeterminate period to a psychiatric institution. Twelve years went by and he was determined to be competent to stand trial for the murder of Bernice Worden. Circuit Judge Robert Gollmar found him guilty of first-degree murder, but during the penalty phase, Gein was declared not guilty by reason of insanity and recommitted. In 1974, he filed a petition, claiming he was recovered and should be set free. His petition was rejected. He died of respiratory failure in 1984 and was buried next to his mother.[2]

Peter William Sutcliffe was not so fortunate. He was arrested in 1981 after a six-year investigation in Britain for the murders attributed to the "Yorkshire Ripper." It began with prostitutes, as letters signed "Jack the Ripper" came to the police, with similar taunts. But these murders were more brutal than Red Jack's, and less frequent. A female corpse discovered in Leeds in 1975 had been found to be battered to death in the head with a hammer, as well as stabbed all over her throat, breasts, and genitals fourteen times. Another victim was found three months later, but then a year went by before there were seven murders in the course of fifteen months. All had been bludgeoned and slashed. In some cases, the killer mutilated the victims' genitals, and while the initial victims were prostitutes, the pool soon included working girls and college students. The Ripper also switched to a screwdriver, stabbing one victim in the eyes. There were survivors who bore extreme disfigurements.

When questioned by police on the suspicion of picking up prostitutes, Peter Sutcliffe, 35, married, and a former mortuary worker, had a ball-peen hammer and two knives in his possession (which he had tried hiding in the bushes). Under interrogation by the Ripper Murder Squad, he gave in and confessed for sixteen hours to twenty mutilation assaults and thirteen murders. In his truck, police found the following note: "In this truck is a man whose latent genius if unleashed would rock the nation, whose dynamic energy would overpower those around him." His "diminished responsibility" defense was based on a claim that God's voice had issued from a grave he'd been digging to order him to kill prostitutes: He'd had a "divine mission" (as well as an agenda of revenge for being cheated by one). Both sides agreed that he had paranoid schizophrenia, but the Crown maintained that he was nevertheless sane during the attacks. He was convicted of murder and sentenced to life in prison.[3]

Seemingly easier to judge was the series of murders associated with Richard Trenton Chase, "the Vampire of Sacramento." He drank other people's blood, he claimed, because he was afraid of disintegrating. He had been institutionalized several times, diagnosed with schizophrenia, and had a history of being preoccupied with any sign that something was wrong with him; he had once entered an emergency room, for example, looking for the person who had stolen his pulmonary artery. He also complained that the bones were coming out through the back of his head and his stomach was backwards. He was diagnosed with a drug-induced psychosis, due to his substance abuse.

Chase began to catch and torture cats, dogs, and rabbits, killing them to drink their blood. Then early in 1978, after he'd shot a man just to see what it was like, he walked into the home of Teresa Wallin, 22, and three months pregnant. He shot her twice and then dragged her body to the bedroom. With a knife, he carved off her left nipple, cut open her torso, and stabbed her repeatedly. He also had cut out her kidneys and severed her pancreas in two. He placed the kidneys together back inside her. Then he got a yogurt container from the trash so he could use it to drink her blood.

On January 27, Chase entered another home and killed Evelyn Miroth, 38, a male friend, and her six-year-old son. Chase also grabbed her infant son from his cradle, smashed the boy's head, and took the body away with him. Back at home, he removed the head and may have consumed several of the organs.

The police closed in and arrested him as he was leaving his apartment. In prison, he told another inmate that he needed the blood of his victims because of blood poisoning, and he'd grown tired of hunting for animals. One might think, with his well-documented history of delusions and disturbed relationship with reality, it would be easy to win an insanity acquittal, but that was not the case. Chase was convicted of six counts of first-degree murder and sentenced to be executed. Instead he died a few years later in his cell from a drug overdose.[4]

Even more apparently obvious was the case in Philadelphia involving Harrison "Marty" Graham. After he was evicted from his apartment due to obnoxious odors, the police found the decomposing corpses of six women, with the disarticulated skeleton of a seventh. Initially, Graham, 28, tried to claim the bodies were there when he moved in, but then he confessed to having strangled them all accidentally during sex. He was usually high on drugs. Despite his insanity plea and his attorney's constant insistence that he was incompetent to have waived his rights, confessed, or stood trial, a judge convicted him in every case, including seven counts of abuse of a corpse. His death penalty was later commuted to life.

But Graham did have a long history of mental deficiency, as attested to by his mother and a foster mother who had him in her care from the age of two to seven. Both insisted that he'd never quite caught on. He was not able to learn much, especially not right from wrong. A former girlfriend claimed that he had frequent conversations with a ragged, dirty puppet.

Yet because he was an articulate man, given to reading the Bible (and later in prison became an ordained minister), the court considered him to be smarter than his associates were claiming. Despite his bizarre ability to live in the same room with putrid corpses, he seemed to grasp that what he had done was wrong.[5]

PSYCHOTIC DISORDERS

Extreme mental illness involves bizarre and disturbed emotions, behaviors, thoughts, and beliefs that may interfere with a person's ability to function in work and relationships; it often isolates the person. In severe forms, it can make people dangerous to others and/or themselves. Since the middle of the nineteenth century, psychiatry has attempted to categorize the types of mental illnesses seen in individuals, and this has been formalized in various texts, notably the *International Classification of Diseases* (ICD) and *The Diagnostic and Statistical Manual of Mental Disorders*, now called the DSM-IV-TR. The illnesses are coded in this manual for health insurers and crystallized in terms of symptoms to facilitate professional dialogue.

The most prevalent of the psychotic disorders, schizophrenia, is marked by a confusion of thinking and speech that is at times chronic. It occurs equally in men and women, and generally manifests between the ages of fifteen and thirty-five. There appears to be a significant genetic component, in that a person may inherit a tendency toward it that can be triggered by an outside stressor.[6]

Schizophrenia often causes sufferers to retreat into delusions and fantasies that disturb their relationship with reality. For example, "Railway Killer" Angel Maturino Resendez, 40, claimed that it was his duty to rape and kill nine people in three states, because they were evil. Resendez also believed that he could travel while asleep, become invisible, and affect weather patterns. He thought that the reason that he had evaded the police for two years was because of his superhuman speed and God's protection. Police tracking dogs, he said, did not want to confront a "wolf-tiger angel with a dinosaur look." The jury rejected his insanity defense and he was convicted of first-degree murder.[7]

Research evidence suggests that the cause of schizophrenia is either a chemical or structural abnormality of the brain. Initial symptoms include a feeling of tension, sleep disturbances, and loss of interest in things. In its worst phases, people experience delusions, hallucinations, or disordered speech. Some people with this disease do develop violent tendencies, especially those who experience command hallucinations such as Mullen and Sutcliffe claimed to hear.

A sadistic killer from the 1930s, Albert Fish, came to the attention of law enforcement when he abducted a young girl, Grace Budd, whom he had taken to "a birthday party." They never returned, but six years later, the Budds received an anonymous note in which the writer described how he had killed and cooked Grace into a soup. Fish was caught and an investigation turned up a bizarre psychological history. He had long been a religious fanatic with an obsession with punishment. He secretly beat himself with spiked paddles, stuck needles deep into his groin (and they stayed there), and lit alcohol-soaked cotton balls inside his anus. He desperately wanted to pull off his fingernails but could not stand the pain. He believed he was the biblical Abraham, and just as God had called Abraham to sacrifice his only son, Fish decided he needed to murder children. It's estimated that he may have molested over one hundred children in twenty-three states (he claimed four hundred) and from one castrated boy he drank blood. He also slaughtered a boy with a knife, eating some parts, but it was the murder of Grace Budd that got him convicted and executed (which thrilled him) in 1936.[8]

Schizophrenia is a lifelong illness with no known cure. Antipsychotic drugs may help to stabilize brain chemistry, but must be taken under close supervision. There are many criminal cases in which a person had stopped taking medication. In fact, some people with schizophrenia have been considered competent to proceed through the various stages of the criminal process, including defending themselves. Colin Ferguson, the man guilty of a spree killing one rush-hour evening on the Long Island Railroad, was one example. Another, who didn't quite get that far but who wanted to defend himself was "Unabomber" Theodore John Kaczynski, who killed three people and injured more than two dozen others with a series of mail bombs. He had also penned a 35,000-word rambling manifesto against the modern world and was arrested in 1996.

In early 1998, Kaczynski was having a difference of opinion with his defense team. They hoped to mount a mental health defense, as Kaczynski had been diagnosed with schizophrenia, but he was not amenable. He wanted to represent himself. While he was considered competent to stand trial, his request to go *pro se* was considered a delaying tactic and was denied. Kaczynski saw no way out of accepting an insanity defense, so he pleaded guilty to thirteen of the crimes in exchange for a life sentence with no possibility of parole.

Yet he continued to seek to set aside his plea and represent himself in court. In 1999, with legal assistance, Kaczynski filed a *pro se* appellate brief. He argued that he had been "railroaded into pleading guilty" and that the plea was "involuntarily made because his defense team threatened to put on a mental-defect defense." The Ninth Circuit U.S. Court of Appeals considered his reasoning but found it less than compelling and denied the appeal.[9]

Another mental disorder that can have psychotic episodes is bipolar affective disorder, once known as manic-depressive disorder. It is a cyclical disturbance characterized by dramatic mood swings between mania and depression, and people suffering from it may have intense periods of high energy in which they seem superhuman. They go without rest for long periods of time, have grandiose ideas, and accomplish an astonishing amount. However, they may then swing into serious depression, sometimes accompanied by delusions and thoughts of suicide. They may hear voices during either phase, but between phases, they may feel normal.

THE OTHER GUY DID IT

Among mental health professionals, the diagnosis of dissociative identity disorder (DID) is the label in the DSM-IV for what prior to 1994 was called multiple personality disorder (MPD). It's commonly been confused with schizophrenia as a split personality. The idea of DID is that a person has fractured into several alter personalities and that two or more subpersonalities share a single body, each with its own identity and each taking turns controlling the personality and behavior. They're believed to emerge as a result of trauma (even this is disputed), such as sexual abuse, and they usually emerge before the age of five. To some extent, as some experts have written, the "alters" arise to protect the "core personality" from overwhelming memories. Some alters appear to form from forbidden impulses as well.

Often during the 1980s and early 1990s, DID emerged in therapy while dealing with repressed memories. Experts indicate that a traumatic memory that is not recalled may still have the energy to emerge in symptoms like depression, numbness, hypersensitivity, and reactions to certain environmental triggers that may touch on that memory. There may also be vague flashbacks. These people may "trance out," feel out of touch with reality, ignore genuine pain, and experience sudden panic attacks. They may also develop eating disorders and other addictions, and abuse others or themselves. Generally, they have trouble with intimacy and may experience any number of sexual dysfunctions and sleep disturbances.[10]

While the authenticity of DID is still debated, a number of criminals have spotted the potential for mitigating their acts, and even to get away with them. Some serial killers have made the claim of having multiple personalities as a way to evade responsibility. For example, John Wayne Gacy, who killed thirty-three young men, attempted to attribute the murders to "Jack Hanley," an alter personality. After he confessed and drew a map of the crawl space beneath his home where he'd placed more than two dozen of his victims, he "tranced out" and pretended that Hanley had actually drawn the map. However, his ploy did not work and he soon dropped it, in preference to another psychiatric diagnosis—that blacking out while drinking had provided conditions for an "irresistible impulse" each time he killed. That did not work for him, either.[11]

"Gainesville Ripper" Danny Rolling attempted to say that he had been under the influence of "Gemini" while he committed five murders in Florida. However, authorities learned that Rolling was a fan of the movie *Exorcist III*, in which "Gemini" emerged from a helpless priest in a psychiatric institution and directed several brutal murders. Rolling was convicted.[12]

The killer most often associated with faking a "bad" personality that made him kill is Kenneth Bianchi, one member of the team known as the "Hillside Stranglers." They emerged in Los Angeles in 1977, and over the course of a few months, nine women were found murdered and dumped along roadways or on the hillside. Witnesses had spotted two males with one victim, whch indicated that more than one killer was at work. The tenth woman was left inside the trunk of her car, but it took solving a double homicide in Bellevue, Washington, to weave together the leads in a way that pointed to Kenneth Bianchi and his cousin, Angelo Buono.

While Bianchi was in prison, his attorney asked psychiatrist John Watkins to examine him. Watkins put Bianchi under hypnosis, got him to admit to several of the murders and implicate his cousin, and then declared that he had MPD. Since he had killed as "Steve Walker," he was not competent to stand trial. Three more experts were convinced of Bianchi's condition as well.

The prosecutor hired his own expert, Dr. Martin Orne, who knew that detectives had discovered that "Steve Walker" was the name of a college student from whom Bianchi had stolen transcripts to set up a fake psychiatric practice. To trap him, Dr. Orne devised a ploy: he suggested to Bianchi that most people with MPD have more than two personalities, and it wasn't long before "Billy" emerged. Bianchi also pretended to touch someone who was not there, but hallucinating is not a symptom, and the authorities knew then that Bianchi was malingering. Under pressure, he admitted to the deception. That gave the prosecutor leverage to get him to plead to seven murders and testify against his cousin. In 1983, the jury convicted Buono of nine murders and gave him nine life sentences.[13]

The issue came up in the trial of Arthur Shawcross, charged with the murder of ten women in Rochester, New York, from 1988 to 1989. Despite his detailed confessions, his attorneys mounted a defense of "not guilty by reason of insanity." To be considered insane in New York State, Shawcross had to demonstrate that at the time of each offense, he suffered from a mental disease or defect such that either he did not know what he was doing or was unable to appreciate that it was wrong.

The defense attorney hired Dr. Dorothy Lewis, a psychiatrist and expert on the effect of organic disorders on violence. Lewis believed that Shawcross had been severely traumatized as a child and suffered from incomplete temporal lobe seizures that blocked his memory. The seizures occurred only under certain circumstances, such as when he was alone with prostitutes at night. Shawcross assisted her by agreeing to hypnosis, which she taped to show in court. Lewis was frustrated with the defense team's inability to get the brain scans she needed to prove her case neurologically. She also was unaware that another defense expert had questioned Shawcross at the same time—which may have influenced what Shawcross told her. Thus, her hope to use him as a good example of her theory became problematic.[14]

Dr. Park Dietz, for the prosecution, stated that Shawcross suffered from antisocial personality disorder, which was not considered a mental disease or defect that thwarted awareness. He had remembered his crimes sufficiently to provide details and lead the police to two more victims. He had also tried to avoid detection and apprehension, so he knew that what he was doing was wrong and could get him arrested. In fact, he'd been in prison before for sexual homicide. After a five-week trial, the jury found Shawcross to be sane and guilty of ten counts of murder in the second degree. He received ten sentences of twenty-five years to life.[15]

No matter whether someone is delusional, egotistical, or killing for thrill, serial killing is often motivated as well by anger and revenge. Let's examine some cases that exhibit this trigger.

NOTES

1. Donald T. Lunde and Jefferson Morgan, *The Die Song: A Journey into the Mind of a Mass Murderer* (New York: W. W. Norton, 1980).

2. Robert H. Gollmar, *Edward Gein: America's Most Bizarre Murderer* (New York: Pinnacle Books, 1984); Harold Schechter, *Deviant: The Shocking True Story of the Original 'Psycho'* (New York: Pocket, 1989).

3. Gordon Burns, *The Story of the Yorkshire Ripper* (New York: Viking, 1985).

4. Ray Biondi, *The Dracula Killer* (New York: Pocket, 1992).

5. Articles from *The Philadelphia Inquirer*, between August 1987 and December 1988.

6. *Diagnostic and Statistical Manual of Mental Disorders-IV* (Washington, D.C.: American Psychiatric Association, 1994; Richard Noll, *The Encyclopedia of Schizophrenia and the Psychotic Disorders* (New York: Facts on File, 1992).

7. Wensley Clarkson, *The Railroad Killer: The Shocking True Story of Angel Maturino Resendez* (New York: St. Martin's Press, 1999).

8. Harold Schechter, *Deranged: The Shocking True Story of America's Most Fiendish Killer* (New York: Pocket, 1990).

9. Marcia Coyle, "Unabomber May Seek to Nullify Guilty Plea," *The Recorder* (Washington), February 10, 1999.

10. Colin Ross, *Multiple Personality Disorder: Diagnosis, Clinical Features, and Treatment* (New York: Wiley, 1989); Joan Acocella, "The Politics of Hysteria," *The New Yorker*, April 6, 1998.

11. Terry Sullivan and Peter Maiken, *Killer Clown: The John Wayne Gacy Murders* (New York: Grosset & Dunlap, 1983).

12. John Philpin and John Donnelly, *Beyond Murder: The Inside Account of the Gainesville Student Murders* (New York: Onyx, 1994).

13. Ted Schwartz, *The Hillside Strangler: A Murderer's Mind* (Garden City, NY: Doubleday, 1981); Darcy O'Brien, *Two of a Kind: The Hillside Stranglers* (New York: New American Library, 1985).

14. Dorothy Lewis, *Guilty by Reason of Insanity* (New York: Ballantine, 1998).

15. Gregg McCrary, with Katherine Ramsland, *The Unknown Darkness: Profiling the Predators among Us* (New York: Morrow, 2003), pp. 37–73.

CHAPTER 7

Rage

It could be argued that people who murder from anger or rage might be classifiable as extended spree killers, since a spree killer's rampage is generally related to a single precipitating incident. Yet for some of these killers, a predatory element invades the act to such an extent that they can just as easily be classified as serial killers. Categories about human nature can never be rigid or absolute.

The killers described and examined in this chapter clearly have an anger-inspired agenda, even if other motives, such as sexual thrill, control, or profit, are apparent as well. Like a mass murderer, who fails to digest life's insults and thus allows rage to build to the point where he (or she) may finally grab a gun with the intent of punishing those who insulted him, some serial killers also keep the embers of rage glowing hot so they can stoke the fire of action when needed, and for them, that often becomes highly satisfying, even erotic.

MAKING THEM PAY

When Pakistani police dismissed a criminal complaint filed by Javed Iqbal against two servant boys who had beaten him, he plotted revenge. He was angry not just by the unpunished attack but by the fact that the police had even accused him of inspiring an act of sodomy. Iqbal was wealthy, with time and resources on his hands to carry out a rather elaborate plan, so he set to work getting the supplies and accomplices that he needed. No matter how much energy he expended on the project, his resolve never faltered. That's because the force of his anger did not die.

When he was ready to act with a vengeance against a world that he had grown to hate, he put his plan into motion.

In 1999, over a period of six months, the thirty-seven-year-old merchant enticed street children to his apartment in Lahore with the promise of a meal and a place to sleep. Three accomplices, including a thirteen-year-old boy, assisted him. Once a targeted child was vulnerable, Iqbal would asphyxiate him with cyanide. Then he would dissolve the body in a vat of acid and dump the liquid paste into a local sewer. He kept a detailed journal of each incident, including the cost incurred. He also included photographs of each victim and saved his clothing and personal effects, so when the time came he could prove what he had done. He knew each of the names and ages of the dead adolescents, and he would regularly count up his tally. Then he reached one hundred. At that point, he had achieved his goal.

Iqbal turned himself in to the Pakistani authorities. In a letter, he explained that he wanted one hundred mothers to cry for their children. He later said that he could easily have killed five hundred without anyone being the wiser, but he had made a pact with himself as to exactly how many he would kill. The police lost no time in arresting this dangerous predator.

On March 16, 2000, the court in Lahore, Pakistan, sentenced Iqbal to be strangled in front of the families of his victims and cut into 100 pieces for the 100 victims, which would be dissolved in acid—an eye for an eye. His accomplices received sentences from forty-two years in prison to execution. Iqbal appealed his death sentence, and the highest Islamic court had agreed to hear it, but four days later, on October 25, 2001, Iqbal used poison to commit suicide in his cell. So did his thirteen-year-old accomplice.[1]

For similar reasons of anger, humiliation, and rage, Saeed Hanaei killed sixteen prostitutes in Iran over a period of two years, strangling them with their own scarves and dumping them in the streets. After Hanaei was arrested, he denied being a crusader against prostitution. Instead, he said he was avenging his wife, who had been mistaken as a prostitute—a humiliating accusation anywhere, but particularly in this society where honor comes before all else. Hanaei had decided that the error had occurred due to the large number of loose women available in Mashad, so he decided he should kill some for creating the conditions that had caused his wife's humiliation. He not only expressed no remorse but said that if he had not killed enough, he would lose sleep. (Oddly, he had utilized their services before strangling them.) The court sentenced him to hanging, which took place on April 18, 2002.[2]

SOMETHING LACKING

Anger arises not just as a reaction to something someone has done but can result from envy and spite. One offender in the Ukraine invaded several homes to slaughter whole families, forcing them to sit together and blasting them with a shotgun. Called "the Terminator," Anatoly Onoprienko terrorized the area, murdering a dozen women and numerous random strangers before he committed wholesale slaughter during the first four months of 1995. Then after taking whatever he could from a family's belongings, he would burn down their home. Sometimes he scattered family photographs, as if the very idea of kinship enraged him, and some experts believe this may have been due to the fact that Onoprienko had been left at an orphanage when he was one year old. His mother had died so his father had made some choices: keep the older son at home and give up the younger one. Onoprienko also killed people nearby or in neighboring houses, as if to eliminate even a potential witness. Some were shot, some bludgeoned to death, a few were attacked with an ax, and four were burned to death.

Over a period of seven years, Onoprienko murdered an estimated fifty-two people, and he would have continued but for his cousin, who feared for his own family after arguing with Onoprienko, and thus alerted the police. They found possessions from the victims in his girlfriend's home. Onoprienko was not remorseful during his confession. In fact, he thought the authorities ought to study him, because he had "powers." He said that "voices from above" had ordered him to kill, but given the rampaging nature of his final months and the generally prickly and vengeful nature of his personality, it seems more likely that he killed in anger.[3]

Studies that indicate that serial killers come from abusive homes have involved too few subjects to be representative, so it's difficult to say whether abuse or neglect have strong causal associations with compulsive killing. But there are many situations that can frustrate a person—abuse or abandonment among them—so let's examine a few of the studies that have explored the relationship of anger to homicide.

THE COMFORT OF ANGER

Given what we have said thus far about the way in which many serial killers (if not most) get their start in their fantasy life, it should be clear that this is the cauldron that blends emotional, cognitive, and behavioral processes. Violent fantasies grounded in anger, which is an aggressive reaction to an unpleasant situation, serve several purposes. They:

- provide a secret world of comfort and narcissistic indulgence
- feed the need to act out
- offer possible scenarios for acting out
- provide a means for recycling frustration and anger into images that feel better
- develop private self-esteem from acts of bravado, control, or revenge

- reinforce a sense of entitlement
- allow indulgence in the most extreme perversities
- fuel momentum when opportunity knocks
- reinforce acts of murder and prepare the way for more
- perfect the *modus operandi*
- provide a way to secretly relive the crime

Since this chapter focuses on rage, let's look at the idea that killers find in their secret fantasy life a place for recycling frustration. Given their general sense of narcissism and entitlement, they will not easily resolve their anger—they don't want to. For some, this is equivalent to being weak or less masculine. Instead, they're more likely to remain angry and to even let it build. They ruminate, get depressed, feel mistreated, dwell on the past experience, and probably minimize their role in it while exaggerating the role of others. Blame is a strong factor in keeping anger alive. Those "others" who caused the distressing situation will now become objects in their fantasy, upon which they will take out their rage.

This kind of anger becomes chronic and forms into revenge scenarios, religious missions, or power plays. The disturbed individuals can envision acting out against a visible target—prostitutes who don't help them sexually perform, women who look like their nagging mothers, children who are at an age at which *they* were abused, patients in hospitals who represent their own frightening vulnerability. Thus, when they do act out under the influence of these compelling drives, the victims are often symbolic punching bags. They bear the brunt of the killers' need and they are forced to feel the pain that the killers have long harbored inside themselves.

Anthony Beech, Dawn Fisher, and Tony Ward found that sexual murderers shared the same implicit theories as rapists, but murder itself derived from a certain combination. These researchers interviewed twenty-eight sexual murderers and identified five ideas that appeared to be motivators to one degree or another for extreme crimes: the world is dangerous, the male sex drive is uncontrollable, women are sexual objects, women are unknowable, and personal entitlement. All five beliefs were found in rapists as well, but only when the first two were combined—the world is dangerous and the male sex drive is uncontrollable—was an individual motivated specifically to rape and kill. If they believed that the world was dangerous but not that the sex drive was uncontrollable, they were motivated to kill primarily by anger and resentment against women, and if they did not perceive the world as dangerous but did view the sex drive as out of their control, they were motivated to rape, but usually only killed to secure cooperation or to remove a witness. Thus, anger itself can be a causal factor in sexual murders.[4]

When interviewed, several killers have expressed rage at women in general or prostitutes in particular. For them, serial murder is a statement as well as a way to express (and derive relief from) their frustration. Despite the fact that their victims are immaterial to their situations, they choose people who symbolize their anger, either due to looks, profession, age, or the way the person treats them. Anger provides an adrenaline rush, and when it's coupled with poor impulse control, there's little to hinder a person's intent on rage-motivated murder. In the moment, it feels good. They've rehearsed this solution to their frustration in their fantasies, so the pleasure from killing has become ingrained in them as a routine response.

Duncan Cartwright studied the predisposing personality of the rage murderer, based on a study of nine offenders, and found that they were able to split reality into an external world and an internal world. A degree of dissociation occurs during the act of murder, which is precipitated by an innocuous external event. In other words, the explosive intensity of rage murder is well beyond what the stimulus should have provoked. While Cartwright focused on sudden murder that was out of character for the offender, he offers insights that we can apply to serial murder.

He describes the origination of murderous impulses from the feeling of internal threat, and the person decides to annihilate the threat. Vulnerability to committing such murders derives from intrapsychic qualities; in other words, it's a defense against damage to an already vulnerable or deficient personality. Aggression functions to preserve the inner world. Early problems in childhood, be they from abuse or an inability to adapt to the world, can make the person inflexible, with a tendency to control (even overcontrol) situations. But their hostility and rigidity set them up for failure, which escalates their desperation to keep their inner world intact. If they can't control, they're going to *be* controlled, but that frightens them. When the triggers are just right, they can react quickly, with extreme violence.[5]

Anger can develop early, due to circumstances and a person's inability to control his or her surroundings. Carl Panzram, self-described as "the meanest man alive," is a good example. Panzram's crime spree during the early part of the twentieth century lasted eighteen years, taking place on at least two continents. Arrested for drunkenness when he was only eight, Panzram lived a hard life. After going to a reform school where he suffered numerous beatings and "learned man's inhumanity to man," he resolved to commit destruction wherever he could. He often retaliated for acts he did not like by burning down buildings.

In his diary Panzram referred to himself as "the spirit of meanness personified" and attributed his foul temper to endless abuse from family, religion, and prison guards. When he experienced a rare period of caring, he wrote, "If in the beginning I had been treated as I am now, then there wouldn't have been quite so many people in this world that have been robbed, raped, and killed."[6] He murdered, raped, and sodomized indiscriminately after luring victims into situations of vulnerability. He thought that killing people was fun, admitting to twenty-one murders, and added that he had sodomized over one thousand men. At trial for burglary, he told the courtroom that if he was released he would kill the judge and jury. Panzram represented himself at his trial, hoping to inspire the jury to give him the death sentence, which he received. Until he was executed, he spent his time reading the philosophies of Friedrich Nietzsche. He hated the whole human race, he claimed, and wanted to kill everyone. In 1930, he was executed.[7]

When killing is cathartic, it has little to do with the actual target victim and will likely continue under similar circumstances. Let's examine a case in which killing appeared to play out as a rigid ritual.

ANGER AND RITUAL

Former investigator Robert R. Keppel states, "Almost all sex offenders, especially signature killers, need to demonstrate a degree of total control over the victim, whether she's living or dead. They have to; anger drives them to do it."[8] He describes a signature killer (one that leaves a personal behavioral imprint at a crime scene) that he had assisted to investigate in Claremont, California, near San Diego, who attacked white women. Early in 1990, this man entered the apartments of three different women and murdered them. A fourth victim turned up in her home, and by September "the Claremont Killer" had attacked a mother and daughter in their home, murdering them both. It was not difficult to link these crimes, as the perpetrator had left a distinct signature—piquerism. That is, he liked to stab and gouge with a sharp implement. In particular, he aimed at the heart and left breast, stabbing deeply in that area many times. Signature analysis, which noted both the overkill and the ritual involved, indicated that this man was angry and felt a need to control his victims.

The Claremont Killer removed most of his victims' clothing, stabbed them multiple times, and left them on their backs, posed provocatively. He also moved in and out of a victim's home with relative ease, left items strewn about, and often discarded the knife he had used right there, as if in a statement of defiance to investigators. From the manner of brutalizing the victims beyond what was necessary to kill them and from the type of deep stabbing he preferred (especially on the breast), it seemed clear that he was stimulated by violence, and since only one victim had been physically raped, the knife was thought to be a substitute for penile penetration.

A failed break-in led to the arrest of a black man, Cleophus Prince, Jr., 25, who had lived in the area. He had joined the same health club as some of his victims, leading to speculation that he'd followed them from there to their homes. He often took a piece of jewelry from them as a trophy.

Keppel believed that the killer was sadistic. He had not stabbed his victims in a frenzy, but had sunk the knife in slowly, with satisfaction. He stabbed to the depth of an erect penis. "The killer was obsessed with the stimulation of penetrating the victims." He left the knife behind at three scenes as if to "show" the police his prowess. Although Keppel does not disclose what Prince admitted to, he indicates that Prince's primary pleasure came from seeing blood flow from the breasts of women.[9]

Yet sometimes the killer does want to talk, and in doing so reveals the source of his anger.

STAND-INS

Edmund Kemper III murdered his paternal grandparents at the age of 15 in 1964. His grandmother had made him angry, he later said, so he'd shot and stabbed her to "see what it felt like" and eliminated his grandfather to "spare" him. Kemper then called his mother, who urged him to turn himself in. He was placed into the California juvenile system, but released in 1969 with a clean record. Soon the six-foot-nine giant with a genius IQ was ready to kill again, his anger and rage not sated with the first two murders.

In 1972 and 1973, Kemper noticed young females out hitchhiking and envisioned things he could do to them. He picked them up, sometimes two at a time. Often he played a game with himself, allowing some to be free while others were shot, stabbed, or strangled. "I'm picking up young women," Kemper explained to the police in a later confession, "and I'm going a little bit farther each time. It's a daring kind of thing.... We go to a vulnerable place, where there aren't people watching, where I could act out and I say, 'No, I can't.' ... And this craving, this awful raging eating feeling inside, this fantastic passion. It was overwhelming me. It was like drugs. It was like alcohol. A little isn't enough."[10]

His first murder involved two girls on May 7, 1972. Mary A. Pesce and Anita Luchessa, both 18, were stabbed, decapitated, and dissected. Kemper got away with it and secretly enjoyed the news coverage as the parts were found. His next opportunity arrived in the form of a fifteen-year-old dance student, Aiko Koo, on September 14. Kemper picked her up, suffocated and strangled her. Then, in the fashion of his more informed fantasies, he removed her head and limbs. Another four months passed without any incident, but then between January and April, Kemper murdered three more young women. All were shot and decapitated. Finally Kemper got into one more fight with his demeaning mother, and he decided that she was the one all along whom he'd wanted to kill. On April 20, 1973, he talked with Clarnell Kemper for a while and then bludgeoned, decapitated, and dismembered her, removing her larynx to shove down the garbage disposal. For good measure, he invited his mother's friend, Sara Hallett, over and killed her as well. He fled to Colorado, but then turned himself in. Once with the police he began to talk, describing how angry he had been with his mother over the years and how each murder was an extension of that.

On November 8, 1973, Kemper, 24, was found guilty of eight counts of first-degree murder. Although he hoped to receive the death penalty (with torture), he was convicted during a time when the U.S. Supreme Court had placed a moratorium on capital punishment, so he received life.

Most of what is known about Kemper comes from his own accounts, so it's not clear how much is accurate, but there is corroborating information that his parents neglected him. His mother insisted that he sleep in the basement, which frightened him, and his father refused to take him in when he asked. As a child, Kemper wished that everyone else in the world would die, and he envisioned killing them himself. He also indulged in tormenting cats. He'd buried one alive, then dug it up to cut off its head.

Kemper got his ideas for how to murder the coeds from his fantasies, and collected tidbits from crime novels about how to give his targeted victims the impression that they were safe. Sometimes he picked up girls and let them go. But finally he felt what he called his "little zapples," and acted.[11]

Dr. Donald Lunde, a psychiatrist who interviewed Kemper at the time of his arrest, thought he exhibited complete awareness and relished the perversions to which he had admitted, including cannibalism and necrophilia. Lunde believed that Kemper's sexual aggression stemmed from a combination of childhood anger and violent fantasies. His ambivalent relationship with his mother was common to sexual sadists, Lunde said; they generally kill their mothers in their fantasy worlds.[12]

Of course, not all rage killers are male. At least one mass murderer was a female, Sylvia Seegrist, and she killed out of anger over people's treatment of her. Also, in January 2006, police in Mexico City indicated that a former female wrestler, charged in the strangulation murders of at least ten elderly women, had acted out of anger at her mother for abandoning her and at a caretaker for sexually assaulting her. Juana Barazza, 48, was caught fleeing from one crime scene and fingerprints tied her to the others. She had taken small objects from the victims as trophies.[13]

While Aileen Wuornos is often classified as a lust murderer, there is no reason to believe that she killed to attain sexual satisfaction. She waffled between her stated motivations, from killing in self-defense to robbery, but it's evident from her patterns that she was an angry woman who targeted men. Having been abused by men much of her life, it seems likely that her crimes were fueled by rage. If she merely wanted to profit, she could have robbed them. But the way she spoke about her crimes, and her demeanor in court, indicates that anger drove her, and the enjoyment was the result of appeasing that anger.

HELL'S FURY

Wuornos has been the subject of countless books, articles, and movies— even an opera. She indicated in an interview before her execution in 2003 that if she were released, she would kill again, and that she had planned the robbery and murder of her seven victims rather than reacting to their abuse of her, as she had earlier stated.

It started in December 1989 when an abandoned car was found not far from Daytona Beach, Florida, with bloody seats. Papers indicated the car belonged to Richard Mallory, known to pick up prostitutes. Two weeks later, Mallory's corpse was found in the woods, shot four times in the chest with a .22-caliber gun.

While this was Wuornos' first murder, it was not necessarily the first man she wanted to kill. According to the story she told to psychologists later, her mother had abandoned her as an infant and her schizophrenic father had been imprisoned for the rape of a seven-year-old. With a murder investigation on, he had hanged himself in his cell. Aileen and her brother had been forced to live with her maternal grandparents, and her grandfather was an abusive alcoholic. When a friend of his (she said) impregnated her when she was only fourteen, she was forced to have the baby and give it up for adoption. Her grandfather then kicked her out of the house, so she turned tricks to survive.

At the age of seventeen, she hitched out to Denver and then Florida. Along the way, as she plied her trade, she was beaten and raped several times. She met Tyria Moore in Florida, who became her lover, and Wuornos also acquired a gun. After killing Mallory, she waited five months before her next victim. In May 1991, David Spears's truck was found along a Florida highway and his naked corpse was discovered about sixty miles away. He, too, had been shot in the chest with a .22. While no fingerprints were found in the car, there was a single strand of blond hair.

Five days later, another male corpse was found, also shot with a .22, and his car was abandoned about sixty miles away. While police did not realize at this point that they had a serial killer, they learned that two women were spotted pulling over in a silver Sunbird and removing the plates. Then they ran into the woods. The car turned out to have belonged to a missing missionary. Then three more male corpses were found, all shot with the same weapon.

Composite pictures were made from witness reports of the two women, and publicized. Several people identified the pictures as a pair of lesbians, Tyria Moore and "Lee"—Aileen Wuornos. She was arrested at a biker bar,

The Last Resort. Police approached Moore, who admitted that Wuornos was a murderer and agreed to get her to talk. On January 16, 1991, Wuornos offered her confession to the murders of seven men. She insisted that she had acted in self-defense. She'd been hitchhiking and they'd picked her up and propositioned her. When they got violent, she shot them.

Wuornos was tried, and defense psychologist Elizabeth McMahon explained that her background had made her paranoid about men, but the prosecutor thought that she lured men with the possibility of sex, and then killed them for their money and possessions. She was a predator. He hammered Wuornos about her motives and she insisted that she was the victim.

Nevertheless, Wuornos was convicted and the jury recommended the death penalty. She called the jury members "scumbags of America." Yet when she went to court in 2001 to dismiss her lawyers and stop her appeals, the judge told her she was now on the "fast track" to the electric chair. At that time she indicated that the prosecutor had been right all along: she was a cold-blooded killer.[14]

Biographer Sue Russell points out that throughout Wuornos' life, she was rejected, humiliated, and abandoned. "Her world was filled with pain, rage, and alcoholism." She sought to be loved by someone, but she inevitably found exploitation and betrayal. "By making a man suffer, Aileen transformed herself from victim to victimizer."[15] She enjoyed the power she felt from dominating them, holding a gun on them, and walking off with their goods as they lay dead. Russell also points out that Wuornos' killing days were preceded by personal stressors, which may have made her feel powerless, so she reacted and regained at least some sense of power. She may also have simply discovered that killing was an easy way to make money. Given the difficulty in pinning Wuornos down to a single explanation, no one really knows, but we do know that Wuornos did feel anger against men and against a society in which she struggled hard to make a living and to find a trusted companion. She may have felt entitled to what she got, given all she had to endure. That, clearly, is rooted in defiance, which feeds off anger.

Given her modus operandi, Wuornos provides a good transition to the next motive, which is profit.

NOTES

1. Harold Schechter, *The Serial Killer Files* (New York: Ballantine, 2003), pp. 108–109.

2. Ibid, p. 28.

3. Michael Newton, *The Encyclopedia of Serial Killers* (New York: Checkmark, 2000), pp. 177–178.

4. Anthony Beech, Dawn Fisher, and Tony Ward, "Sexual Murderers' Implicit Theories," *Journal of Interpersonal Violence*, November 2005, 20(11), 1366–1389.

5. Duncan Cartwright, "The Narcissistic Exoskeleton: The Defensive Organization of the Rage-Type Murderer," *Bulletin of the Menninger Clinic*, Winter 2002, 66(1), 1–18.

6. Thomas Gaddis and James O. Long, *Killer: A Journal of Murder* (New York: Macmillan, 1970), p. 238.

7. David K. Frasier, *Murder Cases of the Twentieth Century* (Jefferson, NC: McFarland, 1996), pp. 354–356.

8. Robert D. Keppel, with William J. Birnes, *Signature Killers: Interpreting the Calling Card of the Serial Murderer* (New York: Pocket, 1997), p. 26.

9. Ibid., pp. 129–152.

10. Interview footage on "Mugshots," *Courtroom Television*, 1996.

11. Margaret Cheney, *Why—The Serial Killer in America* (Saratoga, CA: R&E Publishing, 1992), pp. 134–145; Ward Damio, *Urge to Kill* (New York: Pinnacle, 1974).

12. Donald T. Lunde, *Murder and Madness* (San Francisco, CA: San Francisco Book Co., 1976), pp. 53–56.

13. Mark Stevenson, "Mexican Police Say Anger Spurred Serial Killer," Associated Press, January 27, 2006.

14. Sue Russell, *Lethal Intent: The Shocking True Story of One of America's Most Notorious Female Serial Killers* (New York: Pinnacle, 2002), p. 377.

15. Ibid., p. 378.

CHAPTER 8

Profit

Dr. Morris Bolber ran an insurance scam ring in Philadelphia during the 1930s that involved the successive murders of an estimated fifty men. Bolber and two cousins, Paul and Harman Petrillo, had devised what seemed a foolproof scheme, and for a while, it was. One would seduce a female patient who seemed unhappy in her marriage and persuade her to have her husband insured for a lot of money. The others would kill him and split the money with the widow. Several more accomplices joined the team, including a female poisoner, and they went about this business for five years before one of them boasted about it and got the entire group arrested in 1937, along with a few of the complicit wives. Some widows turned state's evidence, but others went to prison along with the men who had planned the scheme. Two from the original group were executed.[1]

Serial killers throughout the centuries have been motivated by profit, especially during difficult economic times, even if they also derive other pleasures from murder. Aileen Wuornos, for example, appears to have found that while she enjoyed killing, it was also a means for acquiring money and goods. Female serial killers have often killed to improve their circumstances, many of them earning the moniker "black widow," and a woman who murdered even before Jack the Ripper is a good case in point.

BLACK WIDOW

A physician's suspicions about seven-year-old Charlie Cotton proved to be Mary Ann Cotton's undoing. She was among those who poisoned people with arsenic during an era when fatal gastric distress earned a catch-all diagnosis and was generally ignored by doctors who worked among England's poor. But little Charlie's death stood out because it was one among many that were associated with Mary Ann Cotton, and when this boy died, a suspicious doctor decided to perform an autopsy. As it progressed, he noticed signs of malnutrition and he suspected poisoning. However, there was no definitive test for arsenic poisoning at the time, apart from detecting it in the stomach contents, and it wasn't there. So he had no proof against the boy's stepmother.

Yet the villagers in West Auckland knew. Mary Ann Cotton had once poisoned her neighbor's pigs, and acquaintances knew that a lot of people around her had died. Still, she proceeded to collect on the life insurance money, as she had also done when Charlie's father had died. Folks knew that Mary Ann already had another lover—she was even pregnant by him—and they feared for him as well.

The village surgeon was bothered by his findings, so he decided to retest the contents of Charlie's stomach, in case he had made a mistake. This time evidence of arsenic emerged, so he alerted the police. They arrested Mary Ann before she made it to the altar a fifth time, and an investigation into her history revealed a long string of murders, largely done so that she could unburden herself of one family, reap the financial gain, and prepare to "marry up." Each new husband or boyfriend had improved her station in life. Somehow, she had developed the attitude that she was entitled, and that to get what she deserved, it was all right to kill.

Mary Ann had grown up a miner's daughter, but her father died before she was fifteen. By age nineteen, she was married to William Mowbray and was soon pregnant. Over the next several years, they had a daughter and four sons, but all of the boys died of "gastric fever." Mary Ann soon had two more daughters, but both died from the same illness. Another daughter and a son came along, and the son was dead before he reached his first birthday. Then Mary Ann made sure that Mowbray died, and afterward, she danced before her mirror in a new dress.

One more child died, leaving just one girl out of the eight children born to her (so far). To support herself and look for another husband, Mary Ann left the child with her mother and became a nurse. She met George Ward, a patient, and married him. But when he proved disappointing, his end was quick. Thus, by age thirty-three, Mary Ann had killed ten people. She had also collected quite a bit of life insurance. But she was not finished.

A housekeeper for widower James Robinson and his five children, Mary Ann poisoned one boy. Robinson, deep in grief, was vulnerable to Mary Ann's solicitous comfort, and she soon became pregnant. She was ready for a better life, but then her mother requested that she retrieve her nine-year-old daughter. In Mary Ann's mind, there was only one solution to adding this burden: arsenic, for both of them, as well as for two more of Robinson's children. They all had contracted the same painful gastric fever. Mary Ann gave birth to her baby but in less than two weeks, the infant was dead. When she nagged her husband to get his life insured, he became suspicious. So Mary Ann attempted to insure his life secretly. He discovered it, along with his depleted bank accounts, and sent her away, an act that probably saved his life.

It was not long before pretty Mary Ann met Frederick Cotton, whose wife had recently died, leaving him with two young boys. His sister lived with him to assist, so after Mary Ann had seduced Cotton, she poisoned his sister. Then she got pregnant, but rather than marry Cotton, she went to work for Dr. Heffernan. After he caught her trying to poison him, she escaped, taking some valuables with her. Returning to Cotton, and pregnant with his child, she married him, although she had never divorced Robinson. In short order, she insured the lives of the Cotton family, and when another man caught her eye, her fourth husband mysteriously died.

Her new lover moved in and took over as head of the family, but then Mary Ann spotted another man with even greater social standing. Excise officer John Quick-Manning became her lover. Soon, Cotton's oldest son and Mary Anne's own baby with Cotton died within a few weeks, as did her live-in lover—all of them from terrible convulsions. Now she only had little Charlie left—and an unborn child sired by Quick-Manning.

It may seem odd that no one noticed Mary Ann's pattern, but she was described as exuding a strong sexual allure, which can blind men to a woman's true nature. She worked her advantage, finally killing little Charlie, and that's when the physician caught her. While she was in jail, three of the other bodies were exhumed and all yielded findings of arsenic poisoning.

Although Mary Ann was tried for only the death of the boy, the other poisonings were introduced as evidence. Her attorney attempted to convince the court that the arsenic came from the wallpaper paste used in the homes where Mary Ann had lived, but this lame defense did not save her. The jury found her guilty of murder and sentenced her to die. On March 24, 1873, Mary Ann Cotton was hanged, ending an extended, self-enriching, and productive twenty-year killing spree.[2]

"FARMING"

Other women seeking profit via serial murder have attempted to keep some distance between themselves and the victims. Dorothea Helen Puente ran a boarding house in Sacramento, California, and was known to be quite meticulous with her garden. She also had a reputation for assisting elderly men down on their luck (since people did not generally know about her past background of picking them up in bars, drugging and robbing them). During the mid-1980s, this fifty-nine-year-old woman offered low rent in her home, with hot meals, to welfare and social

security recipients. It seemed to be a nice place to live, but neighbors noticed that the turnover was high. What they did not see was the government checks that continued to arrive for the men and women who had
supposedly left for new housing. Puente accepted and cashed them on
behalf of her "tenants," banking the money.

However, she miscalculated with one victim, because a social worker
came to call. This woman had heard about noxious odors at the boarding
house and came to check on one of the boarders. When she failed to get
satisfactory answers from Puente as to where the man was, she filed a
missing persons report with the police. In fact, seven elderly people had
disappeared from the place. The police arrived on November 7, 1988, and
while an officer questioned Puente, others poked around in the yard. They
turned up items of clothing, a leg bone, and a foot bone inside a shoe.
Puente cleverly expressed her distress over this discovery and asked if
she might stay with a relative while the police excavated the yard. They
allowed it, and she took the opportunity to escape.

The police dug up the lawns and gardens and soon discovered the remains of the seven missing people, covered in lime and plastic. One of
them—a woman—had been beheaded, dismembered, and buried sitting
up. The bodies were too decomposed to determine a cause of death, but
more sophisticated tests later proved that the victims had died from a drug
overdose.

While on the run, Puente tried to dupe another man in a bar in Los
Angeles, but he recognized her from news reports and called the police.
An investigation revealed that this "sweet little old lady" had forged sig-
natures on over sixty checks. This was less surprising in light of the discovery that Puente had served prison time in the past for theft and fraud,
and upon her release at that time, she had been considered a danger to the
elderly. Given the circumstances, two earlier deaths with which she had
been associated were revisited, making her a suspect. She claimed she was
only guilty of forgery and fraud. Nevertheless, Puente was tried for nine
murders but convicted of only three because one male juror refused to
agree that she could have killed more. She received life in prison.[3]

Even more ingenious was Belle Gunness, a Norwegian-American
woman who dispatched two husbands and several of her own children
to get insurance payments. With that money, she bought a pig farm in Indiana and then devised a clever scheme for self-enrichment: She placed
classified ads to lure men of means to join her venture, persuading them
to tell no one where they were going, and many of them were never seen
alive again. But then Belle learned that the concerned brother of one of
these men, Andrew Heleglein, was determined to find out why he had not
heard from his brother in three months. Andrew had given him a name
and address, and he was on his way to the farm. Belle's discovery seemed
imminent.

On April 28, 1908, an early morning fire leveled Belle's house and supposedly killed her and her three children, although the charred adult figure appeared to be much too small . . . and it was missing its head. Former handyman Ray Lamphere was arrested, but he claimed that he he was innocent and that Belle herself was still alive. He had even taken her to the train.

Investigators searched the property for the possible remains of Andrew Heleglein, aware that Belle had written letters imploring him to sell everything and come to her. They dug in a soft area and before long turned up a gunny sack containing Heleglein's dismembered body. His legs had been expertly sawed off above the knees, his arms disarticulated, and his head removed, and all of his parts had been shoved into the hole with his torso.

Other soft spots yielded more remains of other victims, and before it was all over twelve to thirteen sets of remains had been removed from the ground. Now the sudden inexplicable death in 1900 of Belle's first husband, Mads Sorensen, who had been insured for $8,500, appeared to have been murder. After that loss, Belle had married Peter Gunness, who had died eight months later when, as Belle reported, a meat grinder and jar of scalding water fell on his head (although no burns were present on the body and the blow to his head did not fit the supposed implement). The situation was ambiguous, since no one could prove that the burned female body from Belle's house was that of Belle Gunness. Had she been a victim or was she a murderess who killed four more people in the fire and escaped?

Lamphere went on trial, but a jury convicted him only of arson. While serving his prison term, he revealed what he knew about Belle's scheme of enrichment from her victims. As for Belle, while she was sighted in many places she was never caught. In 1931 in Los Angeles, an elderly woman named Esther Carlson was charged with killing a man for money but she died before her trial commenced. Two people who had known Belle Gunness recognized her from photos of Carlson in the newspaper. Yet no one could prove that Carlson was Belle.[4]

ENTITLED TO IT

Michael and C. L. Kelleher discuss the profit motive in *Murder Most Rare*, and there are many cases of it. However, because women tend to select people they know or are related to, it's not difficult to spot their pattern of greed. (Even so, they're not always caught.) Often, other family members start to suspect them, but may keep their mouths shut out of fear or loyalty. The Kellehers indicate that these serial killers can get away with their crimes for years, in part because investigators rely on their version of events and in part because there has long been a general social bias against viewing females as killers. Yet as a category of murderers, Black Widows are "among the most active, tenacious, and prolific of criminals."[5] Such women will often marry numerous times in their attempt to enrich themselves.

Candice Skrapec, a professor of criminology, includes "entitlement" as a motive in her survey of motives, and that would explain some of what drives a person who murders as a way to take something for themselves. Feeling as if they're owed something, they target specific victims "in the service of some inexplicable personal need."[6] Quite often, they maintain a distorted perception of themselves in relation to everyone else. Just the fact that Belle Gunness chose to kill and rob was good enough for her. In fact, she believed she deserved to take whatever she could, because *she* had been a victim of an unjust world. She was simply turning the tables and taking her due. The victims symbolize those who need to be punished, so even though they're innocent, as the killer perceives the situation they deserve what they get. Whatever moral rules such predators observe, they apply differently to that person than to everyone else, especially if the end result improves his or her situation.[7]

Serial killers may share a common attitude about victims-as-objects, but the way they exploit victims to acquire and sustain a sense of power seems to be influenced by culture. A comparison of 82 Japanese to 402 American serial killers by Kaori Aki indicated that while Americans were more likely to be sexually motivated, Japanese offenders tended to kill for financial gain and were more likely to have accomplices and to choose male victims.[8]

Several serial murderers have exploited troubled times to kill for profit, particularly during a world at war. Not only is it easier to escape notice, given the chaos and lack of staffing for police, but they may even align with "causes" or suggest other justifications that allow officials to excuse it.

THE LIQUIDATORS

In 1944, Paris was occupied by Nazi Germany, and feelings by the French against the Third Reich were rather bitter, to say the least. Police investigating a fire discovered in the basement of an abandoned building a stack of twenty-seven dismembered and decomposing corpses, with other body parts burning inside a furnace. They identified Dr. Marcel Petiot as the building's owner and went to question him. Unruffled, he explained that the corpses were the remains of Nazis and their collaborators. Officials let him go, appreciative of his efforts for the Resistance. He probably smiled to himself as he continued to kill. But the police continued to investigate him and they realized that his story was probably a cover for something more sinister. They believed he was luring wealthy Jews with the promise of safe passage, and as they brought their suitcases loaded with their most precious goods, he took advantage.

Caught again, Petiot admitted to having murdered sixty-three people, but he denied conning and robbing them. The authorities proposed that he had "inoculated" them with poison and had also subjected them to gruesome experiments, as evidenced by his torture chamber. Jury members who walked through the collection of human bones in Petiot's building quickly convicted him in 1946 and he was executed. Since he had incinerated many victims, his death toll is unknown, aside from his own estimate. The half million dollars he supposedly collected was never found.[9]

Not long afterward in England, another scoundrel, John George Haigh, was arrested for conning victims, killing them, and stealing their goods. In fact, he had once stated that the world was full of people born to be exploited by the likes of him, and without remorse, he took full advantage.

In 1949, Haigh was questioned in the case of a missing woman, Mrs. Durand-Deacon, known to have been on her way to keep an appointment with him. Haigh's first question to the police as they arrested him concerned his chances of getting out of the local mental institution. Quite soon he launched into a detailed confession that involved killing six people in order to drink their blood. He said that he would lure them into a storage area and then hit them over the head to kill them. Then he would cut open an artery in their throat and fill a cup with blood to drink it: Imbibing fresh blood made him feel better. Faced with the need to dispose of a corpse, he would dissolve it in a drum filled with acid. He claimed that he couldn't help himself, and he linked his sick compulsion to dreams he had suffered from a head injury.

However, there's clear evidence that each crime was committed when Haigh needed money and there's no evidence that he had acted under a compulsion or mental defect. Twelve physicians examined him while he was in prison and only one thought he had an aberrant mental condition— egocentric paranoia. The others believed that he was making it all up. In fact, the question he had asked upon being arrested about the psychiatric institution was a signal that he intended to fake having a mental illness so that he might avoid the death penalty.

Haigh was a known con artist. In the past, he had posed as a doctor, a lawyer, and an engineer when it had suited his purposes. An investigation uncovered solid evidence that he had targeted victims with money during times when he was in debt. In the case of his murder of a family of three, he had forged a power of attorney that had allowed him to inherit their estate. Two years later, he murdered a couple and sold off their possessions. However, he gambled away the proceeds and had to find another victim. He picked Mrs. Durand-Deacon, luring her to his "factory" to ask her to invest and shooting her before he dissolved her corpse. Human sludge was found on his property and it was proven that Haigh was the man who had pawned her jewelry. Thus, given his obviously clear-sighted conning, his insanity defense did not work, and he was duly executed on August 10, 1949.[10]

No matter what the motive, there are some killers who have a penchant for more perversity, craving blood, flesh, or mutilation. We turn next to some of the more shocking cases to see how such deviant desires develop.

NOTES

1. Brian Lane and Wilfred Gregg, *The Encyclopedia of Serial Killers* (New York: Berkley, 1992), pp. 62–63.

2. Tony Whitehead, *Mary Ann Cotton: Dead but not Forgotten* (London: Whitehead, 2000).

3. Carla Norton, *Disturbed Ground: The True Story of a Diabolical Female Serial Killer* (New York: Morrow, 1994).

4. Sylvia Shepherd, *The Mistress of Murder Hill* (www.1stbook.com, 2001).

5. Michael Kelleher and C. L. Kelleher, *Murder Most Rare* (New York: Dell, 1998), p. 34.

6. Candace A. Skrapec, "Motives of the Serial Killer," in *Violence and Psychopathy*, Adrian Raine and Jose Sanmartin, eds. (New York: Kluwer Academic, 2001), p. 106.

7. Ibid., pp. 105–122.

8. Kaori Aki, "Serial Killers: A Cross-Cultural Study Between Japan and the United States," Master's thesis, California State University, Fresno, CA, 2003.

9. John Grombach, *The Great Liquidator* (Garden City, NY: Doubleday, 1980).

10. Arthur J. La Bern, *Haigh: The Mind of a Murder* (London: W. H. Allen, 1973).

CHAPTER 9

Blood and Bodies

Joachim Kroll, 43, managed to rape, kill, and mutilate more than a dozen people over about two decades in West Germany. On a whim, he had once tasted the flesh cut from the buttocks of a murdered woman and found that he liked it. Thereafter, he stalked females of various ages that he thought would yield tender meat (he reportedly killed only one man). One of his victims was four years old. When police finally nabbed him in 1976, they found a kettle on his stove boiling carrots and potatoes, along with a tiny female hand. In the clogged toilet were her internal organs, while in Kroll's refrigerator, resting on plates, were more pieces of the victim, and larger parts had been wrapped and frozen.

After his arrest, Kroll apparently commented that meat was expensive, so he went seeking it on his own. He also suggested that his perversion arose from being aroused as a teenager when he'd seen pigs being slaughtered and admitted that after butchering a woman, he would use a doll for sexual gratification. He also used dolls as practice for perfecting his strangulation technique and as bait for children.[1]

Along with murder, some people include an added deviance, derived mostly from paraphilias or deviant fantasies. Their handling of human remains or fluids sets them in a category apart from those who approach murder for greed, power, or sadistic purposes. These cases are among the most difficult to comprehend, the most disturbing, and for criminologists and forensic research psychologists, the most fascinating.

PARAPHILIAS

Paraphilias are disorders that begin in childhood or adolescence and persist into adulthood, most commonly afflicting males. They become strong enduring patterns of behavior based in a preoccupation for sexual arousal on objects, unusual activities, or deviant situations, and are driven by repetitive fantasies. The cause of a specific paraphilia is unclear, and different psychological theories posit different hypotheses. Psychoanalytic theory, for example, holds that an individual with this condition may be fixated on an early-developing sexual habit, while behavioral explanations look to the process of conditioning, that is, an object or a specific act is repeatedly associated with erotic pleasure during the individual's budding sexuality. They come to prefer the object or behavior, sometimes to the exclusion of other types of sexual activity, and will rarely seek treatment, short of the threat of arrest or exposure and humiliation. In secret, the pleasure experienced from the object or activity is highly intense and can trigger compulsive behavior and extreme dependency for sexual gratification.

The most common paraphilias are listed in the *DSM-IV*, and I include a few from a classic work in criminology, *The Sexual Criminal*, by Dr. J. Paul de River:[2]

- Fetishism—sexual arousal from nonhuman objects, such as shoes, underwear, candles, or ropes
- Adamism—the desire to exhibit oneself in the nude
- Exhibitionism—the desire to expose one's genitals to others
- Auto-eroticism—a sexual fixation on oneself
- Frotteurism—touching or rubbing one's body surreptitiously against another person, usually a stranger in a crowded public place
- Telephone scatology—arousal from making obscene phone calls to strangers to hear their reaction
- Pedophilia/hebephilia—the focus of sexual attention involves children, either as pornography, or as molestation or the assault of actual victims; hebephilia is specifically about prepubescent girls
- Masochism—gaining sexual pleasure from being hurt or humiliated, via verbal abuse, bondage, and even being beaten, whipped, or cut.
- Necrophilia—gaining sexual arousal from handling or having intercourse with corpses
- Necrofetishism—being aroused by corpses as a fetish
- Partialism—sexual arousal from some body part, such as the arch of a foot
- Piquerism—arousal from stabbing with a sharp instrument
- Pygmalionism—sexual desire for statues or dolls
- Zoophilia—sexual arousal with animals as the focus

- Apotemnophilia—sexual attraction to amputees
- Coprophilia—sexual excitement over the taste and smell of excrement
- Urophilia—sexual arousal from urine
- Klismaphilia—sexual arousal from receiving an enema
- Sadism—the acquisition of sexual pleasure from dominating, torturing, or abusing others via such activities as verbal abuse, whipping, burning, stabbing, raping, choking, and killing
- Gerontophilia—arousal from elderly persons of the opposite sex
- Infibulation—desire for self-torture
- Transvestitism—cross-dressing by heterosexual males, from wearing a piece of female clothing to dressing entirely as a female, and even passing as one
- Triolism—a form of exhibitionism in which a person wants to perform a sexual act with several partners or in the presence of several people
- Lycanthropy—the idea that one has become a werewolf
- Vampirism—excitement over drinking blood
- Scoptophilia (voyeurism)—deriving sexual pleasure from watching others from a clandestine position, such as peeking in windows where someone may be undressing or sleeping
- Fire-water Complex—after lighting a fire, one exhibits oneself and then has a strong desire to urinate

These are the types of objects, images, or situations that urge people to act, and when the activity involves nonconsenting partners or damage to someone else's property, it becomes a crime. Many serial killers are triggered by paraphilias, and they force their victims to do things that will enact their specific fantasy and satisfy their craving. All of the following cases involve some type of paraphilia, but let's first look at a peculiar fetish that led to serial murder in Texas.

Between 1990 and 1991, three prostitutes were murdered, and their eyes had been skillfully removed. On a tip from a woman who'd escaped, Charles Albright, 57 and married, was arrested. A hair and fiber analysis on debris from his vacuum, a blanket, and the victims were linked to him. Yet he was anything but a typical serial killer. Highly intelligent and friendly, Albright was fluent in several languages, coached baseball, and had taught biology. No one who knew him could believe he had this hidden viciousness. He could also paint and play musical instruments, and was skilled in taxidermy. Even so, he had an extensive criminal record that even his wife did not know about, frequenting prostitutes and admittedly enjoying bludgeoning women. He was a skilled liar who clearly had an obsession with eyes, which by some reports he maintained even in prison by drawing eyes and hanging them around his cell.[3] Albright also subscribed to a magazine about iridology and got a copy of the first issue of *Omni* magazine from 1978, the cover of which features a large eyeball.[4] As bizarre as this behavior seems, no expert on sexual deviance can pinpoint just how Albright (or anyone) would became so obsessed with a body part that he needed to kill to get it.

We'll see something similar with those killers who felt an overwhelming desire to eat human flesh.

CANNIBALS

In Barcelona, Spain, a child led police to a "witch" who had held her captive and forced her to eat pieces from a deceased human. They arrested Marti Enriqueta, who had kidnapped several children to kill and dismember for use in her potions. She also consumed parts of them. Her victim count was unknown, but by 1912 at least six children had been subjected to this treatment.[5]

Throughout World War I, Georg Karl Grossmann, a former butcher in Berlin, was caught with the dismembered remains of four women. Authorities learned that he had brought prostitutes to his house for sex (looking particularly for plump women), but sometimes he would kill them. Often he sold the flesh at cut rates to the hungry and also consumed it himself. He was caught when neighbors heard him struggling with a woman who was fighting him off. It's estimated that Grossmann killed around fifty women, although he was charged with only fourteen murders.[6]

Karl Denke, the "Mass Murderer of Münsterberg," killed homeless people in Silesia (now Poland) and guests at his inn (who were often people with no place to go), cooking parts of them and reportedly pickling their remains for later. Strangely, he kept detailed records of their weight. The fact came out after his arrest that in an open courtyard where neighbors could see him, he would pour buckets of blood, and yet no one suspected something quite so lurid as murder and cannibalism, because they viewed him as a kind, God-fearing man who gave what he could to people in need. In 1924, a man he'd attacked with a hatchet survived long enough to identify him, so Denke was arrested, whereupon he admitted that he had lived on human flesh for at least three years and had eaten parts from as many as thirty-one people. In fact, police found many of those parts in storage. Apparently knowing that the authorities would find evidence of even more deviant practices, such as suspenders made of human skin, Denke committed suicide in jail.[7]

At times, cannibalism is committed for practical reasons, at others because it's arousing, which we can see more clearly when it's combined with the delusion of lycanthropy.

WEREWOLVES

Girls tending sheep in the south of France encountered a thirteen-year-old boy who appeared to be hungry. He introduced himself as Jean

Grenier, the son of a priest, but said that he had sold his soul to the Devil. He claimed to have a wolf-skin cape that changed him for an hour at dusk into a wolf, whereupon he romped around the countryside with a gang of nine others like him. Grenier told this same story to others around the village as well.

After he hinted that he attacked and ate little girls, the authorities undertook an investigation. Grenier was no priest's son, they discovered, but the offspring of a poor laborer. He'd been hired to watch sheep but had often neglected his duties. Taken before the courts, Grenier continued to state that he could take the form of a wolf. He told a story about a neighbor who had introduced him to M. de la Forest, a dark-skinned man in the woods who gave them both a salve and a wolf-skin cape. Thereafter, according to his delusion, Grenier had found himself able to transform into a wolf. He admitted to going into a house, grabbing a baby, and killing it so he could consume it. In two other villages, he said, he had killed and eaten pieces from little girls.

Grenier's account matched details from reports of missing children, and his father and stepmother were questioned. They agreed that Grenier believed himself to be a wolf. Some children who'd been attacked but had survived bore wounds that were just as Grenier had described. The next day, Grenier told his story in his father's presence, changing nothing. The court decided he was an imbecile who was hallucinating, and he was sent into the care of monks at a monastery at Bordeaux. There he loped around the courtyard like a wolf. After seven years, an official visited him and Grenier admitted that he still craved raw flesh and had twice seen the Lord of the Forest. His case was dismissed as lunacy, and when he was twenty, he died at the monastery.[8]

R. E. L. Masters, former Director of the Library of Sex Research, with writer Eduard Lea composed a comprehensive history of sexual violence in *Perverse Crimes in History: Evolving Concepts of Sadism, Lust-murder, and Necrophilia—From Ancient to Modern Times*. The authors discuss the notions of vampirism and werewolf psychosis in terms of "necrosadism," or as erotic gratification from death-related acts or fantasies. As an example, they describe a Parisian woman in 1890 who was found dead in her home, with her son sleeping next to her. She had been raped and then thoroughly disemboweled—by him—and he had managed this by reaching into her vagina, puncturing the organs and pulling the intestines back out by the same route. He'd thrown them over her shoulder and then went to sleep beside her corpse. That's how authorities found them. The autopsy revealed that the mother had died before any of the mutilation had occurred. The son, it seems, had ravaged her corpse.[9]

Dr. Richard Noll, a clinical psychologist, edited *Vampires, Werewolves, and Demons*, which includes reports of lycanthropy from the clinical literature. Noll states that since 1975 there have been eighteen documented cases. Six of them involved delusions about wolves and the rest featured other animals. The diagnosis most commonly given to the behavior of these people was bipolar disorder, but some were diagnosed as suffering from delusional depression and schizophrenia. Noll believes that lycanthropy more closely resembles zoanthropy, "the delusion that one has been transformed into an animal," which he says may be better described as a dissociative disorder.[10]

One could combine such a lycanthropy delusion from the list of paraphilias with cannibalism to get the next serial murderer, one of the most deviant on record. In 1990, the Russian government announced the capture of a man wanted for nearly a decade for the murder and mutilation of dozens of women and children. The crimes of the *Lesopolosa* Killer, also dubbed the Maniac, were first noted as a series in 1982 with three corpses found in wooded areas in quick succession. The first victim was a young girl, and it appeared from her postmortem posture that she had tried to fight someone off. Two ribs were broken, and they evidenced numerous stab wounds into the bone. A knife had apparently cut into her eye sockets, too, and similar gouges were viewed in the pelvic region.

Although the authorities officially treated the murders as unrelated incidents, claiming that serial killers were nonexistent in the Soviet Union, investigators knew better. The killer showed evidence of overkill and sexual deviance—the incision of the bodies and removal of certain parts. Viktor Burakov headed the investigation, and more bodies soon turned up. A little girl preserved by winter conditions showed a clear pattern of knife wounds. Her skull was punctured, as were her chest and stomach. The knife had been inserted dozens of times, as if in a frenzy, moving the organs around in the body cavity. The killer had especially targeted the heart, lungs, and sexual organs. And as with the others, the offender had attacked the eyes.

Burakov realized that this man spent a considerable amount of time with his victims as they were dying and after they were dead. On girls and women, he had stabbed the breasts and destroyed the vagina, uterus, and bladder. On boys, he'd often mutilated the penis, scrotum, and anus, and once had even chewed out a tongue.

The Russian team determined that the killer had AB blood, which helped to eliminate suspects (but which turned out to be an error that eliminated the actual killer). Burakov asked psychiatrists for help and Dr. Alexandr Bukhanovsky agreed to study the killer's behavioral patterns to develop a report, and he offered the following suggestions: The killer was twenty-five to fifty years old. He thought the man suffered from sexual inadequacy and may have blinded his victims to prevent them from looking at him. He was a sadist and had difficulty achieving orgasm without inflicting cruelty on another person. He was also compulsive and would be generally depressed until he could kill. He was not retarded or schizophrenic, but an organized loner, ordinary and unassuming, not a transvestite, homosexual, or overt sexual pervert.

Eight years passed before the investigation got a genuine break. Suspecting that the killer was picking up victims at train stations, Burakov posted undercover officers to keep watch. Andrei Romanovich Chikatilo, 54, a man who had previously been a suspect but was released, had been at the Donleskhoz train station. He was seen coming out of the woods, where another victim was soon found brutally murdered.

Burakov's team learned that Chikatilo had resigned from his post as a teacher, due to reports of molesting students. He also had been fired from another position, but while unemployed, he found solace in train stations. During the time he had been detained in 1984, there had been no murders, and his travel records coincided with other murders in those areas to where he had traveled.

Chikatilo was brought in for questioning. In his bag detectives found Vaseline, rope, dirty towels, and a kitchen knife. They needed a confession, since that was the Soviet way, but Chikatilo refused to admit to anything. When it appeared that they might have to release him, they had Dr. Bukhanovksy read his report. As Chikatilo listened, he broke down and admitted that he was guilty of the thirty-six crimes listed. Yet he said that his first murder had occurred in 1978, earlier than police realized.

He had grabbed a nine-year-old girl and tried to rape her. When he could not achieve an erection, he used a knife as a substitute, killing her. He had blindfolded her during the ordeal because he was afraid that an image of him would remain in her eyes—a common superstition.

Soon he became obsessed with reliving the crime. In 1981, he killed a vagrant girl looking for money, biting off and swallowing her nipple. When he cut her open, he found sexual relief. He took her sexual organs away with him. With this and many other crimes, Chikatilo offered the details of his modus operandi. He even showed the police on a mannequin what he had done to victims. Some he had watched carefully but most had been victims of opportunity who were easily lured into a position of vulnerability. They were often just kids who were wandering around train stations. The stabbing, he said, was in place of the sexual intercourse that he could not perform, and he needed violence and a struggle for arousal. With male victims, Chikatilo would imagine them as his captives.

He also admitted to cannibalism. At least once, he had removed a uterus and placed his semen inside it, then chewed on it as he walked away from the corpse. Or he might bite off a part and swallow it. He loved the way the victims screamed, the way they bled, and their agony. Even as it excited him it also relaxed him, and after it was all over he always craved more. In all, Chikatilo admitted to fifty-six murders, although there was corroboration for only fifty-three.

In trying to understand the savage nature of crimes like this, psychologists inevitably search through such a killer's childhood for specific erotic associations, as well as for sources of anger and hatred. Chikatilo was no real mystery in that regard. He had been a lonely child, mocked by others for his clumsiness and sensitivity. As a result, he had inwardly seethed with anger. His first sexual experience as an adolescent involved ejaculating as he struggled with a ten-year-old friend of his sister's. Later in life, as he experienced difficulty achieving erections, the images of this erotic wrestling helped him to become aroused. So later, as an adult he had made many of his victims struggle.

The real source of his need to act out, it seems, arose from the humiliation he repeatedly suffered at the hands of women. As a young man, he entered the military, but when he came home and tried to develop a relationship, he could not perform sexually, and the girl with whom he had failed told this to others; thus, she entered his fantasies as someone he wanted to bite and pull apart. Thanks to her and to his mother, who was scornfully critical, he held out little hope of getting married. Thus, his inner torment became more pronounced, along with his anger against women. Chikatilo became a schoolteacher and his sister took pity on him and assisted him with meeting someone suitable for marriage, although after he married, his wife, too, belittled him throughout their marriage. Reportedly, he was able to conceive children only by ejaculating outside her and pushing his semen inside by hand.

After his mother died in 1973 when he was 37, Chikatilo began gradually to molest young girls. This made him feel powerful, and when incidents were reported, his Party membership protected him from prosecution. Yet for true satisfaction, he needed violence, so he turned to murder. His savagery and cannibalism have often been associated with incidents to which Chikatilo was exposed growing up. During the early part of the twentieth century, after Stalin crushed private agricultural concerns, the Soviet Union went through several devastating famines. Millions died from starvation and many desperate people removed flesh from newly dead corpses. Supposedly, Chikatilo's mother told him that he once had an older brother, but when the boy was ten, hungry villagers had killed and eaten him.

He apparently turned this incident over and over in his mind, along with what he had witnessed of the Nazi occupation and of German bombing, with bodies blown up in the streets, and these things had both frightened and excited him. Between his humiliations, being bullied and feeling alienated, he developed a quiet, smoldering rage. To entertain and empower himself, he told investigators, he had devised images of torture, and these had become instrumental in his killings later in life.

Chikatilo was sent to Moscow's Serbsky Institute for two months for psychiatric and neurological assessment, and it was determined that he had brain damage from birth, which had affected his ability to control his bladder and his seminal emissions. He also had deviant fantasies. However, he was found to be sane and turned back over to the court.

Convicted of numerous counts of molestation and murder, Chikatilo shouted "Swindlers!" His case was appealed but the appeal was denied. So this former teacher with a university degree in Russian literature, a wife, and children, and no apparent background of physical abuse, clearly had a savage heart. He described himself as a mistake of nature. It's unfortunate that a better biopsychological analysis was never performed, and all hope of that was lost when on February 15, 1994, Chikatilo was quickly executed.[11]

Besides human flesh, some killers derive erotic enjoyment from blood or other bodily fluids to such an extent that they will murder people to possess it. Their own blood won't do, although sometimes they will kill animals. Mostly, the ultimate experience for them is to gain access to another person's vital fluids, and to be fully satisfied they may even drink it. That's why they're known as vampire killers.

VAMPIRES

Ahmad Suradji, 45, was an Indonesian sorcerer with a supposed ability to grant wishes. In 1997, he was arrested after an investigation turned up twenty-six skeletons on his sugarcane plantation. The victims were prostitutes who had asked to be made more beautiful. Suradji confessed to forty-two murders, saying that he had planned for thirty more at the behest of his deceased father, also a sorcerer, who had come to him in a dream. But on his own, Suradji had added a strange twist: after strangling the women, he drank their saliva.[12] The idea for offenders with such obsessions is that taking their victims' fluids gives them mystical control over that person, because they're ingesting the water or blood required for the person to survive. The secret exchange can be so arousing that it begs for more.

With Suradji, at least the victims had died first. Another "vampire" did not wait. Fritz Haarmann, a butcher in Hanover, Germany, and a practiced child molester, noticed the many young men drifting aimlessly around after World War I, so he devised a plan to make them vulnerable. He teamed up with a handsome male prostitute to lure these men to his home. There he fed his intended victims until they felt sleepy and then he overpowered and raped them. Haarmann later described how he would lose himself in a frenzy and chew into their necks, sometimes devouring their throats until the head was practically severed from the body. As he tasted their blood, he achieved orgasm. He would then cut the flesh from their bodies, consume some of it, and sell the rest as butchered meat. Whatever remained, he dumped in a nearby canal.

In fact, it was a sack of bones found there that led the police to his door in 1924. Bloodstains on the wall and clothing from missing men incriminated Haarmann, as did a prior arrest for molestation. He confessed to his deeds, claiming some fifty victims, although authorities charged the "Hanover Vampire" with only twenty-seven. Haarmann was not flustered with a death sentence. Indeed, he reportedly seemed pleased. Haarmann also apparently enjoyed putting his deeds on paper, as he described his bloody offenses in meticulous detail. Just before he died, he declared his execution to be his "wedding day."[13]

Another so-called vampire was Peter Kürten, who could charm people with his mild manner but who could also become so agitated that he would bludgeon grown men with a hammer or drink the blood from a child. When he was nine, he had set up an "accident" in which two other boys died. In 1913, he entered an inn at Koln-Mulheim in the Rhine River Valley and murdered a ten-year-old girl. There were two incisions on her throat, one shallow and the other deep, and the autopsy found less blood in her body than should have been the case. Leads were chased down but her killer was not found.

In fact, Kürten was imprisoned for sixteen years for petty crimes, and when he was freed, the incidents resumed. An eight-year-old girl was stabbed thirteen times and stuffed under a hedge. A week later, a forty-five-year-old mechanic was found dead next to a road, bleeding from twenty stab wounds. Six months went by before two girls were murdered at the fair grounds. The five-year-old was manually strangled and her throat was cut. The fourteen-year-old was also strangled but also beheaded.

There were other assaults, with survivors who could not identify their attacker, but then an adolescent girl was raped and battered to death with a hammer. Six weeks later, a five-year-old child disappeared and a letter came to a local newspaper, apparently penned by her killer. He offered a map and police soon found the strangled, battered body, stabbed thirty-six times. The letter also described the location of the corpse of another young woman who had been missing for several months.

After Kürten allowed a rape victim to go free, she led the police to his door, and he confessed. He had committed numerous assaults and thirteen murders, he said, and admitted to drinking the blood from many of his victims because blood excited him. About the incident years earlier at the inn, Kürten described how he broke into the room, choked the girl, and cut her throat. The blood had spurted into an arch over his head, which had excited him to orgasm, and then he drank some from her throat.

At his trial, defense psychiatrists who had studied him declared him insane, but the jury ignored them. He was sentenced, based on nine counts of murder, to be executed in 1931. Just before dying, Kürten expressed a desire to hear his own blood bubble forth after the blade came down. He could not imagine a better experience.[14]

Among other infamous blood-drinking serial killers are Martin Dumollard, who killed several girls in France in 1861; Joseph Vacher in France, who when caught in 1897 said he'd drunk blood from the necks of a dozen murder victims; and Marcello de Andrade, 25, who sodomized and killed young boys, reportedly drinking their blood as a means of taking on their beauty. A female, too, got into the act. Magdalena Solis participated in a blood-drinking cult in Mexico. She helped to convince villagers in Yerba Buena that she was a goddess and she orchestrated sexualized blood rituals that involved numerous murders.

Most of the killers described here did not do much with the remains once they had torn the bodies apart, tasted them, or taken the blood. A more intriguing deviance involves keeping bodies around for comfort, control, or pleasure, and for that we examine several notorious offenders.

NOTES

1. Moira Martingale, *Cannibal Killers: The History of Impossible Murders* (New York: Carroll and Graf, 1993), pp. 51–59.

2. J. Paul de River, *The Sexual Criminal: A Psychoanalytic Study* (Springfield, IL: Charles C. Thomas, 1949), pp. 5–185.

3. Skip Hollandsworth, "See No Evil," *Texas Monthly*, May 1993, 21(5); *Charles Albright v. the State of Texas*, 05-92-00005, Fifth District, May 19, 1994; John Matthews and Christine Wicker, *The Eyeball Killer* (New York: Kensington, 1996).

4. Eric Hickey, *Serial Murderers and Their Victims*, 3rd edn. (Belmont, CA: Wadsworth, 2002), p. 29.

5. Harold Schechter, *The Serial Killer Files* (New York: Ballantine, 2003), p. 40.

6. David Everitt, *Human Monsters* (Chicago: Contemporary Books, 1993), pp. 79–81.

7. Martingale, *Cannibal Killers*, pp. 34–45.

8. Adam Douglas, *The Beast Within* (New York: Avon, 1992), pp. 180–183.

9. R. E. L. Masters and Eduard Lea, *Perverse Crimes in History* (New York: The Julian Press, 1963), pp. 115–130.

10. Richard Noll, *Vampires, Werewolves, and Demons* (New York: Brunner/Mazel, 1992), pp. 83–138.

11. Robert Cullen, *The Killer Department: Detective Viktor Burakov's Eight-Year Hunt for the Most Savage Serial Killer in Russian History* (New York: Pantheon Books, 1993); Richard Lourie, *Hunting the Devil: The Pursuit, Capture and Confession of the Most Savage Serial Killer in History* (New York: HarperCollins, 1993).

12. Michael Newton, *The Encyclopedia of Serial Killers* (New York: Checkmark, 2000), p. 212.

13. Everitt, *Human Monsters*, pp. 84–85.

14. Karl Berg, *The Sadist: An Account of the Crimes of Serial Killer Peter Kürten: A Study in Sadism* (London: Heineman, 1945).

CHAPTER 10

Living with Death

Not all killers-in-the-making devise fantasy scenarios where they imagine hitting back, empowering themselves in a fit of anger or ego, or attacking in a savage frenzy. Some who grew up lonely simply wanted company, and they took extreme measures (murder) to force people to remain with them. Others felt morbid desires about corpses that they knew would be socially condemned, and they believed the only way to satisfy these desires was to do so with someone whom they either had to kill or who was already dead. While the motivation in any of these situations was clearly about control over others, the need for keeping bodies close by issued from desperate isolation or the attempt to keep their secrets under wraps. All of these predators had in common a high tolerance for the smell of death, handling corpses, and being in the presence of decomposing flesh; they also all derived a certain satisfaction, sexual or psychological, from keeping their victims in their homes for as long as possible.

While there's no clear syndrome through which to understand all of the killers who have collected bodies, their desires are among the most perverse known to humankind. We'll see below how one theorist has devised a concept, the "necrophilous character," to encompass the various manifestations. A few murderers derive a sexual attraction from the dead, so they would be viewed as outright necrophiles (from the list of paraphilias in the previous chapter), while others enjoy experiencing a death during sex and then keeping the corpses as erotic reminders. We've already discussed psychotic killers who were oblivious to the bodies that had collected around them, but each of the following men was found to be sane and perfectly aware of the bodies—even excited by them for one reason or another. Let's look first at a killer who used murder as a sexual aphrodisiac and his home as a gruesome way to put notches on his belt.

INSIDE THE WALLS

No one had a clue about what had been going on for several years in Number 10 Rillington Place, in London—not until 1953, that is, when Beresford Brown sublet the place. Brown disliked the smell coming from a wall, so he tore off the wallpaper. In the process, he uncovered an alcove, and to his shock, inside was the decomposing body of a nude woman. He summoned authorities and as they carefully removed the corpse, they found two more dead women squeezed in the same small space. All had been oddly diapered and one had been placed head down, while another was tied by the neck to a third victim. An autopsy indicated that all of them had been sexually molested and strangled.

The police looked for Christie, the former tenant, but he had disappeared. In the meantime, they discovered that his home contained yet more human remains, including Christie's dead wife, Ethel, who had been killed and placed beneath the floorboards. In the garden were the skeletons of two more females, with a thighbone used to prop up a trellis. It was a bizarre collection that evidenced a long-standing series of murders, and authorities set about to learn the identities of these victims.

The papers posted headlines about Christie's "house of horrors" even as he wandered the streets in a daze. Eventually the police nabbed him and he confessed to the murders. In order to become sexually aroused, he admitted, he had needed the women to be unconscious, so he had used a homemade contraption that dispensed a poisonous coal gas. As they passed out, he raped them while strangling them and then collected their pubic hair in a tin.[1]

Christie had lived with these corpses in his home (one can only wonder what he told his wife about the obvious stench, since she was the last to die), and had even handled their remains while digging in his garden. Unlike the killers mentioned in Chapter 9, Christie wasn't seeking blood or the need to tear someone apart. He wasn't aroused by the idea, image, or experience of corpses. Instead, he sought control over women, which he gained through trickery, and as his victims died, he was so aware of his power over each one that it sexually aroused him. That is clearly a distorted mingling of the life instinct with death, feeling more alive as the other person expires. While many killers describe that experience, Christie enhanced it by keeping his victims in his home to remind him of what he had done.

That's not quite the same as someone who gets aroused by a dead body.

THE NECROPHILE

Necrophilia is an erotic attraction to corpses, with the most common motive cited by psychologists as the attempt to gain possession of an unresisting or nonrejecting partner. The activity fits the *DSM-IV* psychiatric diagnosis of "Paraphilia, Not Otherwise Specified." Social philosopher and psychoanalyst Erich Fromm believed that "necrophilism" was the result of social evolution, occurring as societies evolved toward the spiritual destruction of greater mechanization. In *The Anatomy of Human Destructiveness*, he states that people suffering from a "necrophilous character" are guided by a set of values influenced by social circumstances that move them toward embracing images of death and demolition. These people appear to crave absolute control, which arises from a chaotic childhood. The more they seek it, however, the less they can appreciate the evolving and unpredictable nature of life.

Fromm makes a distinction between the natural instinct of benign aggression, developed from an automatic need for self-protection, and malignant aggression, that is, a failure of character. The latter involves the desire to make a distinct mark on one's world in a destructive manner. The extreme manifestations of this are sadism—the passion for unrestricted power over another person—and necrophilia—attraction to all that is dead.

Necrophilia, in Fromm's theory, can be either sexual (as in the list of paraphilias) or nonsexual. The former involves a desire to have sex with a corpse and the latter is simply the need to be near or to handle or dismember a corpse for psychological reasons. Necrophilia, says Fromm, can be actual or it can be symbolic. The cruder manifestations grow from necrophilia as a character-rooted passion, and in the symbolic sense, "necrophilous characters" yearn for life to be finished; they often have dreams about dismembered parts or rotting remains. When they desire a world where there is no life, their drive for control can make them dangerous. Fromm cites Hitler as a good example.

Among the traits of the necrophilous character are an inability to relate to living people, lifeless conversations, a tendency to wear light-absorbing dark colors and to dislike bright colors, the belief that resolving conflict involves force or violence, an interest in sickness, a lack of spontaneity, and the compartmentalization of emotion and will, with a resulting insensitivity to tragedy involving loss of life.[2]

Since Christie was emerging into the nuclear age, having witnessed two world wars, he might well have sought a means of control that involved an attraction to killing women and keeping them there with him. Only when he lost everything and despaired did he sign his own death warrant by giving up his home and waiting for the police to arrest him. By then, he had no more will to keep going.

According to Dr. Jonathan Rosman and Dr. Phillip Resnick, in psychological theory there are three basic types of "true" necrophilia:

1. Necrophilic homicide, which is murder to obtain a corpse
2. Regular necrophilia, the use of corpses for sexual pleasure
3. Necrophilic fantasy, envisioning the acts but not acting on them

In their study of 122 cases, more people fit the second category, and more than half of them worked in a morgue or some other aspect of the funeral industry. Supposedly (if one can judge such a secret activity), necrophiles are primarily male (about 90%), but one female apprentice embalmer claimed that during the first four months of her employment, she had devised a pump contraption in order to have sex with a number of corpses.

Contrary to common belief, say Rosman and Resnick, most necrophiles are heterosexual, although about half of the known necrophiles who have committed murder were gay. In only about 60 percent is there a diagnosed personality disorder, with 10 percent being psychotic. The most common occupations through which necrophiles in their study came across corpses included being employed as a hospital orderly, morgue attendant, funeral parlor assistant, cleric, cemetery employee, and soldier—although the majority of people thus employed are *not* tempted to violate a corpse.[3]

Masters and Lea, in *Perverse Crimes in History*, describe a "platonic necrophilist" as someone who never touches the dead but finds sexual gratification merely from looking at them. But others can be dangerous. Their fantasies might turn from corpse mutilation to outright murder in order to acquire a corpse to mutilate. Yet the lust killer who also engages in sexual activities with a corpse, Masters claims, is not considered a true necrophile. He says that sexual violation is only an extension of what the lust murderer will do as part of the overall crime. A true necrophile is only interested in the corpse, not in the living person. If he kills, it's only to acquire a corpse. He's often incapable of even making a sexual approach to the living. It's a fine distinction, to be sure, but it's an important one, if we're concerned with the precipitating fantasies as factors in murder.

Masters and Lea say that it's surprising how often the corpses that necrophiles violate are not fresh but rather are dug up from the grave in a putrefied or mummified condition. Some even like only the bones. Those who actually feed on decaying dead bodies are known as necrophagists, as opposed to cannibals, who prefer fresh meat or who consume dead loved ones for spiritual purposes (anthropophagy). One man merely wanted to eat the nail trimmings from a corpse, another to lick the sexual parts. One woman whose family had mostly died would go into the family crypt to devour the genitals of her male relatives.

With such people, the concept of sexuality is infantile. Psychologically healthy people participate in human relationships by receiving and giving pleasure, but with a corpse, only one person derives pleasure, indicating a narcissistic ego.[4] Yet sometimes the person who has kept the dead nearby has indulged in torture while the person was alive and necrophilia after death. No one seems to have an adequate category for that.

DARK CORNERS

In December 1978, a team of police officers began a gruesome excavation in the crawlspace beneath the house at 8213 Summerdale Avenue in Des Plaines, Illinois. After an officer had noticed the odor of death coming through a heat duct in the home of John Wayne Gacy, a contractor associated with the disappearance of a missing teenager, Rob Piest, he had requested a search warrant. Investigators brought up twenty-eight separate bodies of young men in all different states of decomposition—the parts of some of them even intermingled with others. Several more were dredged up from the river, including Piest, and Gacy was charged with numerous counts of first-degree murder. The final official total of his victims was thirty-three. He is an example of a man who tolerated close proximity to a collection of malodorous decomposing corpses. He wasn't necessarily aroused by corpses, but he did love the sense of power that he derived from a prolonged session of sexual torture and murder. Like Christie, he enjoyed the satisfaction of knowing that these young men were dying at his hand, but he also had sexual contact with at least a few of the corpses. Some analysts indicate that he was aroused by healthy young men but possibly hated his own homosexual urges, so he killed his victims as a punishment—of them and of himself.

To put together a solid case and to bring closure to families who had been waiting as long as six years for news of a missing relative, investigators undertook the painstaking task of identifying the bodies. Some desperate families offered photos, X-rays, and dental records, and in other cases, driver's licenses and other forms of identification to find out if their missing loved one was among the victims. Yet because there was so much discussion of homosexual acts in the media, it was thought that families were hesitant to come forward and thus some of the bodies remained unidentified. When after six weeks the officials had succeeded with identifying less than half of the bodies, they hired forensic anthropologists Charles P. Warren and Clyde C. Snow to assist, and they employed in turn a forensic sculptress, Betty Pat. Gatliff, to reconstruct badly deteriorated skulls into recognizable faces. Forensic odontologists were ready to help with the identification of teeth. Since Gacy had piled some bodies on top of others in the crawlspace under his home, the team's first task was to sort and separate individual bones. In the end, it was determined that Gacy's typical victim was a Caucasian male in his teens or early twenties; one had been a marine and another had even been married. Those who worked on these crews were nauseated and disgusted by the idea that a person could live with all this fetid flesh.

Gacy was tried and convicted of the murders, and given the death penalty. In 1994, he was executed. But many questions remained. While he was killing and burying boys in his crawlspace, the odors were obvious even to neighbors. Yet his second wife and his mother lived for a time in the home early in his killing career. He killed when they were away. Gacy had assured everyone that he just had a septic problem, nothing that a little lime couldn't fix. But it never did get fixed, and yet no one alerted the authorities.

At times, Gacy killed two victims in a single night, and he was always faced with what to do with the bodies. Only when he ran out of space beneath his house did he start tossing them in the Des Plaines River. When Gacy talked about how he had killed his victims, he admitted at times to keeping the corpse close to him for a few hours. "After sleeping in bed next to the corpse all night, Gacy got up at 6 A.M. and moved it to the attic."[5]

As infamous as Gacy was for his perversion, he doesn't hold a candle to two killers who shared a common modus operandi. They figured that the best way to keep a companion around was to kill him. Both manifested a form of necrophilia, yet in different ways.

KEEPING THEM CLOSE

Jeffrey Dahmer and Dennis Nilsen were both quiet, ordinary young men who became lethal. Dahmer dreamed of creating a living zombie as a sex slave—a person who would always obey him and stay with him—and Nilsen similarly craved someone who would never leave. Like many murderers, they viewed other people as objects to be used for their own purposes. Let's look first at Nilsen.

He lived in London and picked up his victims in pubs. Before he ever killed, he had already experienced an erotic attraction to death, so he would spend hours lying in front of a mirror, glimpsing himself pretending to be dead. There was something about the vulnerability of that position, in himself and in others, that stirred in him an intense hunger. He had invited a few lovers on occasion to role-play his fantasy, but he had difficulty asking people to do this. Like all secret fetishes, he felt ashamed. However, that did not diminish the intensity of what he craved.

In 1978, Nilsen invited a man he had met in a pub back to his apartment. They drank a few beers and when Nilsen realized this man would eventually leave, he came up behind him and strangled him with a necktie. To his surprise, he found the act of murder erotic, especially the feeling of complete control. He kept the body for a little while until it began to smell and then placed it beneath the floorboards of his apartment.

Nilsen continued to invite men to his home. A few he let go, but he strangled others. Once he got used to having bodies around, he liked how good it felt to have them completely in his power. He would bathe them and even get into the bathtub with them. Sometimes he put them into his bed. He admitted to attempting to have sex with the bodies, but said that he often found it difficult. On occasion, he would just position them somewhere in his apartment so he would not feel alone. Finally, when the decomposition got to be oppressive, Nilsen would dismember them in his living room. Some parts he kept nearby and others he would dump in garbage somewhere or burn in his garden. In his later confession, he indicated that his favorite part of these rituals was the first night when the body was fresh. He was enraptured with the fact that they couldn't get up and leave. He enjoyed playing with them as if they were dolls: he might store them in a cupboard, sit them in a chair, dress them, or cut them up—whatever his whim at the time.

With experience as a butcher, Nilsen had no trouble dissecting the corpses and boiling the flesh from their skulls in a large soup kettle. To him, the entire procedure was a loving act, the last one that these men would know, and that idea gave him satisfaction.

However, he eventually moved to another apartment that did not have a garden, so he had to devise a better way of disposing of his victims. He cut pieces of flesh from them and threw them into the toilet to flush, but when the septic system clogged in the entire building, an investigation led straight to Nilsen. Aware of what they sought, he pointed out a closet where police found the dismembered parts of two different men. Another torso was found in his tea chest, along with a number of old bones, and he was arrested. He then confessed to killing fifteen men over a period of five years. In prison, he entertained himself with drawings of their corpses and body parts.

Nilsen believed that his troubles could be pinpointed to several experiences. Because his father had left when he was a child, he'd been raised by his grandfather, Andrew Whyte, but when Nilsen was six, Whyte died. Nilsen's mother had him look at the corpse, and that experience triggered a sense of devastating loss. Then two years later, he nearly drowned in the sea, and was rescued by an older boy. This boy must have been aroused by Nilsen's prostrate body, for he removed his clothes and apparently masturbated onto him. Nilsen awoke to find a sticky white substance on his stomach.

In 1961, Nilsen had enlisted in the army and became a cook, which is how he learned butchery. He relied on alcohol to stave off loneliness, and during these years, he would lie in front of a mirror in such a way as not to see his head and pretend to be unconscious. The "other body" aroused him and he would masturbate. Around this time, he developed a close friendship with a man who was not gay but who agreed to pretend to be dead while Nilsen took home movies of him to play later for his own enjoyment.

Once he was a civilian again, Nilsen fell into a life of casual pickups, but he wanted something more solid and lasting. His mirror activities developed more bizarre qualities, as he now viewed the "other" body as being dead. He even used makeup to achieve a better effect, including applying fake blood to make it appear that he had been murdered.

Nilsen tried for an insanity defense, but he was convicted and given life in prison. He has kept a prison journal and attempted to publish a book, but so far he has been prohibited from that enterprise. Nilsen is an example of someone who gradually came to love death and to be sexually attracted to corpses, but who desired a companion. In murder, he was able to blend these desires—to retain a companion "forever" and to have sexual contact with a corpse—but oddly, he denied having had intercourse with his murdered victims. He supposedly just liked having them around for a while.[6] Much more sexually involved with dead bodies and more clearly necrophilic was Jeffrey Dahmer, who wanted a living zombie to do whatever he required.

EXPERIMENTS

Richard von Krafft-Ebing, the German neurologist who published *Psychopathia Sexualis* in 1886, was the first to formally describe necrophilia. Among his many cases, he includes Sergeant Francois Bertrand, who as a child liked to dissect animals and who developed violent torture fantasies as he grew older. In 1849, he dug up fresh corpses with his bare hands from the grounds of Pere Lachaise and Montparnasse Cemeteries in Paris in order to have sex with them. Once he saw the corpse, he would go into a frenzy. He'd disembowel them, hack them with a spade, sometimes chew on them, and leave the parts strewn about the cemetery. Although he was caught and convicted on fifteen counts, he served only one year in prison. He claimed that he could not control his behavior.[7]

von Krafft-Ebing believed that necrophilia may be simply a matter of having no hindrances to sexual satisfaction. Perfect subjugation, such as one might experience with a corpse, is erotic for some people, and that certainly seemed to be the primary fantasy for infamous Milwaukee killer Jeffrey Dahmer.

He came to the public's attention in July 1991, admitting to police that he had murdered seventeen men before one near-victim ran away from him and brought back the police. They went through his apartment and noticed the smell, then spotted Polaroid photos of dead men, mutilated and dismembered. A look inside the refrigerator revealed human heads, intestines, hearts, and kidneys. Around the apartment investigators found skulls, bones, rotting body parts, bloodstained soup kettles, and complete skeletons. There were three torsos in a large barrel, and chloroform, electric saws, a barrel of acid, and formaldehyde in various places. In all, investigators were able to find the remains of eleven different men. Dahmer told them about six more.

His first murder happened when he was only eighteen years old. His parents had abandoned the family home, going their separate ways, and for several weeks, Dahmer had the place to himself. While out driving, he spotted an attractive hitchhiker named Steve Hicks. He lured the man home with the promise of getting high. Hicks stayed a few hours and when he got up to leave, Dahmer smashed a barbell against the back of his head and then strangled him. "I didn't know how to keep him there," he later said to former FBI profiler Robert Ressler.[8] He discovered then that he was intensely aroused by the captivity of another human being, and when he cut the body into pieces for disposal, this activity excited him as well, so he masturbated over it.

Later he moved in with his grandmother, but felt the compulsion grip him once again. Going to the funeral of a young man, he made plans to go to the cemetery at night and dig up the body, but thwarted in that, he began again to pick up men. He would drug and strangle them, and have sex with the corpse. After that he would dismember them. While living with his grandmother, he killed four people and cut them up in her basement. Twice she had complained to his father about the odor, and Dahmer's father had searched the house, but Dahmer had always managed to talk his way out of discovery.[9]

Then he got his own apartment. In an effort to create zombies to do his bidding, he tried drilling holes into the heads of his unconscious victims and injecting acid into their skulls. One victim actually survived for two days after this treatment. Dahmer also tried to cut off the faces of his victims and to preserve them as masks, but they deteriorated too fast. As some sort of homage to his fantasies, Dahmer designed an altar made of skulls, which he hoped to build one day when he'd killed a sufficient number of men. He believed that from it he might gain special powers that would help him to better his life socially and financially. While he was careless at times, allowing victims to get out and outsiders who might notice the smell and the paraphernalia to come in, so were the police, who bought his stories on several occasions when a victim tried to get help. That allowed Dahmer to repeatedly get away with murder.[10]

Robert Ressler talked with Dahmer for two days to learn more about his motives. Dahmer was both articulate and willing to provide details, and Ressler had the impression that his subject was attempting to shock him. He came away aware that Dahmer trivialized the lives of his victims and thought only about his own needs; he had even seemed to take a certain amount of pride in his grisly workmanship. All the while he had protested that he'd wanted to change and had even purchased a mannequin to satisfy himself so he would not hurt anyone—an item that his father had discovered in his closet. This admission seemed disingenuous in light of the rest of Dahmer's confession.

"There's murder and there's murder," Ressler said. "There's the kind of murder that I think the average person can understand as not justified but nevertheless understandable. For example, a man kills someone during a felony. He wants to get away. Or two guys fight in a bar and a knife comes out. There are all sorts of homicides along those lines. But when you get pure unadulterated repetitive homicide with no particular motive in mind and nothing that would make it understandable as a gain, that indicates that you have something above and beyond rational motivation. You just have evil incentive and evil tendencies. I've had the feeling in interviews with these people that there's something beyond what we can comprehend.

"There's no rational motivation and when they're stalking people looking for a victim, and capturing them and taking them and locking them up—some of them would keep them for days and weeks—the emotion is gone. It's a cool-headed decision to do all this. It's very methodical. There's no rage and the goal is just to get the victim and use the victim in various ways and then eliminate them. Dahmer killed because he was lonely. Well, a lot of people are lonely and they don't kill other people. His solution to his loneliness was to get someone to his house, drug him, kill him, and keep the body for days at a time. Even though his defense was along the lines of insanity, I think in fact he did understand a lot of right from wrong. He went to lengths to conceal what he was doing. He did it in a manner that was designed to keep himself out of harm's way with law enforcement. It was pretty evident that Dahmer knew what he was doing and knew it was wrong, and yet at the same time he had this element of fantasy that drove him to dismember his victims and experiment with them by putting acid into their brains. He went way beyond the realm of what a person could understand."[11]

Dahmer's attorney, Gerald Boyle, in an attempt to show his insanity, opened his case with, "Jeffrey Dahmer wants a body. A body. That's his fantasy. A body." It seemed to him incomprehensible that anyone could view that as anything but psychotic. Yet Dahmer's clarity of mind in lying to police and the care he took not to get caught indicated that despite a peculiar paraphilia and compulsive sex drive, Dahmer was not a messy, disorganized individual. He had known what he was doing and that it was wrong. In fact, he had changed his plea to guilty just before the trial began, leaving the jury to determine the appropriate sentence—prison or a psychiatric facility. That's why his state of mind became relevant.

The court learned that by the age of fourteen, Dahmer was already pondering the use of a corpse for sex. He would ride around in a car with a friend who enjoyed hitting dogs, and he viewed his first murder the way many other men thought of their first sexual conquest. When he went to a funeral of a young man, he had a fantasy of stealing the body from the cemetery, and he learned from taxidermists how to preserve animals. He could only get an erection, he had said, if his sexual partner was unconscious. He needed that sense of complete control but did not wish to have to reciprocate by subjecting himself to others' desires. He claimed to have eaten body parts because he believed the victims would return to life through him. So that he could continue to have sex with them, he left his victims lying around for as long as possible (sometimes even showered with them in the tub) and when he finally had to dispose of them, he felt a loss. He disliked seeing their lives reduced to parts in garbage bags. There were times when he did feel evil, but the feeling eventually disappeared, especially once he got another victim under his control.[12]

Ressler, among other mental health experts, believes it would be best to devise a way to study these people who fall into the gray areas between uncontrolled psychosis and obvious sanity. Some people who do know that what they are doing is wrong, and who can even exercise control when threatened with unmasking, may nevertheless be so ill that their understanding of right and wrong is itself perverted. Several psychologists testified to this possibility with Dahmer. Yet the courts want things simple, as do juries, so the nuances of mental illness are generally unappreciated. Not only that, the justice system still accepts notions about mental illness that date back to the 1843 M'Naughten standards. For all the money some states spend to execute these killers, society might be better served by training people to study and more clearly identify just how serial killers with bizarre manifestations tick. Several researchers hope the answer lies somewhere in the brain, but for now, no one really knows. If they did, they might be able to address why some killers appear to act for no reason at all.

NOTES

1. John Eddowes, *The Two Killers of Rillington Place* (New York: Little, Brown, & Co., 1994); Jesse, F. Tennyson, ed., *Trials of Timothy John Evans and John Reginald Halliday Christie* (London: William Hodge & Company, Ltd., 1957); Ludovic Kennedy, *Ten Rillington Place* (New York: Simon & Schuster, 1961).

2. Eric Fromm, *The Anatomy of Human Destructiveness* (New York: Owl Books, 1992), pp. 362–367.

3. Jonathan Rosman and Phillip Resnick, "Sexual Attraction to Corpses: A Psychiatric Review of Necrophilia," *Bulletin of the American Academy of Psychiatry and Law*, 1989, 17(2), 132–145.

4. R. E. L. Masters and Eduard Lea, *Perverse Crimes in History* (New York: The Julian Press, 1963), pp. 115–130.

5. Terry Sullivan and Peter Maiken, *Killer Clown* (New York: Grosset & Dunlap, 1983), p. 176.

6. Brian Masters, *Killing for Company* (New York: Dell, 1993) (Originally published as *The Case of Dennis Nilsen* in Britain in 1985).

7. Richard von Krafft-Ebing, *Psychopathia Sexualis with Especial Reference to the Antipathic Sexual Instinct: A Medico-Forensic*, rev. edn. (Philadelphia, PA: Physicians and Surgeons, 1928).

8. Robert K. Ressler, *I Have Lived in the Monster* (New York: St. Martin's Press, 1997), p. 116.

9. Lionel Dahmer, *A Father's Story* (New York: William Morrow, 1994), pp. 124–127.

10. Anne E. Schwartz, *The Man Who Could Not Kill Enough* (New York: Birch Lane Press, 1992); "Jeffrey Dahmer: Mystery of the Serial Killer," *American Justice*, Arts & Entertainment, 1993.

11. From an interview with the author, published on www.crimelibrary.com, 2002.

12. Robert K. Ressler, *Whoever Fights Monsters* (New York: St. Martin's Press, 1992), pp. 276–281.

CHAPTER 11

No Particular Purpose

SHORT-RANGE PLANS

As the year 1950 drew to a close, ex-convict William "Cockeyed" Cook, in his black leather jacket and "hard luck" tattoos, came out of the Missouri State Penitentiary and home to Joplin. Once abandoned by his father (who'd raised him and his seven motherless siblings in an abandoned mineshaft), this twenty-one-year-old began another crime spree, but this time much more serious. Near Joplin, he hijacked a car but when the driver got away, he abandoned that one for a car in which a family was riding. He made the father drive him from one state to the next. Apparently he simply enjoyed the fact that he could force people to do his will. In the meantime, the first driver had reported the hijacking incident and the police had found a receipt with Cook's name on it.

Back in Missouri from the long drive, Cook continued to keep the family hostage but when a police officer drove by, he panicked and shot the three children, the parents, and their dog. Then he drove around in their car with their corpses for a while, as if he had not thought out a plan. Finally, he took them to an abandoned mineshaft, not unlike the one in which he'd been raised, and depositied them.

Although Cook now had a car at his disposal, he walked away from it, providing the police with a way to pick up his trail, and they were able to link the two hijackings, although they worried over blood found in the second car. Since he had abandoned both vehicles, clearly Cook was not out to steal a car. The police realized that they probably had a drifter on their hands with nothing much to do but harass people . . . perhaps worse. They looked for someone who fit that description.

But Cook had already forced a salesman to drive him to California, where he then killed the man for no apparent reason. He was unaware that his identity was known and a manhunt was on for him across the Southwest. He kidnapped several other people, letting them go, and took two men hostage in Mexico, but the authorities there recognized him from the warning they had received from the States. They grabbed him before he could harm his next intended prey. Cook was convicted in Missouri of the murder of the family of five, but California also convicted him for the murder of the hapless salesman and on December 12, 1952, he was executed in the gas chamber. He never offered a reason for why he had killed, and his pattern seemed so random that no one else could pinpoint a sensible reason for it, either.[1]

MANY REASONS, OR NONE

A number of predators have killed for a variety of motives and cannot easily be viewed as having had a clear drive, like Jeffrey Dahmer did, or a single-minded goal, as Dennis Rader expressed. For example, H. H. Holmes killed for sexual excitement, self-enrichment, and to silence witnesses, as did Pee Wee Gaskins, who claimed more than one hundred victims along America's southeastern coastal states. When the reasons they offer are clearly instrumental, such as to eliminate witnesses, there's not much more to say. The reason is obvious: they wanted to get away with whatever they had done and not leave any means of discovery behind. But the more disturbing killers are those who just did it, for no apparent purpose, and who murdered repeatedly. Gary Gilmore, for example, simply killed two men in Utah because he had not adapted well to being outside prison, was feeling powerless and without a sense of direction, and apparently just got an idea. While some experts would not include Gilmore as a serial killer, the only reason he did not kill a third time (and more), by his own admission, was because he was caught directly after his second murder. He stated in prison that if he were free, he would continue to kill. As such, the psychology of his aggression is relevant to this study.

On Monday, July 19, 1976, Gilmore entered a service station and saw no one around but the attendant. He walked up to the man, whose nameplate read "Max Jensen" and pulled out a .22 Browning Automatic. He instructed Jensen to empty his pockets, which the young Mormon quickly did. Then he told Jensen to go into the bathroom and lie down on the floor with his arms under his body. Jensen obeyed. Inexplicably, Gilmore placed the muzzle right against Jensen's skull and shot him twice—one for himself and one for his estranged girlfriend. He left the gas station without even noticing the wad of cash on the counter. He then went to a movie, undisturbed by what he'd done, as if he had done nothing more than pick up a six-pack.

The next day, Gilmore had trouble with his new truck, so he took it to a gas station. Upon learning that a fix could take twenty minutes, Gilmore walked down the street and spotted the City Center Motel. Once again, he got an idea, so he entered the lobby. Ben Bushnell asked Gilmore what he wanted, and Gilmore ordered him to give over the cash box and get down on the floor. Before Bushnell could obey, Gilmore shot him in the head.

Gilmore was not difficult to track, and his cousin turned him in. At first he denied killing anyone, but Bushnell's wife had seen him, so he finally confessed. He said that he did not know why he had killed the two Mormons. He didn't have a reason, and he admitted that had he not been caught, he would likely have continued killing.

Gilmore is a good example of a person with the predatory impetus to be a serial killer, as per the standard definition of at least three murders in three separate incidents, but he was caught before he managed a third. Given his lack of inhibitions and the ease with which he was able to shoot the two men without remorse, he was probably correct that he would kill at whim, again and again. Gilmore was sentenced to die and had to fight to get the state of Utah to go through with it. His claim to fame lies in the fact that he was the first person executed after the United States had reinstated the death penalty after a moratorium. Asked for last words, he said, "Let's do it."[2]

Another killer who offered no insight into his motive was David Edward Maust, 51, who was sentenced in Indiana to three consecutive life terms in prison on December 18, 2005. He had murdered three boys, and after the sentencing, he agreed to speak about all five of the murders he had committed. He knew a lot about the victims and the circumstances of their deaths, when asked, but he was unable to say why he had done it. He likened the feeling of murder to when his mother would punish him by taking things from him that he wanted.

"They were good, nonviolent, innocent young people who did not deserve to die," Maust said of his victims in jailhouse writings that were published in the press. "None of them did nothing wrong. They had nothing I wanted except for them to be my friend, and they took nothing from me. But I still killed them for no reason... I cannot blame the places where I was raised, my fall as a four-year-old, my environment, my genes, or my parents."

There was nothing about Nicholas James, age 19, that stood out to Maust. They had worked together in a trophy shop. On May 2, 2003, Maust invited James to his rental home and bludgeoned him in the kitchen with a baseball bat. He then coated the body in paint and placed it into wet concrete in the basement. Later that year, in September, Maust strangled James Raganyi, 16, and Michael Dennis, 13. He had first brought them to his home from a pool two months earlier in July and they had spent the night. During the time they were there, Maust had fantasized about stabbing them, but he'd held himself back because he wanted someone to hang out with. But then, a few days before they returned in September, Maust dug a hole in the basement in preparation. The two boys were apparent runaways, Maust said, who had sought shelter with him. (Others insisted that he lured them there.) He gave them whiskey, killed them within three hours of each other, wrapped them in plastic, and poured concrete over them.

But Maust had also murdered two other boys before that year. In 1972, when he was stationed in the army in Germany, he killed Jimmy McClister, 13. The army convicted him of involuntary manslaughter and court-martialed him. Maust received a three-year prison sentence. He'd had other adolescents in mind, he later said, but at that time McClister became his only victim. It was a crime, he said, born of general frustration.

In 1981, back in Illinois, he stabbed and drowned fifteen-year-old Donald Jones. Convicted, he received thirty-five years, but served only seventeen. Upon his release in 1999, he sought to be classified as a sexually violent offender so he could be housed in the Sheridan Correctional Center, but his request was either denied or ignored.

Arrested in December 2003 after three bodies were found in his basement, Maust remained silent for two years until after his sentencing—three life terms in exchange for a guilty plea. His attorney blamed the way he was handled as a boy by neglectful parents, who had placed him in a mental institution when he was nine. He'd remained there for four years (although Maust claimed that he had liked it there). Supposedly due to these circumstances, Maust grew to hate himself, and he had externalized that hatred against others. When asked to provide some reason why he had decided these boys should die, he said, "I think the answer is you got to put my whole life together, look at the sequence of events." Which, of course, is no answer at all. He did mention that if he had known that his last victim was thirteen, he would not have hung out with him, because "I had already killed a thirteen-year-old." Comments like that, along with Maust's general inability to offer a motive, indicate that he probably killed on impulse, perhaps based in rehearsal fantasies. "Being lonely is what destroyed me," he said. None of the victims had been sexually assaulted, because, as Maust says, he was looking for affection, not sex. Shortly after his sentencing, he hinted he would soon die, and he committed suicide in prison by hanging himself with a bed sheet.[3]

JUST TO DO IT

When three members of the Groene-Mckenzie family were bludgeoned to death in their home in Idaho on May 15, 2005, and young Shasta and

Dylan Groene were kidnapped, it became national news. Thanks to the nationwide Amber Alert program, several people recognized Shasta in a restaurant and called the police. She told them that over the course of several days, she and her nine-year-old brother had been repeatedly sexually assaulted. Then their kidnapper had taken Dylan away, tortured and shot him, burned his remains, and fled with her. (Dylan's remains were found in Montana.)

Their abductor was James Edward Duncan III, a convicted child molester. His criminal history included a long string of assaults against children, as well as at least one other murder, giving him a total of six murders in three different incidents, although he is a suspect in several as-yet unsolved murders (in his online blog, he alluded to having committed more). Duncan, 42, officially began his criminal career in 1978 when he was fifteen by forcibly raping a nine-year-old boy at gunpoint. Apparently he told a therapist that he had assaulted at least a dozen boys in a similar manner, six of whom he'd bound. Only two years later, he was in prison for raping a fourteen-year-old boy.

Duncan remained in prison for fourteen years, and his parole conditions stipulated that he stay away from children. Yet he reportedly admitted to FBI agents that he was involved in the abduction and murder of Anthony Martinez in Riverside, California, in 1997. He'd attempted to grab Anthony's brother as well, but that boy escaped.

In April 2005, Duncan was charged in Minnesota with molesting a six-year-old boy and attempting to molest his friend. Bond was posted and, as if in retaliation, Duncan purchased a shotgun, a claw hammer, and ammunition. He stole a Jeep Grand Cherokee and fled the state, arriving in Idaho. He apparently spotted the Groene children in their yard and staked out the home for a few days until he determined the right time to go grab them. Although he has not confessed to this, a reconstruction indicates that this is a likely scenario.

But instead of taking the children from the yard at an opportune moment, Duncan apparently decided to enter the house and kill the three people inside. Rather than just shoot them, he chose to bind them and use the claw hammer to bludgeon them to death. He also described to Shasta and Dylan, after taking them, what he had done to their family and recorded his treatment of them for his later enjoyment. So it seems that he made a decision to kill the rest of the family because he wanted to, not because he had to or because he wanted to steal something, and he turned the same meanness against Dylan. Shasta was probably his next victim, but she was rescued in time.

Duncan, 42, reportedly whined about his treatment as a sex offender in a blog journal he kept online, labeled "The Fifth Nail," a reference to the nails used on Jesus Christ during his crucifixion. In some entries, he discussed the idea of right and wrong and his awareness that he did not know the difference. He blamed demons for his desires. "My intent," he wrote, "is to harm society as much as I can, and die."[4]

RATIONALE AS AN AFTERTHOUGHT

Sometimes a motive develops after a predator has seen his own patterns mapped out by the media. In 1984, Richard Ramirez entered the home of a seventy-nine-year-old woman in Glassell Park, California. He slashed her throat and stabbed her several times after she was already dead. He killed twice more over the next eight months before the police got a description from the survivor of an intended double homicide. A man had entered the condominium she had shared with her murdered friend. She indicated that the killer, dressed in black clothing, had bulging eyes, a narrow face, curly dark hair, a terrible odor, and bad teeth.

The murders and rapes continued, with some people suffering more than others. Vincent Zazzara was attacked in his home and killed, while his wife was shot and then stabbed to death. The assailant removed her eyelids, carved out her eyes, and took them with him. Not long afterward, two elderly sisters were bludgeoned and their attacker left Satanic symbols on the thigh of the one who died, in the form of a pentagram. While the Los Angeles area murders continued at random, the "Night Stalker" also killed a couple in San Francisco. But he'd left behind a fingerprint. Running it through a database, the police turned up the name of Richard Ramirez, a reputed Satanist who had a long record for traffic and drug violations.

Ramirez's picture was published in the newspaper and when he tried to steal a car on August 30, he was recognized and beaten by a group of citizens, who then held him for the police. He was ultimately charged with thirteen murders and thirty other criminal counts, including rape and burglary. As for his motives, he had told one of his guards that he loved watching people die.

Ramirez reportedly enjoyed all the references to Satanism and his penchant for the Dark Side, and it's unclear whether he actually acted for "Satanic" purposes or simply adopted the persona as a way to stand out, taking the idea from what the press had written about him. At a preliminary hearing, he praised Satan and flashed a pentagram that he'd had tattooed onto the palm of his hand. When he was convicted, his lawyers warned him that he could get the death sentence. He didn't care. "I'll be in hell, then," he said, "with Satan." He was sentenced to death and he now sits on California's death row. Whether he had any motive other than the one he adopted to play up his notoriety is unknown, although some experts who have studied the crimes attribute his impulse to kill to religious motives and/or to experiences he had as a child.

The young Ramirez had admired an older cousin named Mike, who had become a role model. Mike loved to prove how tough he was. As Richard hung out with him, absorbing Mike's life philosophies, he learned a tougher outlook. Mike had survived the rigors of Vietnam, and when he returned with brutal stories, he became larger-than-life in Richard's eyes. Mike told Richard that killing made him feel like a god. He bragged that he had raped and murdered a number of women. Richard viewed Polaroid photos of Mike in sexual activity in which a woman was a helpless victim and of Mike murdering these same women. Mike even bragged about them, and the adolescent Richard no doubt was excited by the degraded women. In addition, Mike taught Richard the art of hunting as a predator, and on one occasion, Mike shot and killed his wife in front of the boy. So Ramirez's exposure to violence associated with manhood could have influenced his developing fantasies.[5]

Even so, no one knows the exact ingredients that transform a boy into a predatory murderer. Another killer thought to be involved in occultic practices refused to accept what others said about him, and indicated that he really had no reason to kill. This case began shortly after Ramirez was caught and just before his trial began.

FATAL SIDE EFFECTS

In April 1988, Chris Bryson jumped from the second-story home of Robert Berdella and ran for help. He wore only a dog collar and had trouble opening his eyes. The story he told was difficult to accept, but it turned out to be true. He had been knocked out in Berdella's home and had revived to find himself on a bed, tied spread-eagle to the posts. He had no clothes on and as he passed out again, he felt Berdella place a dog collar around his neck. When he came to, Berdella was dabbing a substance with a strong odor into his eyes. It stung badly, but Bryson had no choice but to endure it. Berdella then used an iron rod to smack at Bryson's bound hands and attached an electrical device to Bryson's testicles and thighs. Bryson felt a strong jolt of electricity which sent the pain in his hands snapping through his body. As he reacted in agony, he saw a flash of light and heard a whirring noise. Berdella was taking pictures.

Bryson's torture continued over the course of several days, including having his throat injected with drain cleaner, but one day Berdella left the house and Bryson managed to free himself by burning the ropes with discarded matches and he escaped. Others had not been so lucky. As a form of psychological torture, Berdella had shown Bryson photographs of other men who appeared to be dead. Indeed, they were, all six of them.

While searching Berdella's home, the police discovered a log full of notes in which Berdella had described what he had done to victims and had recorded their reactions. In a peculiar type of shorthand, he had jotted the times, a victim's slightest movement, whether a victim was aware of things being done to him, and sometimes an ominous notation, "DD" or "86." After that, for that person, there was nothing more.

Three years earlier, Berdella had been investigated over the disappearance of two young men, Jerry Howell, 19, who went missing in July 1984, and James Ferris, 25, who vanished in September 1985. A man named Todd Stoops had informed the police that he had seen both men with Berdella. Eventually he, too, disappeared. There had been no evidence at the time linking Berdella to these men, but now the tables had turned. Human remains found in the backyard were difficult for Berdella to explain.

Berdella agreed to make a full confession in exchange for a life sentence and he offered details about his sadistic assaults. In a small conference room in the basement of the Kansas City jail, he started talking and the final report came to 717 pages. Berdella considered influences that might have been factors, and among them was a film, *The Collector*, that he had seen as a teenager (mentioned earlier by another killer as a significant influence). Based on the novel by John Fowles, the film features a character driven by the need to capture a woman and keep her imprisoned in a building on his property while he develops a relationship with her. She resists him, but as it dawns on her that she will never escape, she attempts to accept the situation. Eventually she dies and he decides that this unfortunate development was her fault. He ponders what he needs to do with the next captive to make it a better experience for him and then goes in pursuit of her. Berdella said that this movie gave him a framework for feelings he was already having about controlling other people for sexual purposes, and inspired him to try something similar.

Yet since it was the torture rather than the actual murders that had given Berdella pleasure, he was asked why he had killed the men. He said that he didn't really have a reason, at least not consciously. He had just thought that since he had not been caught after the first murder, what difference did it make if he killed again? His attitude about it was clear when he described putting the remains of some victims outside on the curb in bags for the garbage collector.[6]

SUBTLE INFLUENCES

Adrian Raine, from the University of Southern California, researches the neurological correlates of violence. He and his colleagues have identified several areas of brain deficit that appear to contribute, specifically the limbic system (known to be the emotional center) and the prefrontal cortex. These deficits may make people impulsive, fearless, less responsive to aversive stimulation, and less able to make appropriate decisions about aggression toward others. They may also seek out sensation-stimulating activities.[7] This research suggests that some people are more predisposed toward impulsive violence than others in virtue of brain structures, and that can affect their fantasy life as well.

Seeking a more philosophical answer, criminal justice professor Candice Skrapec from California State University at Fresno indicates from qualitative research that serial killers use their murder to give meaning and purpose to their lives. She finds evidence of basic human needs in what they do, albeit distorted or exaggerated. From interviews, she discovered that male serial killers of the predatory type often feel like victims themselves, so they strike back to make others pay. That seems to be the case for Duncan in the examples above. He, like the others, seemed to view himself as exempt from any moral code and entitled to do whatever he wanted. When serial killers gain momentum from their violent fantasies, they may feel more able to kill. Enacting the fantasy protects them by offering them the rehearsal of being in control. It may also make them feel special, because they're achieving something that few people can do.

The killing thus provides a sense of vitality, which produces euphoria that is followed by a sense of calm or relief from pressure. Then when their murders are covered in the media, it affirms their sense of power. It isn't difficult to sexualize the aggression, even if sexual predation is not the original motive. Given their limited range of evaluation—everything is black or white with no in-between—their acts must be all or nothing. The killings make them feel complete. "In the end," says Skrapec, "what appears outwardly to be offensive behavior is essentially defensive."[8]

While this may not fully explain why a specific individual commits senseless murder, it does give us a better understanding of why they may keep going. It may also shed light on why some of them start so young. Those who engage in torture, as opposed to the more instantaneous "blitz" killing, have shown deficits in their ability to feel anything for the victim, which inhibits distress or guilt over what they are doing. Thus, if they desire power, control, and domination, they will continue to seek opportunities for them after the effects of prior incidents wear off. Likewise, if they seek a higher level of sensation, they will need to repeatedly renew the experience. Some get started on that as adolescents. So we turn now to aggressively violent children who have killed more than once.

NOTES

1. David Everitt, *Human Monsters* (Chicago: Contemporary Books, 1993), pp. 146–148.

2. Mikal Gilmore, *Shot in the Heart* (New York: Doubleday, 1994); Norman Mailer, *The Executioner's Song* (New York: Random House, 1979).

3. Ruth Ann Krause, "Serial Killer Talks One Day after Being Sentenced to Three Consecutive Life Terms," *Post-Tribune*, December 18, 2005; Ruthann Robinson, "Interview with a Serial Killer," *Northwest Indiana News*, December 18, 2005.

4. Taryn Brodwater and Becky Kramer, "Transcripts Detail Murder, Kidnapping Case," *The Spokesman Review*, October 22, 2005.

5. Cyril Wecht, Greg Saitz with Mark Curriden, *Mortal Evidence: The Forensics behind Nine Shocking Cases* (Amherst, New York: Prometheus Books, 2003), pp. 239–270; Tom Jackman and Troy Cole, *Rites of Burial: The Shocking True Crime Account of Robert Berdella, the Butcher of Kansas City, Missouri* (New York: Pinnacle, 1992).

6. Philip Carlo, *The Night Stalker* (New York: Kensington, 1996); Articles from the *Los Angeles Times* during the Ramirez trial in 1988.

7. Adrian Raine, "Psychopathy, Violence and Brain Imaging," in *Violence and Psychopathy*, Adrian Raine and José Sanmartín, eds. (New York: Kluwer, 2001), pp. 35–58.

8. Candice Skrapec, "Motives of the Serial Killer," in *Violence and Psychopathy*, Adrian Raine and José Sanmartín, eds. (New York: Kluwer, 2001), pp. 105–122.

CHAPTER 12

Early Aspirations

While a number of male serial killers began their careers during adolescence, it's a female who holds the record thus far as the world's youngest serial killer. Can we spot the budding serial killer in children? While there are as yet no definite predictors of violence, we do know about traits associated with what has been called the "fledging psychopath." In addition, some children actually make becoming a "serial killer" their life's ambition. Their cases offer hope for better understanding.

BAD SEEDS

On May 25, 1968, four-year-old Martin Brown was strangled in New Castle, England. His aunt learned the news from little Mary Bell, who breathlessly came to tell her that there had been an "accident." Over the next few days, Mary and her thirteen-year-old friend, Norma Bell (no relation), came repeatedly to ask the woman whether she missed Martin. Mary also turned up at the Brown's house to ask if she could see the body in its coffin. No one believed then that the tragic death had been a murder.

Two days after the boy was found, several scribbled notes claiming responsibility, two signed by "Fanny and Faggot," were left at a nursery school. A chilling message indicated the killer was not finished: "I murder so that I may come back." However, the police believed it was just a sick prank.

Then two months later on July 31, another boy, Brian Howe, was killed. He was only three years old and had been strangled and sexually mutilated with a sharp instrument. His killer had also used a razor to carve

"M" in the flesh of his stomach. The two deaths were linked and neighborhood residents feared a predator. They kept their children close.

Again, Mary and Norma had been involved. They had even helped worried relatives search for the boy, leading his sister right into the area where the body turned up. When Howe was buried, Chief Inspector James Dobson observed Mary Bell waiting outside the family's house to watch the coffin be carried out. She rubbed her hands together and laughed. He realized, quite beyond belief, that he might have a child murderer on his hands—a girl. And she was only eleven; in fact, the first murder had occurred one day before her eleventh birthday, so she had been only ten. It seemed impossible, but he had to investigate before she killed again. (She apparently tried strangling Norma's sister but Norma had intervened.) Dobson took Mary and Norma in for questioning.

Each immediately accused the other, and both were held for trial. Mary gave a detailed statement to the police that was unsettling in its nonchalant delivery. When the girls were brought to the courtroom, the press focused on the notion of a "bad seed," or a child born evil. Mary, with her indifferent expression, seemed to fit the bill, both for the press and the prosecutor. While she was "clearly" a vicious, aggressive mastermind with cunning and intelligence, Norma was a simple backward girl of subnormal intelligence. It was no surprise that Norma was acquitted, but Mary was convicted of manslaughter and sentenced to an all-boys' institution. The press called her a bully, a liar, and a callous murderess, capable of acting on her own. The public consensus was that Mary Bell, her youth notwithstanding, was evil incarnate.

However, years later, Gitta Sereny, who had covered the trial, located Bell after her release. Sereny learned a startling story of how Bell's mother, a prostitute, had subjected her to repeated child abuse, making her engage in sexual acts with men when she was only five. Apparently the woman had even tried to kill Mary on several occasions. These revelations put her past aggression in a new light.[1]

No such explanation is available for Craig Price, who committed his first murder in 1988 in Warwick, Rhode Island, when he was thirteen, making him the youngest known American serial killer, and the youngest male. He had stabbed a woman in her home fifty-eight times. Yet no one realized his criminal disposition until two years later when he climbed through a kitchen window into the home of Joan Heaton to slaughter her and her two daughters. They were all stabbed and slashed multiple times—more than 120 wounds among them.

Price had cut his own hand during the struggle, and since blood that had not belonged to the victims was found in the home, it was not difficult to link him to these murders. However, no one would have suspected him. Although he was one of the few black children in a predominantly white neighborhood, he was athletic and friendly, from a respected family. Yet it turned out he had a record of breaking-and-entering, and theft. The fingerprints from the refrigerator door at the Heaton home matched Price's, and he failed a polygraph test about how he had cut his hand on a broken car window. There was also no evidence of broken glass where the car had been parked.

This became a major case in Rhode Island, because under their law, Price couldn't be tried as an adult, so he'd get out when he was twenty-one. Afraid of having him back in their midst, they rewrote their laws. In 1995, the judge gave Price seven more years for another offense, and then he assaulted two prison guards and got an extra twenty-five.[2]

More than a century earlier in 1874, the next youngest killer had committed his crimes. A ten-year-old girl went missing in Boston and the mystery of her whereabouts was solved only after fourteen-year-old Jesse Pomeroy confessed to killing and mutilating Horace Mullen, aged four. Mullen had been found near a swamp on the outskirts of the town, stabbed and slashed so savagely that he was nearly decapitated. Pomeroy, already known for his cruelty toward other boys, was brought to the body to see it. When pressed, he admitted he had done it.

Pomeroy got his start as a criminal at the age of twelve. He had lured other boys into the woods to beat and torture them, so he'd been sent to reform school. His aggression may well have been influenced by bullying, since he had the kind of appearance that draws out nasty behavior from other children: a sloping misshapen head and a milky-white eye. It wasn't long before the missing girl was also found dead, buried in the cellar where Pomeroy's mother had a shop, and he confessed to that murder, too. He said he just liked the act of killing. Dubbed by the press "the Boston Boy Fiend," Pomeroy was convicted and sentenced to death. During his sensational trial, moralists blamed his violence on lurid dime novels. Some accounts say he confessed to over two dozen more murders, and that more mutilated bodies were unearthed, but these accounts proved untrue. Pomeroy ended up in solitary confinement for most of the rest of his life.[3]

COLD AMBITIONS

In *A Violent Heart*, psychologist Gregory Moffatt says that one of the most important variables among the variety of factors involved in the development of aggression is choice. In the case of younger people with limited cognitive abilities, their choices are contained within those limitations. They're often also immature in their outlook and ability to understand the consequences of their behavior.[4] One young man offered an open window into his fantasy life by keeping detailed journals. While he was stopped before he could kill a third time, his ultimate goal was clear.

In Texas in 1993, Jason Massey, 20, committed the double homicide of a teenage boy and girl whom he had lured out one night. After he was caught, it became clear that throughout the course of his adolescence, he had harbored fantasies of extreme violence, and had killed small animals as practice for what he wanted to become. In fact, Massey had told a friend that if he ever heard about a serial killer in the area, it would be him, Massey.

Two years earlier, Massey's mother had taken him to see Dr. Kenneth Dekleva, a state psychiatrist. She had found two notebooks that contained Massey's journals, kept since 1989, and was disturbed by their violent content, especially his list of names of girls he wanted to kill. Dekleva learned through the journals that Massey had an obsessive fantasy life and was enamored of the idea of becoming a serial killer. He described it as a "sacred journey" and a way to "engrave his name on society." Apparently, he wanted to cause as much sorrow and suffering in others as he could. Massey had actually made plans and purchased weapons, which increased the danger that he would act out and possibly kill someone. Dekleva concluded that Massey posed a threat to others, so he was committed to the Dallas Psychiatric Intensive Care Unit for further observation, although Dekleva knew there was no real treatment for antisocial personality disorder. Other doctors examined the young man, eighteen at the time, but they did not agree with Dekleva's prognosis, so Massey was released.

During Massey's trial, a former classmate from seventh grade, Anita Mendoza, told the court that as early as 1989, Massey made threatening phone calls to her, harassing her with vile language and notes, and telling her that he had dreams about killing her. In fact her dog had been killed and mutilated in her driveway the day after she refused to meet him, its blood smeared on her car. She believed he had done it. He had also sent her a magazine photograph of a woman that he had beheaded with scissors, telling her that this is what she would eventually look like.

Even as the jury learned about the brutal double homicide, Massey's journals were found in the woods by a hiker, along with a red cooler that contained the decapitated skeletonized heads of thirty-one small animals. The journals, bagged in plastic, were labeled, "The Slayer Book of Death. Volumes 1–4. The thoughts of Jason Massey." There were over five hundred pages of entries, from 1989 until 1993, the month in which the victims had been murdered. Inside, among other things, Massey admitted to killing a girl's dog and smearing its blood on her car.

In these pages, it was clear that Massey had picked out one young girl after another, all between the ages of ten and thirteen, to be his "first." He had claimed undying love for them and the need to possess them, which he could only do if he killed them. It was also clear that he was determined to do what he claimed he would do, because that was the way to "be a man," and he needed to be the best at whatever he set out to do. Ultimately, his violence welled up from the feeling that "the Master"—Satan—was watching him at all times. He wanted to do something significant, like an all-out massacre. He worried that if he did not act soon, God would come and take "his girls" away from him.

The defense attorneys used the journals to show passages where Massey described being lonely, having doubts, and wanting to turn away from all this and be good. He had described being sexually abused by a babysitter when he was around five and being hit by a father who'd left him and his mother when he was two. The attorney also put Massey's sister on the stand to describe their difficult lives as children. However, the mitigating circumstances failed to outweigh Massey's own admissions.

He had kept track of his animal abuse, killing forty-one cats, thirty-two dogs, and seven cows, removing their heads to keep with him to remind him of his violence. It was clear that had he not been stopped in July 1993, he would have killed again. His greatest ambition, he wrote, was to become America's most famous serial killer. "My goal is 700 people in twenty years." In the entry for January 19, 1991, a Sunday, Massey indicated that he had tried and failed to kill his girlfriend and "I'm tired of feeling like shit for not being able to kill." He looked forward to really "losing his virginity" as a killer. He wanted to physically eat some girl's brain and heart, and drink her blood. He wanted bones to cry to him from the earth, bones of victims that belonged to him and him alone. Three days later, he made a notation that officially marked his "sacred journey." His master was Satan, who had called out to him in the woods, and Massey believed that once he began, he would be unable to stop.

The jury lost no time in convicting Massey of the double homicide, and after hearing from psychiatrists that there was no hope for rehabilitation, they gave him the death penalty. He was executed in 2001.[5]

Children who grow up without stability, as Massey did, have difficulty forming emotional attachments to their caretakers and others in later life. Jason, who never knew his father, was then deprived and forced to live in an environment of uncertainty and random violence, at the mercy of a mother who reportedly treated her children as if they were a bothersome appendage. Not only did she foster a transient and unpredictable environment, but also added a certain amount of neglect, starvation, and random punishment. It should come as no surprise that Massey, feeling disempowered and needy, might develop a love/hate relationship with women. His mother never saw what she was creating. First, she was an influential role model who showed her children that violence was the way to resolve life's problems. Second, she inspired in at least one of her children the feeling that he had to create his own center of stability, and for a male that meant finding some image that would make him feel powerful rather than weak. Unfortunately, Massey looked up to *killers* as images of strength and manhood.

While this kind of parenting and childhood experience would not necessarily cause maturing boys to find their role model in criminals, it apparently had some influence on Massey's choices about what gave life meaning. Feeling angry and afraid, he developed violent fantasies, and his perception of females was formed by an ill-tempered mother who was anything but nurturing. When he learned from experience that violence against others empowered him, it was inevitable that his fantasy life would become more textured with these images, and eroticized, especially as he moved through puberty.

He roamed the woods in search of his own private cemetery, viewing himself as serving some "Master" and building altars to a demon. He killed animals out here under the moon and became obsessed with specific girls he saw. He even wrote that he wanted to decapitate a girl and have sex inside her neck. Thus, he would gravitate toward others who had found the same kind of solace or solutions in violence, notably people such as Charles Manson, Ted Bundy, and Henry Lee Lucas. They were *somebody*, because they were famous, and he thought that if he became one, he'd no longer be a nobody. Everyone would remember him, people would write about him, and he'd be in criminology textbooks, offered as an example of real dangerousness. Thoughts like that were powerfully erotic to a lonely, disturbed boy who had few social skills.

Psychologist Donald Black believes that antisocial personality disorder such as that manifested by many killers affects up to seven million Americans, with eight more times the likelihood of appearing in males than in females, and he believes the evidence suggests that some people are just born bad. There are warning signs, he says, which include a reactive and resistant personality, failure to care about the difference between right and wrong, and a lack of empathy or remorse.[6] His work is similar to that being done by people interested in the precursors of criminal psychopathy.

THE FLEDGLING PSYCHOPATH

A sixteen-year-old boy (not named in the press) assisted serial killer Douglas Moore to dismember and dispose of two of the bodies of his victims in Mississauga, Ontario, in Canada. Although his attorney argued that the boy was under Moore's influence and was therefore confused and afraid, the judges found that he exhibited "some initiative" and was thus criminally responsible as an accessory to murder after the fact.

Moore killed Robert Grewal and Joseph Manchisi in his garage in November 2003. The teenager disposed of the knife that was used to dismember the bodies without Moore asking him to, and he admitted to holding the heads of the victims as Moore cleaned his car in a car wash before burying them and the dismembered hands in separate holes in the woods in Quebec. He drove the car to Quebec and apparently also stole drugs and money from Moore, who had believed that his victims were responsible. The boy was aware that Moore intended to kill them because of their thievery and did nothing to stop the killings. Moore already had a conviction as a pedophile and was a suspect in the death of another teenager in the area. The boy claimed he had viewed Moore as a father figure. He received only six months in prison for his part, and even that he fought (unsuccessfully) through appeals.[7]

While adolescent misbehavior is often labeled as a conduct disorder, with the hope that it will pass, along with the instability of teenage issues, Frick and his associates have found the concept of psychopathy in children to extend beyond conduct problems. They view the salient factors in young offenders for detecting the personality structure of a budding psychopath as impulsive/conduct problems and callous/unemotional attitudes. They assessed ninety-five clinic-referred children and found that psychopathy and conduct problems are independent yet interacting constructs in children, similar to the way criminal behavior and psychopathic traits interact in adults. These children exhibit grandiosity, irresponsibility, and susceptibility to boredom. The researchers also discovered that children with or without conduct problems but with low anxiety (approximating what is found to be true of psychopathy) participated in more trials of an activity that had an increasing ratio of punishment to reward. Those with low anxiety and conduct problems had the highest reward dominance response. In other words, they responded largely to external cues and were not thwarted by punishment.[8]

Donald Lynam seems to have done the most extensive work with this population. He showed that psychopathy has common antecedents with oppositional defiance disorder, callous disregard, and hyperactivity. He believes there is a neurological deficit that manifests as a lack of behavioral restraint, such as with hyperactive and impulsive children. In adulthood, these become irresponsible and impulsive behaviors. Psychopathy was assessed in 430 boys, aged twelve and thirteen, by using reports from caretakers. Childhood psychopathy fit the framework of adult psychopathy, and children with psychopathic personalities were shown to be stable offenders prone to the most serious offenses. Childhood psychopathy has proven to be the best predictor of antisocial behavior in adolescence.[9]

Lynam also developed and tested a hypothesis about the developmental relationship between the adult psychopath and children with symptoms of hyperactivity, attention deficit, and impulsivity (HIA), and concurrent conduct problems (CP). He divided a population of adolescent boys into four groups: non-HIA-CP, HIA-only, CP-only, and HIA-CP. They were compared on measures thought to determine psychopathy. As he

126 Inside the Minds of Serial Killers

predicted, the HIA-CP boys most closely compared with psychopathic adults. Of the four groups, they were the most antisocial, disinhibited, and neuropsychologically impaired.[10]

In a study of eighty-one boys in a residential treatment program, symptoms of aggressive conduct disorder, along with lying and stealing, were predictive of adolescent psychopathy in those aged fourteen to seventeen. In other words, if they had a conduct disorder and also had acted in some antisocial manner, it was more likely than not that they would become adult psychopaths.[11]

As we have already seen in Chapter 3, psychopathy in adults is characterized by such traits and behaviors as conning, exploitation, manipulativeness, lack of remorse, impulsivity, unreliability, narcissism, and lack of empathy. As offenders, they tend to repeat their crimes more often and to be more criminally diverse. Some children with conduct problems may become chronic offenders, so researchers have translated assessment instruments into age-appropriate devices for studying children who may become adult psychopaths. With these measures, says Lynam and his research colleagues, juvenile psychopathy shows the expected relationship to offending, and can be assessed in a juvenile population through a five-factor model of personality (with the factors being stable over time), which can then be used to predict how they will be as adults:

1. Extraversion (sociability)
2. Agreeableness (positive interpersonal strategies)
3. Conscientiousness (control of impulses, ability to plan)
4. Neuroticism (emotional adjustment and stability)
5. Openness (preference for new activities and emotions)

Psychopathy, Lynam points out, consists of a mix of low agreeableness and conscientiousness, mostly high extraversion, and low on the neuroticism factors that involve anxiety and fear. With some refinements in the research, it could be expected that children can be tracked through this more generalized personality theory rather than via studies that negatively label them as antisocial or psychopathic.[12]

To sum this up, the presence of traits and behaviors that could be diagnosed as childhood psychopathy has proven to be the best predictor of increased antisocial behavior in adolescence, especially in boys who were egocentric, hyperactive, impulsive, callous toward others, and suffered from attention deficits. Additionally, certain personality factors remain stable over time and can be used to predict antisocial behavior in adulthood.

In picking out items from several studies, we can see that the commonalities in the background of psychopathic children include:

- a mother exposed to deprivation or abuse as a child
- a transient father
- a mother who cannot maintain stable emotional connection with the child
- lack of attachment to adults or friends
- failure to make eye contact when touched
- low frustration tolerance and low anxiety
- sense of self-importance
- transient relationships throughout childhood, or close association with another like him or her
- cruelty toward others
- animal abuse
- impulsivity
- self-centeredness
- lack of remorse for hurting someone
- lack of empathy in friendships

But we need a broader theory that includes both biology and environment.

VIOLENCE FEEDS VIOLENCE

Dr. Helen Smith, a forensic psychologist, has evaluated thousands of mentally disturbed children and adults. She objects to the way many experts blame such things as television, mental disturbance (the "bad seed"), or edgy music for what children do. Violence, she states, derives from the accumulation of many distorted thoughts and stressors that finally send a child over the edge. It's found in the manner in which a child processes what he or she sees, hears, and experiences. Smith finds that adolescents who use violence to solve a problem have already had a number of violent thoughts. They perceive their environment and their situation in such a way that violence seems the best mode of action. They may have role models in relatives or peers who have demonstrated this to them, which is to say that children who kill become gradually predisposed to kill. They don't just snap; they develop their readiness to act out over time. They have a restricted view of other people's rights and at some point they come to feel that they must bring their situation to a dramatic conclusion. Violence is the first thing they think of.

Some children who appear to be normal may just be going through the motions in order to fit in; they aren't necessarily feeling normal or good about anything. If a kid gives off any signals of approaching violence, or even warns someone that he might explode, people tend to look the other way or interpret it in the most positive light. Suburban kids who kill often are narcissistic. They think they're great and they value only their own rights. Sometimes they torture animals or other kids, and often they'll exhibit an obsessive fascination with guns or explosives. Another conspicuous trait is the feeling of entitlement, especially coupled with a tendency to blame others. When they kill, they want the world to know how angry they are. Often, a retrospective analysis finds that they've had obsessive thoughts about violence.

Violent girls, Smith found, are different from violent boys. Girls are usually less direct about their anger because they have discovered that expressing it is less socially acceptable. A girl might have her boyfriend kill for her and then feign innocence. Girls also prefer knives to guns, and they're more likely to kill in revenge or to cripple a rival.

Smith indicates that childhood violence comes largely from the environment, especially from lack of positive community cohesiveness, but even more influential is a lack of critical thinking skills, which help kids to understand the consequences of their actions. Because they don't think well, they don't know how to manage their anger and disappointment.[13]

Debra Niehoff, a neuroscientist, indicates that both biological and environmental factors are involved in the creation of a violent person, and each modifies the other such that processing a situation toward a violent resolution is unique to each individual. In other words, no particular type of trigger is going to cause violence in every instance. Niehoff indicates that the brain keeps track of a person's experiences and interactions through chemical codes. Each new experience brings either new information or information that reinforces what the brain has already stored. Everything experienced is then processed through a neurochemical profile, which is influenced by attitudes that have been developed about whether or not the world is safe. It shows up in behaviors and attitudes, and as others react, the individual processes that reaction, updating the profile.

If the person develops the sense that the world is threatening and needs to be approached with aggression or violence, he or she may take refuge in fantasies that will one day become actions. The fantasies provide mental rehearsal and if they're strong and repetitive, they will affect the composition of the individual's neurochemical profile. Niehoff found that there were different patterns of violent behavior and that certain physiological differences are associated with each pattern.[14]

We can see how this may have played out in the case of juvenile killer, Harvey Robinson. His story unfolded after he was caught in Allentown, Pennsylvania, in 1993, trapped in a home by a police sting operation. Over a fourteen-month period, starting when he was seventeen, Robinson had committed five known sexual assaults, killing three of his victims.

Robinson was biracial and his alcoholic father had been convicted earlier in life of manslaughter. His father and mother frequently quarreled, and sometimes his father hit his mother. They divorced when he was a child and he remained with his mother. A review of his background makes it easy to see how the world might have felt unsafe for him. His older brother had also gone to prison. Robinson was an impulsive child with little ability to focus and a quick temper. By the time he was nine, he had been arrested for a juvenile crime. Over the next eight years, he was arrested more than a dozen times, mostly for burglary or property crimes. He was known to fight with authority figures, had a history of substance abuse, and was diagnosed with antisocial personality disorder. Yet each time he committed a crime, he ran home and hid.

When he began to stalk and rape, he was awaiting a hearing in juvenile court for yet another burglary. He looked for white older women who were overweight, similar to his mother. He spotted his first victim through her window, undressing for bed. He broke in and bludgeoned her to death with three dozen blows, after which he stole a pair of panties and left. Put into detention for eight months, once he got out, he started where he'd left off. Robinson grabbed a fifteen-year-old girl off her bike, raped her and stabbed her, leaving her in a park.

Six weeks later, he entered another home, but saw the targeted woman with her boyfriend, so he attacked her five-year-old daughter, raping her. She was found unconscious but alive. It took only a month before Robinson struck again. Yet when he entered a home, the female homeowner was alerted by the noise and ran outside. He overtook her and raped her but was interrupted, so he fled. The papers reported that she was alive and so the police believed that the rapist might revisit her to silence her as a witness. Bravely, she allowed them to place someone in the home to watch during the night.

But Robinson had moved on to his fifth victim, raping and strangling her. Then he returned to the fourth woman to attempt to finish the job. There, a police officer was waiting for him. Nevertheless, he escaped, cutting himself on a broken window. Because the cut was serious, he went to the hospital, where he was finally caught. He insisted that he was innocent.

On November 8, 1994, Robinson was convicted on three counts of murder and sentenced to death. Five months later he was convicted of raping and attempting to murder Cindy Thompson. He pled guilty for the fifth rape and attempted murder. A judge threw out two of the death penalties because of improper jury instruction, but the third one remained intact. It's currently on appeal.[15]

While we cannot say what actually caused Robinson to rape and murder, or why he kept on doing it, we can see that he grew up with disadvantages that could have influenced his perception of the world and other people. Biracial, with a criminal father who then abandoned him, a criminal brother, and a disciplinarian mother, it's little surprise that he turned to antisocial acts himself. Caught repeatedly, he became reactive and resistant to attempts at reform. He simply grew angrier, and with each failure he probably filled his fantasies with scenarios of things he would do to empower himself and get back at the system. It's likely he adopted an attitude that became a self-fulfilling prophecy. Thus, each time he broke a law and was caught, each time he harmed or killed someone, he updated his perceptions of the world, viewing a route to power via burglary, rape, and murder, while perceiving the cops and courts as the source of threat and disempowerment. So he would of course return to silence the only adult victim who might be able to identify him and put him into prison—a place representative of helplessness.

If the theory about the stability of specific personality factors holds true, then Robinson would have continued to act out with violence, especially toward authority figures, as represented by women who resembled his mother and officers of the legal system. He may have been born physiologically with a reactive temperament or absorbed it from his violent father. He then made meaning of the world through how others reacted to him, and the combination may have seemed, for Robinson, to be primarily negative.

Since we're discussing serial killers who start early, let's turn now to repetitive murder that seems to run in families, or is guided by the family unit.

NOTES

1. Gitta Sereny, *Cries Unheard: Why Children Kill: The Story of Mary Bell* (London: Macmillan, 1998).

2. Gregg McCrary, with K. Ramsland, *The Unknown Darkness: Profiling the Predators among Us* (New York: Morrow, 2003), pp. 84–88.

3. Harold Schechter, *Fiend: The Shocking True Story of America's Youngest Serial Killer* (New York: Simon & Schuster, 2000).

4. Gregory Moffatt, *A Violent Heart* (Westport, CT: Praeger, 2002), pp. 97–120.

5. Bill G. Cox, *Born Bad* (New York: Pinnacle, 1996); "Pure Evil," *Forensic Files,* Courtroom Television, 2003; *Massey v. State*, 933 SW2d 141 (Tex. 1996).

6. Donald W. Black, *Bad Boys, Bad Men: Confronting Antisocial Personality Disorder* (London: Oxford University Press, 1999), pp. 1–15.

7. Louie Rosella, "Teen Appeals Jail Term for Aiding Killer," *The Mississauga News*, December 2, 2005.

8. P. J. Frick, B. S. O'Brien, J. M. Wootten, and K. McBurnett, "Psychopathy and Conduct Problems in Children," *Journal of Abnormal Psychology*, 1994, 103, 700–707.

9. Donald R. Lynam, "Early Identification of Chronic Offenders: Who is the Fledgling Psychopath?" *Psychological Bulletin*, 1996, 120, 209–224.

10. Donald R. Lynam, "Pursuing the Psychopath: Capturing the Fledgling Psychopath in a Nomological Net," *Journal of Abnormal Psychology*, 1997, 106, 425–438.

11. R. Rogers, J. Johansen, J. J. Chang, and R. T. Salekin, "Predictors of Adolescent Psychopathy: Oppositional and Conduct-Disordered Symptoms," *Journal of the American Academy of Psychiatry and the Law*, 1997, 25, 261–271.

12. Donald R. Lynam, A. Caspi, T. Moffitt, A. Raine, R. Loeber, and M. Stouthamer-Loeber, "Adolescent Psychopathy and the Big Five: Results from Two Samples," *Journal of Abnormal Child Psychology*, August 2005, 431–443.

13. Helen Smith, *The Scarred Heart: Understanding and Identifying Kids who Kill* (Knoxville, TN: Callisto, 2000), pp. 69–184.

14. Debra Niehoff, *The Biology of Violence* (New York: Free Press, 1999), pp. 31–53.

15. Articles from the Allentown, Pennsylvania *Morning Call*, 1993–1994.

CHAPTER 13

Related by Blood

As we've just seen, the father of three-time murderer Harvey Robinson was also a killer. The Hillside Stranglers, Kenneth Bianchi and Angelo Buono, were cousins and they killed nearly a dozen women together in Los Angeles in 1977 and 1978. Henry Lee Lucas and Bobby Joe Long, discussed earlier in this book, were also related, but their murder sprees had no association. While researchers close in on the genetic factors involved in extreme violence, there has been only one known instance in which two serial murderers from the same family emerged quite separately to start their rampages.

SINISTER SIBLINGS

In 1964, Larry Ranes went hitchhiking across the country. He had grown up in Michigan in an abusive and unstable home, and was a year younger than his brother Danny. They were close, but they also competed to the point of violence. Larry went into the military and ended up in the stockade for the latter part of his stint before he was discharged. Then at the age of nineteen, feeling that his life might not last very long, he started to wander, crossing into Ohio, Kentucky, and Indiana. He made it all the way to Nevada and back in about three months, and killed several people along the way. After accepting a ride, he would sometimes shoot the driver to rob him or he'd shoot a gas station attendant. From his fourth victim in Plymouth, Michigan, school teacher Larry Smocks, he stole the man's shoes and watch. In fact, he was wearing them when the police came calling. He confessed to killing five men, but he was only charged in the Smocks murder.

For that one, he said that he had placed the man in the trunk of his car and told him to be quiet. When the man started thumping to make himself heard, Ranes had stopped the car, tied him up, and shot him in the head. He then drove to Indiana, killed a gas station attendant there, and returned to Kalamazoo. He was actually waved through a police roadblock set up to find the person who had killed the attendant, and Smocks was still in the trunk of his car.

Ranes pled not guilty by reason of insanity, and psychologists testified that he had committed murder during periods of temporary insanity, brought on by rage against a father who had beat him mercilessly. In fact, Ranes's father had once been a gas station attendant, which supported this defense, as did the fact that his victims resembled his father in appearance, but Ranes was nevertheless convicted and given a life sentence. He appealed it, claiming that the prosecutor's psychiatrists had examined him before he was properly represented by counsel, and won a new trial but when it became clear to him that his insanity plea was not very strong, he pled guilty and received a new life sentence. He was to be allowed to change his name, and he chose "Monk Steppenwolf," based on a novel by Herman Hesse that had impressed him.

By this time, it was his older brother's turn. Danny seemed to be equally angry from the abuse received at the hands of his father. In their home in Kalamazoo, they were the middle two children of four; the oldest and youngest were girls. Their father was an alcoholic who reportedly got mean when he drank and would hit whoever was close by. Each of the kids took a share of the abuse before the man finally walked out, but by that time plenty of damage had been done. The father had modeled the use of violence to resolve situations and get through life, and the boys used this approach to take out their frustrations on each other.

Danny, the older boy, went to prison for assault and was paroled early in 1972 when he was twenty-eight. Within a month, he committed another crime, kidnapping a woman and her infant son. He raped the woman and stabbed her to death, leaving her son to wander aimlessly until someone found him. Danny struck again on July 5. He was at work at a service station when two nineteen-year-old girls, Linda Clark and Claudia Bidstrup, pulled in for service. He persuaded his buddy, fifteen-year-old Brent Koster, to help him abduct them in his van. They forced the two girls to go with them, raping them in the van and then strangling them. Their decomposing bodies were found about two weeks later near the Kalamazoo River.

They repeated their act on August 5, kidnapping eighteen-year-old Patricia Fearnow. Both of them raped her and then put a plastic bag over her head to suffocate her. But Ranes had not chosen his cohort carefully. Koster was bothered by what they had done and eventually confessed to the police. He showed them Fearnow's body, not yet found, and it proved to be about a mile from where the other two girls had been dumped. Koster named Danny Ranes as the instigator.

They arrested Danny, who protested that he had done nothing of the kind. He was put into a maximum security cell in the same county jail where his brother was awaiting his retrial (having not yet pled guilty). But unlike Larry, Danny was not one to capitulate. Nevertheless, he went to trial for two of the murders, with Koster testifying against him, and a jury convicted him twice of murder. He was sentenced to life on each count and then pled no contest to the other two murder charges.

Larry agreed to talk with an English professor, Conrad Hilberry, about his family history, on the condition that it be a serious study about the inner workings of his mind. Hilberry spoke to both brothers, a woman whom both had married at separate times, and the legal personnel involved. He learned that Larry, the youngest boy in the family, was a loner who had developed a sense of distance from life. When the family dog was run over, he felt nothing. His mother worked fulltime on the evening shift in a paper factory, and though Larry and the others rarely saw her, he recalled that she was ill-equipped to deal with a family or an alcoholic husband. The father apparently enjoyed tormenting the boys, beat their mother, and destroyed household furniture, as well as picked fights with other men.[1]

Yet a comparison between Gary Gilmore's family of four siblings, an equally abusive and tyrannical father, and similar economic circumstances (as well as a colder mother) shows that of four boys, only Gary became a killer. In fact, the youngest son went on to be the award-winning writer, Mikal Gilmore. That both Ranes boys committed serial murder, selecting entirely different types of victims and showing much different patterns, cannot be attributed solely to poor parenting or economic conditions. Larry's biographer was an English professor with no background in psychology, and the psychiatrists who testified about insanity for Larry offered only weak ideas about his motives, so we have no access to a sophisticated analysis.

Another set of brothers killed together, but when the going got tough, they turned on each other. In February 1978, three people were shot multiple times with a .22 rifle in the home they shared in Columbus, Ohio. The same gun was implicated through ballistics tests in four more shootings (including a man and his four dogs), after which the police matched it to bullets found the year before in two female murder victims in Newark, Ohio. They had been shot while walking down the street and were found frozen in a snow bank. One more man was shot before Gary Lewingdon was arrested for credit card fraud. In his possession were items that had belonged to the last victim, including his credit cards. Under interrogation, he admitted his part in the killings but claimed that his brother, Thaddeus Charles Lewingdon, had been the mastermind.

When Charles was arrested, he admitted to the shootings but accused Gary as the one who had urged them to continue. Both were convicted of multiple counts of first-degree murder (Charles got nine and Gary eight, despite ten shootings) and given multiple life sentences. Gary eventually became psychotic and was transferred to a psychiatric institution. While Charles died in prison from cancer, Gary escaped from the forensic hospital where he'd been held, but was recaptured.[2]

There have even been sisters associated with serial murder. Three Southern women, known as the "Sisters in Black" for the black dresses they always wore, set about killing some of their relatives in the first decade of the twentieth century. Virginia, Caroline, and Mary Wardlow, daughters of a judge, either married or found a profession but remained in close proximity to one another. Inseparable during childhood, they were known to scheme together to hurt people. One of their children, a boy, was found burned to death, which paid off in insurance money (they claimed it was a suicide). Then a husband died from acute stomach pain and a malnourished daughter "drowned" in a bathtub. Money was handed over in each case, and finally the sisters were arrested. One starved herself to death in prison, one was committed to a mental institution, and the third one was acquitted for lack of evidence.[3]

In another family, a pair of identical twins was involved in unrelated fatal incidents, but only one became a serial killer. We started the book with him, so let's return to the case of Robert Bruce Spahalski in Rochester, New York. He turned himself in to the police on November 8, 2005, claiming to have committed four murders, and two months later he was indicted for all four.

During his police interview, he worried about being labeled a serial killer and indicated that he'd had different motives for each. One was a dispute over money for sex, while another was supposedly caused by hallucinations; a third occurred during an argument and subsequent robbery, and the fourth happened when he "snapped" during a sexual encounter. Three had occurred in 1990 and 1991, while the fourth took place years later, three days prior to turning himself in. The victims' ages ranged between twenty-four and fifty-four. Two were strangled, while two were bludgeoned (and one of those was also strangled).

Spahalski had operated a male escort service and worked as a hustler; he had served time in prison for several burglary offenses, sometimes in the same prison as his brother. He claimed to have a mental disorder— post-traumatic stress from being in prison, as well as hearing voices. When he went in to confess, according to the police statements, he said of his most recent murder, "I saw a demon." He also indicated that he had prayed daily for the male victim from years earlier and felt terribly guilty.

He had confessed to clear his conscience and was feeling suicidal over his actions. His usual strategy was to try to forget the things he had done to others, but he believed he had a fatal illness and wanted to set his affairs in order.

Spahalski also had a twin brother, Stephen, who had, when he was sixteen, killed a forty-eight-year-old man, allegedly because the man approached him sexually, and he pled guilty to manslaughter. (Initially, police had suspected Robert as the killer and were surprised when Stephen confessed; they suspected that Robert had been there as well.) Journalist Gary Craig for *The Democrat and Chronicle* tracked Stephen down in Attica for an interview, though Robert would not talk. Stephen was imprisoned for eight years, but upon release committed a burglary and kidnapping, which sent him right back. A second release resulted in him being incarcerated again in 1999. He is gay, while his brother has been sexually involved with both sexes. Both had been skilled gymnasts. Their parents had divorced when they were twelve, and neither twin attributed his violence to his upbringing. Both had a history of criminal offenses.[4]

Then there were the notorious "brothers" who actually were cousins.

CRIMINAL COUSINS

The first documented case of serial murder in America involved a team of cousins, Micajah and Wiley Harp (changed from William and Joshua Harpe). They grew up together and passed themselves off as brothers. After they fought in the Revolutionary War on the side of the British (and deserted), they perpetuated a string of brutal crimes. Growing up in an immigrant family from Scotland, Big Harp and Little Harp had planned to run a plantation in North Carolina, but the American Revolution changed their direction. They left the army in 1781 and kidnapped two women to become their wives as they made their way into the American wilderness to set up a homestead. When their wives inevitably gave birth, they ruthlessly slaughtered the babies.

While historical records are spare on the details, thanks to a history of Tennessee from 1842, we know about some of the Harps's actions. Crossing through the Kentucky and Tennessee territories, the two men killed strangers at whim, racking up between twenty and forty victims. According to this account, they would put stones inside the abdomens of victims and dump them into rivers, or mutilate the bodies and leave them in the wilderness for the animals to scavenge. They made no distinction among children, women, or men as their victims, or between free men and slaves. They simply raped, thieved, and killed as opportunities arose. The Harps eluded justice several times, escaping from prison before they were finally stopped. Big Harp was captured first in 1800 for the murder of a mother and child, and he confessed to twenty murders before his head was removed to be displayed at a Kentucky crossroad. Little Harp survived four more years before making the error in Mississippi of seeking bounty on another man's head. After he came into town, he was recognized, hanged, and decapitated.[5]

More recently, cousins David Alan Gore and Fred Waterfield hunted in Florida for women during the early 1980s. Gore was employed as an auxiliary sheriff's deputy, which facilitated their "hobby." Waterfield offered Gore money for each pretty girl he brought back, and Gore used his badge to persuade girls to get into his car. His first "prey" was a teenage girl he grabbed as she got off a school bus, driving her home to get her mother. On his own, he raped them both, and when Waterfield arrived, he tied up the mother so tightly that she choked to death. He then raped the teenager and murdered her. When it was over, Waterfield told Gore to get rid of the bodies, and he apparently did so without complaint.

Next, Waterfield wanted a blond, so Gore surreptitiously disabled Judith Daley's car and offered her a ride. He and Waterfield raped her, killed her, and then dumped her in a swamp for the alligators. Soon they grabbed a pair of female hitchhikers, who were raped and shot. They tried it again with two more hitchhikers, but one of the girls escaped and went running naked down the street. Gore ran after her and shot her. A neighborhood boy witnessed this incident and went home to call the police.

At the house, the police discovered the girl's body in the trunk of Gore's car. He surrendered and showed the officers to the attic, where a fourteen-year-old girl was bound to the rafters. She told them how she and her friend had been kidnapped and sexually assaulted. Gore confessed to five other murders and turned on his cousin, describing their criminal history. Waterfield was caught, both of them were convicted of multiple counts of rape and murder, and Gore received a death sentence while Waterfield got four life sentences.[6]

While we can understand a bond among siblings or cousins around the same age, even one that involves murder if both are similarly depraved, it's more difficult to imagine entire families that participate in serial killing. Yet there are several on record.

FAMILY FIENDS

A gang of five, known as the "McCrary Family," rampaged from Florida to California in 1971 and 1972, grabbing young women from stores to rape and shoot, and dumping them along highways. The family included husband and wife, Carolyn and Sherman; daughter Ginger; her husband, Raymond Taylor; and their son, Daniel—three generations. Initially, Sherman and Raymond committed armed robberies together to get money, but then turned to kidnapping and extortion. Once they had a hostage from a bank or store, they raped and shot her, and left her corpse along the road.

The female members supported the murders, as they appeared to be in it for profit, but the three males were the primary perpetrators. Finally in California they were stopped after a shoot-out with the police and, thanks to work by the FBI, were convicted of ten of the twenty-two suspected cross-country murders. All received prison time.[7]

Just as notorious were the "Bloody Benders" in southeastern Kansas during the 1870s. Travelers passing through this frontier area received a warm welcome and roadside entertainment in the Benders' way station. Daughter Katie, twentyish and buxom, posed as a spiritualist who could read futures and summon ghosts. It did not take her long to engage the attention of men after dinner, who would be asked to sit in a certain spot in front of a canvas curtain, and while she spun her yarns to keep their attention, Old Man Bender used a sledge hammer to dispatch them. Ma Bender, Katie, and John Jr. would then remove the victims' money and shove the bodies down a trap door to the crawl space beneath the house, to be buried later in the orchard. A few of the victims were men who came specifically to see Katie, having watched her spiritualist show in a nearby town (one of the ways she lured people to the homestead).

Eventually their scheme was discovered in 1873 when the brother of Dr. William York came looking for him. The Benders deflected him temporarily and then packed up and left, but when a heavy rain showed the clear outline of several graves in the orchard, the entire place was dug up. Eleven bodies were exhumed altogether, including York's. This story became a national sensation, adding the "Hell Benders" to the tales used to frighten would-be settlers. The Benders were identified in various locations, but history offers no record that they were caught. It's estimated that they fleeced their victims of around $10,000.[8]

PREDATORY PATRIARCH

A case of a child forced to support murder by a parent was the father/daughter team in Brussels, Belgium, who were convicted in 2002. The father, Andras Pandy, a Hungarian-born minister, brutalized his daughter, Agnes, and had been raping her since she was thirteen. She feared him, so she went along with whatever he demanded, including three years worth of murders of family members. Finally, she'd had enough and went to the police.

She told them about Pandy's murders of his first two wives and four of his children and stepchildren. Some had been shot and some bludgeoned to death with a sledgehammer. Then, she said, she and Pandy had hacked the corpses into pieces and wrapped them in plastic. Some were dumped outside the home, while others were immersed in an acidic drain cleaner, which dissolved them.

The police investigated, but DNA analyses indicated that the body parts and sets of teeth pulled from the basement and refrigerators on one of

Pandy's properties actually belonged to people *other* than the victims Agnes had described. That meant there were potentially more victims. While authorities suspected Pandy in the deaths of at least thirteen people, they could not identify to whom these particular remains belonged. All they had were missing relatives and Agnes's testimony. Pandy objected to the investigation, claiming that the relatives in question were still alive and he was in touch with them "through angels."

At the conclusion of his trial in 2002, the *"Pastor Diaboloque"* was convicted on five counts of first-degree murder, one count of attempted murder, and three counts of rape, getting life in prison, while Agnes, 44, got twenty-one years on five counts for her participation.[9]

Yet just how genetics may impact the temperament for murder is not clear, especially since the familial manifestations are so varied. Some families do share poor economic circumstances and thus collude together to murder for enrichment. There are even instances in which a mentally ill patriarch will infect the entire family system and thus influence other members to accept his delusions or paranoid dictates and engage in his type of criminal behavior. Since there are so few families that act together in behavior as extreme as serial murder, it's difficult to study them and identify specific causal factors. Other types of crimes appear to be involved, such as substance abuse and theft, and there may be criminality in earlier generations. In general, a family that, as an entity, becomes a criminal enterprise (and even in a family where only a parent and one child show a similar penchant) is generally unsocialized in several ways, and their values, along with the modeling of violence as a way to get through life, appear to fuel violent behavior in successive generations. Role models do have an influence on certain dispositions.

Such fatal teamwork, however, is not limited to people who are related. We'll look now at people who initially were strangers joined together to kill.

NOTES

1. Conrad Hillbery, *Luke Karamazov* (Detroit, MI: Wayne State University Press, 1987); articles from the *Kalamazoo Gazette*, 1972.

2. Brian Lane and Wilfred Gregg, *The Encyclopedia of Serial Killers* (London: Headline, 1992), p. 238.

3. Jay Robert Nash, *Bloodletters and Badmen* (New York: M. Evans & Co., 1995), pp. 653–654.

4. Gary Craig, "Mirror Images Reflect Twin Lives of Violence," *The Democrat and Chronicle*, December 15, 2005; Gary Craig, "Spahalski Pleads Not Guilty," *The Democrat and Chronicle*, January 4, 2005; *New York vs. Robert Spahalski*.

5. J. W. M. Breazeale, *Life As It Is, or Matters and Things in General* (Knoxville, TN: James Williams, 1842), pp. 136–151.

6. Bernie Ward, *Innocent Prey* (New York: Pinnacle, 1994).

7. Michael D. Kelleher and C. L. Kelleher, *The Female Serial Killer* (New York: Dell, 1998), pp. 217–221.

8. Robert Alderman, *The Bloody Benders* (New York: Stein & Day, 1970).

9. "Pastor and His Daughter Have Been Jailed after They Were Convicted of Murdering Six Relatives and Dissolving Their Remains in Chemicals," *CNN.com*, March 6, 2002.

CHAPTER 14

Matches Made in Hell

Oliver Stone's film *Natural Born Killers* features a fictional couple who indulge in random violence to vent anger and exercise power. The film demonstrates how couples can develop a murderous drive together, blending their impulses into a spate of violence. Responsibility is spread between two or more people, relieving whatever guilt may exist and finding affirmation—even more ideas—from another's actions. Whenever two (or more) people go on a killing spree together, the question arises as to whether either of them alone would have behaved in this manner. In other words, can one person influence another, nonviolent person, to commit acts he/she would not otherwise commit? Or does something else occur?

We've had all-male killer teams, all-female killer teams, and a mix of both. We've seen two together, three, and even five or six. Sometimes it's a married couple or lovers, other times just friends or associates with similar goals. In each case, the brutality was typically guided by a dominant partner, with weaker accomplices doing whatever it took to remain with that person. In some cases, the dominant partner did not even commit the murders but lived out his (or her) fantasies through one or more accomplices.

TILL DEATH DO US PART

During the summer of 1991, a young woman in Gloucester, England, made an allegation of sexual abuse against her father, Frederick West, who seemed to his neighbors to be an ordinary family man. People liked him and his wife, Rosemary, yet the girl insisted that "Rose" had actually assisted Fred in raping her. When she declined to testify in court, the investigation was dropped.

However, the process had turned up some irregularities. Social workers who had visited the West home had spotted sexual items and learned that Rose prostituted herself via magazine ads. Some of her eight children had been fathered by men other than Fred, and there were hints of incest and voyeurism. The social workers recommended that the West's youngest child be removed. Yet corrupting the moral atmosphere proved to be the least of their sins. The children told an investigator that they once had a sister, Heather, who had disappeared seven years earlier, and their parents often threatened them with being buried under the patio "like Heather." Investigators learned that Heather had supposedly left home when she was sixteen and the Wests had not heard from her since.

Then another item also surfaced: twenty years earlier in 1972, when Rose was just nineteen, the couple had been arrested for a sexual assault on another girl. They had invited her to move in with them as a nanny for their three children. Yet when Fred made overtures and described the abortions he could perform, the girl left. Sometime later, they spotted her, grabbed her, and subjected her to hours of sexual abuse. Once they let her go she went to the police. Investigators persuaded her to forego a trial, so the Wests were only fined. Nevertheless, the girl's testimony was on the record, and there was one item of note: the Wests had threatened to bury the girl under the backyard paving stones. Two such reports, along with a missing girl, raised suspicions.

In 1994, the police arrived to look beneath Fred West's concrete patio. Soon after they started the job, Fred confessed to killing Heather. Rose reacted in horror and surprise, but this was soon revealed to be an act she had prepared. Investigators kept digging and soon found human remains, which dental records proved belonged to Heather. However, there was another body as well. Fred admitted that he had killed two more girls—one of them pregnant—and buried them in the yard. When the police made plans to take up the floors in the home, he conceded that they would find more bodies. Now they really had a house of horrors.

The remains of six more young women, most of them bound with ropes, were uncovered from square graves under the cellar floors, mostly beneath where the Wests had placed the beds of their children. Bones from the hands and feet were missing, apparently kept as souvenirs. Fred also confessed that he had killed his first wife, his stepdaughter Charmaine, and two other women. While the remains of three of those four victims were found, Charmaine's murder was proven with careful forensic analysis to be attributable to Rose. Apparently Fred was covering for her.

She denied any involvement in murder and renounced her husband, but no one believed he could have killed and dismembered so many young women right there in the home without his wife's knowledge. Finally Fred conceded that he had not told the whole story, but then on New Year's Day in 1995, he committed suicide, leaving everyone to speculate about what he might have added. Rose was charged with ten murders and convicted on all counts.

There were several survivors of the couple's sadistic teamwork who were allowed to testify against her, including one of the West's children, Anne Marie. Her father had impregnated her and, with Rose, had subjected her to repeated sexual abuse. Such testimony, along with the evidence that many of the dead girls had been bound, clearly indicated that Fred and Rose had sexually tortured numerous young women before killing them.

While criminologists point to childhood histories of incest, sexual abuse, and neglect for both Fred and Rose, the extent of their crime spree over a span of two decades suggests the influence of another phenomenon. British forensic psychologist Paul Britton labeled their behavior "combined depravity," or mutually supportive sadism. The Wests apparently galvanized their rape-murders with what each offered to the other in terms of cooperation and reinforcement. In other words, the more depraved they got, the more they encouraged each other. They were similar to other such couples who inspire the worst in each other and encouraged its most extreme expression.[1]

Some teams kill in a spree, some over long periods, while others kill their victims all at once. From post-arrest interviews, some team members have admitted that soon after meeting, they had sensed the potential for such a depraved partnership and had moved eagerly toward it. Either they had felt a strong romantic attraction or they had soon established an intimate familiarity that allowed them to share secret fantasies—even violent or deviant ones.

The emotional tone of a relationship is generally set from the start. In such teams, a dominant partner eventually seduces or commands the other to act out a specific fantasy. For example, James William Miller insisted he killed only to keep the love of Christopher Robin Worrell. During the late 1970s in Australia, Worrell would make Miller pick up girls, and after he had sex with them and killed them, he'd instruct Miller to help him dump the bodies. Miller claimed complete innocence in the murders, although it was clear that in most instances he had known what Worrell planned to do. These men killed seven women before Worrell was killed in a car accident. Thanks to a tip from Worrell's girlfriend, police arrested Miller and he broke down and showed them three of the body dump sites. But he believed there was a mitigating factor: He had loved Worrell and thus could not turn him in, so he had done whatever Worrell asked.

Other mental health experts who have studied criminal collaborations indicate that when one is psychologically dominating, the other is usually easy to manipulate and may even be mentally ill. Among the mental disorders frequently attributed to the weaker partner is schizotypal personality disorder—a malleable, superstitious person with emotional instability, excessive social anxiety, paranoia, patterns of magical thinking, and constricted emotions. If the team succeeds, the dominant partner feels euphoric, while the submissive one may experience some guilt but will nevertheless continue out of fear or from some deep-seated need to be with the other person.

Several females have knowingly lured victims for their male companions for rape and murder. Charlene Gallego ensnared ten female victims for her husband, and Australia's David and Catherine Birnie worked together on four victims in their home. Karla Homolka murdered her own sister with an overdose while giving the fifteen-year-old over to her husband, Paul Bernardo, as a Christmas present, so he could rape her. They also killed two other young girls together in their home in Canada, dismembering one of them.

Each couple worked as a team to savage innocent victims and many experts have speculated that with different partners, the female would not have acted thus. Some call these women "compliant accomplices." Former FBI Special Agent Robert Hazelwood and Dr. Janet Warren, a professor of clinical psychiatric medicine, conducted a six-year study on twenty women who had been the wives or girlfriends of sadistic sexual predators. Seven of the men in their study had killed people, and four of the women had participated to some degree. The women were found to be middle-class and most had no criminal record. They were not mentally ill, although many were from backgrounds that included some degree of physical and sexual abuse. Once merged with their sadistic partners, Hazelwood and Warren determined, they were unable to form their own identities because "the sadistic fantasy of the male becomes an organizing principle in the behavior of the women." The study concluded that the males had targeted females with low self-esteem, then isolated them and gradually reformed their thinking. Hazelwood identified a five-step process that turned these women into accomplices:

- Identification: Identifying a vulnerable, easily controlled person
- Seduction: Getting the woman to fall in love
- Reshaping the woman's sexual norms: Introducing her to sexual images and acts that may offend or frighten her but which she must do to please the man and keep him involved
- Social isolation: Cutting her off from family and friends
- Punishment: Physical, verbal, and sexual, which further erodes the woman's self-esteem and ability to act on her own

The girls were so thoroughly demoralized and manipulated, the study concluded, that they couldn't help but do what they did.[2]

Yet psychiatrists who evaluated some of the same women on a regular basis, not just a single-session study, concluded that they could be dangerous even on their own. Their acts might not have evolved from team chemistry but from psychological resonance to men who share their desire to harm others and who were able to put their fantasies into action.

Most criminal teams fall apart fast. Typically, they make a mistake, such as leaving a witness alive, quarreling, or going further in brutality than one partner can stand, so that person ends it. When the investigation begins or an arrest is made, the most narcissistic person will save himself and let the other person take the fall. Fred West was unusual in how long he protected Rose, but in the end, when the cards were on the table, he left her to her fate.

Michael Newton states that around 13 percent of all serial killers are male–female teams,[3] while criminologist Eric W. Hickey places that percentage around fifteen. He did a study involving over three hundred serial killers, indicating that "for some multiple killers, murder must be simultaneously a participation and a spectator endeavor; power can be experienced by observing a fellow conspirator destroy human life, possibly as much as by performing the killing. The pathology of the relationship operates symbiotically."[4] Perhaps what they could not do alone, they were able to do within the chemistry of a dangerous association.

According to Hickey, 74 percent of team killers are white; female killers participate with males around one third of the time; and the majority of cases involve only two offenders working together. When females are involved, it's generally the male who masterminds the homicides, unless the female is dominant, such as in a mother–son team. There is nearly always one person who maintains psychological control, although there may be power struggles at times among the participants.

MUTUAL GOALS

The most dangerous teams involve male/male pairings, and of those, the most aggressive are equals who realize they now have a partner as depraved as they are. With no moral boundaries, they work together to affirm and expand their range of criminal creativity.

Roy Norris and Lawrence Bittaker met in prison, where they discovered a common taste for sadistic sexual torture. Once released, they bought a van in Los Angeles, which they dubbed "Murder Mac," and used it to seek young females. They grabbed Cindy Schaeffer, 16, on June 24, 1979, and repeatedly raped her before strangling her with a coat hanger and dumping her body. The next victim received an ice pick through the brain, and following that attack, these predators tortured and killed two teenage girls together before dumping their bodies over a cliff.

Then they raped a girl and released her. She turned them in. In custody, Norris confessed, implicating Bittaker as the ringleader, and showed the police where they had dumped the bodies. Both men were charged with five counts of murder. Norris got immunity from the death sentence for his testimony and was sentenced to forty-five years, while Bittaker went on California's death row.[5]

And then there were three. In Texas on August 8, 1973, law enforcement learned about a trio of males who had been killing together for some time. One of them, seventeen-year-old Elmer Wayne Henley, called to turn himself in, admitting that he had just killed the leader Dean Corll, 34, known locally as the "Candy Man." Henley said he had shot the man (six times) in self-defense and agreed to show the police the location of several mass graves. In the process, he implicated David Brooks. The young men had lured potential victims to a boathouse for $200 per pickup, where Corll would bind them to a torture board, rape them, and then murder them. Sometimes, Henley added, Corll even chewed off their genitals or castrated them. Henley claimed that he had shot Corll in "self-defense." By the time the exhumations and confessions were done, they had unearthed twenty-seven bodies—including a nine-year-old.

The end had come when Corll decided to kill Henley and some of his friends. Henley, bound to the board, persuaded him not to, and when freed, he shot his former employer. Brooks and Henley both received life sentences for their participation.[6] As horrific as their involvement was, they apparently did not engage in the torture in the way that another team of accomplices did.

Robin Gecht had once worked for John Wayne Gacy, the contractor who had murdered thirty-three young men. During the 1980s, according to the confession offered later by one member of the gang, Gecht led a group of three men known as the "Ripper Crew" or "Chicago Rippers" in killing an estimated seventeen women. Gecht had an ability to draw others to him and get them to do his bidding. No matter how sick or disgusting his ideas were, he inspired others to get involved. During adolescence, he developed a keen interest in Satanism and its secret rituals, believing that they offered power over others.

When Gecht was thirty, he met Ed Spreitzer, 21, and the teenaged Koko-raleis brothers, Andrew and Thomas. All three were easily taken in by Gecht's charismatic personality, and together they roamed Chicago at night in his van, hunting for women. When they got one, they raped her, beat her up, tortured her, and strangled her. They also cut off a breast to take to Gecht's secret altar. One participant in this unholy ritual admitted that they consumed pieces from it while Gecht read verses from the Bible.

The gang got away with this for several years, but were caught when a survivor identified the van. However, Gecht was never convicted of murder, because he was not the one who had killed; he had merely inspired the others. Two of them received the death sentence and the third man got seventy years in prison. In 1999, Andrew Kokoraleis was executed, while Spreitzer's sentence was commuted to life.[7]

THE HELPERS

Much has been written about Charles Manson, whose cult in California was suspected in as many as thirty-seven murders, but Manson did not actually get convicted of any murder he may have committed himself. Instead, he directed others to kill at his behest. As such, he presents another rare combination: like Gecht above, he was able to persuade others to follow his vision, which included murder. His gang is most famous for the Tate–LaBianca murders that occurred, respectively, on August 9 and 10 in 1969. The first one took place in the home of film director Roman Polanski, with five people slaughtered, including pregnant actress Sharon Tate, Polanksi's wife. All were stabbed multiple times, as were a married couple, the LaBiancas, the following night.

Then in October, one of the cult members, Susan Atkins, who was in jail for unrelated crimes, admitted her part in the murders to a cellmate. That led the police to her associates, hippies living on Spahn ranch outside the city. Charlie Manson, their "leader," was among them. They arrested Susan Atkins, Leslie Van Houten, and Patricia Krenwinkel, along with Manson and a drifter called "Tex" Watson. It became clear that Manson had urged several of the cult members to go on a killing spree, telling them to make it look like the job of black militants. His disciples were known as "the Family," and his vision of "Helter Skelter" meant that blacks would rise up to massacre whites and reclaim the earth.

Prosecutor Vince Bugliosi made the case in the 1970 trial that since Manson was the group mastermind, he was culpable. The jury convicted Manson, Susan Atkins, and Patricia Krenwinkel of seven counts of first-degree murder. Leslie Van Houten was convicted on two counts, and in a separate trial, Watson was convicted for his part.[8]

There have also been female masterminds. In Japan, Kau Kobayashi went to the gallows for three murders that she had plotted and perpetrated. In 1952, her husband was her first victim, killed at her behest by her lover. Eight years later she and another lover plotted death for that man's wife, and for this they paid a homeless man in money and sexual favors. He then became Kobayashi's new lover, and together they killed her second lover and co-conspirator in the first murder. It wasn't long before she found yet another accomplice to help her dispatch the third guy, but before that occurred, they were arrested.[9]

An even more deviant couple was based in California. Around 1:00 PM on Thursday, June 12, 1980, a Caltrans worker picking up trash along the Ventura Freeway came across the nearly nude body of a teenaged girl. She had been shot in the head with a small caliber weapon. Not far away, another girl around the same age lay dead, also shot. They were identified as Gina Marano, 15, and Cynthia Chandler, 16.

Soon a call came from a woman who implicated her boyfriend in the killings but who refused to say how to locate him. She knew details that had not been released to the media, and her report that she and her boyfriend had recently washed the car, inside and out, was consistent with the way a killer who wished to remove evidence would act. But the switchboard cut her off and she did not call back.

Eleven days passed and two more females were found shot in a similar fashion. First on June 23, someone discovered the body of prostitute Karen Jones, 24, on Franklin Avenue. Then the headless body of a woman believed to be in her twenties was discovered nude beside a steel trash bin. The victim was identified as twenty-year-old Exxie Wilson, also a prostitute—and a friend of Karen Jones. A thorough search of the area failed to turn up her missing head, but four days later, a man found an ornate wooden box with the head inside.

It wasn't long before snake hunters in the San Fernando Valley on June 30 discovered the mummified remains of a fifth victim, shot and hidden under an old mattress. She was linked to the series, which had acquired a name in the news, the "Sunset Strip Murders." She turned out to be seventeen-year-old Marnette Comer.

Then a male victim was found on August 9, five days after he had been killed and left in his van. His headless corpse was blackened and decomposing, and he'd been viciously stabbed nine separate times and slashed across the buttocks. He was identified as country singer John "Jack" Robert Murray, 45.

On August 11, Carol Bundy, 37, told coworkers that she had taken lives, so they called the police. When they arrested her, she handed them three pairs of panties that she said belonged to recently found victims, as well as a photo album of Doug Clark in compromising positions with an eleven-year-old girl. Bundy also admitted that while she had only assisted with the other murders, she had killed Jack Murray herself.

Another team arrested Clark at work. One of his coworkers found his two .25-calibre Raven automatics and the police lab linked one via ballistics tests to five victims. Clark was charged with these murders.

As often happens, these two killers turned on each other, attempting to place blame for the murders on anyone but themselves. Eventually, Bundy told the details of their sordid story. She had met Clark in a bar in 1979 and they became lovers. Eventually Clark introduced into their lovemaking his fantasies of torture, captivity, and necrophilia. In the spring of 1980, Clark came home covered in blood. He lied about its source but on another occasion Carol discovered a bag of bloody women's clothing in the car. Doug then told her about Gina and Cynthia, the two girls found dumped off the freeway.

Bundy was intrigued by this kind of kinky sexual escapade, so Clark showed her where he had dumped a prostitute after shooting her. Bundy had also accompanied Clark on his Hollywood area cruising and in a parking lot he made her lure a young prostitute who used the name "Cathy" to the car. Bundy climbed into the back seat, ostensibly to "watch" Cathy perform oral sex on Clark. Bundy was supposed to signal whether or not she wanted to go ahead and shoot the girl herself, but Clark apparently grew angry at the hooker and shot her in the head.

Then Clark brought home the head of a dead victim. He placed it in the freezer to preserve it for their use as a sex toy. Carol put makeup on it so Clark could penetrate the mouth for a form of necrophilic oral sex. They continued to use it in this way for three days before placing it in the box in which it was found.

Then on August 5, Bundy sought out former lover Jack Murray for some companionship. She dropped hints about what she had been doing with Clark, and according to her, he mentioned the police. That was not what Bundy had intended, so she lured Murray into his van, forced him to lie on his stomach, and shot him in the head. But he was not dead, so she stabbed him. Afterward, she removed his head.

Their nasty demise was as predictable as their relationship had been in terms of the dynamics of dominance and submission. Yet there's a popular misunderstanding about such relationships that the dominant one runs the show and makes all decisions, and the submissive one has no choice but to obey. In fact, both partners have strengths and weaknesses, both manipulate, and both complement the other. To make the dance work, they each need the other.

The dominant person finds pleasure in mastery while the submissive one enjoys the surrender. They help each other to explore their fantasies. The experience pushes them both closer to a high, which reportedly creates an intense flow of energy. Oddly enough, a paradoxical equality is achieved.

The most extreme form of this dynamic is sadomasochism, which involves consensual violence. The "master" inflicts pain and humiliation to help the "slave" reach emotional catharsis. Sadomasochism, according to practitioners, eroticizes mental and physical pain. The rituals make the fantasies they both enjoy concrete and become a means for gaining a powerful psychic orgasm.

Clark had his own version of the story. He said that Bundy imagined herself to be the wife of Ted Bundy. She had engaged Jack Murray in this delusion and they had killed the victims together before Carol had finally turned her wrath on Jack. But the police had collected plenty of physical evidence that implicated Clark, and none that involved Murray.

Bundy and Clark were both analyzed and one professional described Bundy as condescending and controlling. She was not brain-damaged and showed no overt psychopathology. Clark, too, was not found to be organically damaged or psychotic.

The chief witness against Clark at trial was Bundy, promised "use immunity." She dressed like a proper housewife and spoke articulately about being under Clark's spell. Although she claimed to be a compulsive truth-teller, she undermined herself with a letter she had written explicitly stating that she could not be trusted to tell the truth.

Nevertheless, Clark was found guilty of six counts of murder and one count of attempted murder. He kept insisting he was innocent, but nevertheless when he took the stand to once again display his arrogant attitude, he urged the court to sentence him to die in the gas chamber. They were willing to oblige. On March 16, 1988, Douglas Clark received six death sentences.

Carol Bundy pled guilty to killing Jack Murray and accepted a plea deal that spared her the death penalty. Despite her testimony against Clark, she continued to write to him.[10]

While all-female teams have also been documented, they are rare and have occurred largely in the role of caretakers. We've already seen one such team when we discussed lust murder, and we'll cover another in the following chapter.

NOTES

1. Brian Masters, *She Must Have Known: The Trial of Rosemary West* (London: Transworld Publishers, 1996); Howard Sounes, *Fred and Rose: The Full Story of Fred and Rose West and the Gloucester House of Horrors* (London: Warner, 1995).

2. Janet I. Warren and Robert R. Hazelwood, "Relational Patterns Associated with Sexual Sadism: A Study of Twenty Wives and Girlfriends," *Journal of Family Violence*, March 2002, 17, 75–89.

3. Michael Newton, *The Encyclopedia of Serial Killers* (New York: Checkmark Books, 2002), p. 214.

4. Eric Hickey, *Serial Murderers and Their Victims*, 3rd edn. (Belmont, CA: Wadsworth, 2002), p. 183.

5. Ronald Markman and Dominic Bosco, *Alone with the Devil* (New York: Doubleday, 1989).

6. Jack Olsen, *The Man with the Candy: The Story of the Houston Mass Murders* (New York: Simon & Schuster, 1974).

7. Jaye Slade Fletcher, *Deadly Thrills* (New York: Onyx, 1995).

8. Vince Bugliosi and Curt Gentry, *Helter Skelter* (New York: Norton, 1974).

9. Kaori Aki, "Serial Killers: A Cross-Cultural Study between Japan and the United States," Master's thesis, California State University, Fresno, CA, 2003.

10. Louise Farr, *The Sunset Murders* (New York: Pocket, 1992).

CHAPTER 15

"Care" takers

At the end of 2004, Nurse Charles Cullen was caught mishandling medications and, upon his arrest, he admitted to multiple murders in ten different institutions. A year later, a British investigation into convicted killer Doctor Harold Shipman revealed that he may have been responsible for at least 250 deaths among his patients. People in such positions have been exploiting trust and killing people for centuries, but more recently their murders have come to light in increasing numbers around the world, with their motives more critically scrutinized. Healthcare serial killers, known to experts as HCSKs, may be any type of employee in the healthcare system who uses his or her position to murder at least two patients in two separate incidents, with the psychological capability of committing more. This is not about euthanasia; it's far more selfish and sinister.

In the past thirty years, there have been more than eighty cases of HCSKs in developed societies (nearly half in the United States), with more than 2,000 fatalities and many suspicious deaths that could not be fully investigated.[1] A rare few HCSKs enter the profession as predatory "angels of mercy," while most transform into killers on the job—sometimes from initially benign motives. The most susceptible patients are very young children and the elderly or critically ill. In other words, the ones least likely to tell someone what a nurse has done.

DOCTORS

While HCSKs who are physicians are rare (around a dozen known), the available cases indicate that doctors often kill from the desire to experience a godlike sense of power over patients or from experimental curiosity. They view themselves as superior and thus their decision to kill involves fantasies of entitlement. One of the most notorious physicians to have murdered patients is Harold Shipman in England; he holds the record for the number of murders to date in this subcategory of serial killer.

Shipman was initially believed to have begun his killing career after he joined a general practice in Todmorden in 1974, but then investigators examined patient deaths prior to that time, inspired by reports from a student nurse at a facility where Shipman worked in 1971. A special commission reexamined 137 patient deaths and found Shipman present in at least one-third of the cases that he had certified, compared to an average of 1.6 percent for other doctors. That raised red flags, as did the fact that an unusually high percentage of the deaths had occurred between 6:00 PM and midnight.

In his later years, Shipman had made house calls to the elderly (mostly women), and had taken advantage of the easy pickings among such patients, but he had preyed on other types as well. His first victim was probably Margaret Thompson, 67, who was recovering from a stroke. She died in March 1971, and records indicated that Shipman had been alone with her at the time. Then he killed three men between the ages of 54 and 84. When the Commission looked for possible causes for Shipman's behavior, they learned that Shipman had watched his cancer-ravaged mother die in a morphine-induced coma and had himself become addicted to pethidine, so he may have developed a fascination with drugs. There was evidence that he liked to test the boundaries of certain forms of treatment. Since some of the patients would have died anyway, perhaps within a few hours, it seems that Shipman had used the opportunity to experiment on them, thereby accelerating their demise. His experiments were usually performed on the evening shift when few other personnel were around.

Despite Shipman's reputation among his house-bound patients as a gentle and good man, the investigation found that Shipman had often mocked his victims and used derogatory codes for them, such as WOW—Whining Old Woman—and FTPBI—Failed To Put Brain In. He exhibited arrogance at his trial and a complete lack of remorse for his actions, which included attempting to make himself the beneficiary of one patient's will. He went to prison and in 2004, he hanged himself in his cell with a bed sheet—a gesture of apparent defiance.[2]

While there are female physicians who have killed, as yet we know of no female serial killers in that group.

MALE NURSES

Nurses often feel undervalued, and male nurses in particular have expressed to colleagues a sense of powerlessness and disrespect. Killing sprees among nurses of both genders appear to be fueled by motives such as gaining attention, finding a small realm of power and control, assuaging depression, paying back an unfair system, relieving frustration, or reducing their burdensome workload.

In 2003, Charles Cullen was arrested on the suspicion of murdering one patient and attempting to murder another at a hospital in New Jersey. Both had been given a heart medication, digoxin, which records showed they should not have received. Cullen, 43, was a common factor between them, as he was in four other cases of patients with high levels of insulin or digoxin. It turned out that he had also been suspected of administering medication to deceased patients at other hospitals, but no proof was forthcoming in those cases. (HCSKs know how difficult it is to detect certain medications, especially after a person has been embalmed and buried.) Whenever he moved on, which he did frequently, those institutions let the matter drop.

At a court hearing for the two suspected victims, Cullen admitted that he had indeed attempted to overdose these patients, but then shocked the court and the reporters covering the hearing: Over the past sixteen years in ten different institutions in New Jersey and Pennsylvania, he admitted, he had done the same thing to between thirty and forty patients. He declined legal representation but then accepted a public defender, who said Cullen would offer names of victims in exchange for avoiding the death penalty.

Detectives in New Jersey interrogated Cullen for seven hours on December 12, 2003, and he talked about how easy it had been to move on from one facility to the next, as soon as suspicions were voiced. He pointed out that this was a problem with the system, allowing people like him to operate quietly, without being noticed. One of his methods was to acquire medications from patients' drawers or closets, because, initially, no one tracked the drugs. When electronic drug tracking was put in place, he learned how to manipulate computer records. He left "tracks," but no one checked, and the nurses were not held accountable for the drugs they ordered. In another place, a storage room for drugs was never locked, so he'd pilfered at will. He said that some of his bosses knew the errors he'd made that had harmed patients, but had overlooked them. In some places, he simply got fired, "written up," or was pressured to leave. He did not get reported to the state boards, although he knew this was always a risk. Yet he also knew that hospitals needed evidence or they could be sued.

Cullen claimed he killed to end suffering. He'd had a difficult life as the youngest of nine brothers and sisters. His father had died when he was an infant and his mother while he was in high school. Two of his siblings had also died, and he had cared for one of them. By 1988, he was working at a hospital. He got married and had two daughters, but the marriage was rocky and they were soon divorced. In 1998, Cullen filed for bankruptcy, with debts and back payments in child support of over $65,000. Due to reported neglect, the animal protection agency also confiscated his dog.

Despite Cullen's professed motive, many of the patients that he'd killed had not been suffering and some were even getting better when he decided to take their lives. It seems, from a longitudinal analysis, that Cullen was killing during times of personal stress, perhaps from feelings of failure. When the going got rough, he acted out. In 1993, his wife had filed for a restraining order against him, frightened that he might endanger her and their children. She said he had spiked people's drinks with lighter fluid, burned his daughters' books, and was cruel to family pets. Then his wife served him with divorce papers, and a few weeks later he was arrested for stalking a girlfriend. He broke into her home, then taunted her, and subsequently admitted himself into a psychiatric facility. On two occasions that same year, he tried to kill himself. At the places where he worked during this time, he killed patients, and the record shows that when things went wrong, Cullen often reacted with aggression.

As of January 2006, Cullen had admitted to twenty-nine murders and six attempted murders. For the families, he had named names and claimed to be sorry.[3]

Male nurses are disproportionately represented among caretakers who harm patients. While there are many more cases, quantitatively, of females who indulge in this behavior, Beatrice Yorker, Dean of the College of Health and Human Services at California State University, Los Angeles, cited a striking statistic: the 146,000 male registered nurses represent only 5–7 percent of nurses and yet are responsible for about one-third of those nurses in the United States since 1975 who have killed patients.[4]

Donald Harvey holds the record. In 1987, he pled guilty in Indiana, Kentucky, and Ohio to thirty-seven counts of murder and several counts of attempted murder, mostly by poisoning or smothering (although he had initially confessed to around eighty). A psychiatrist who examined him said that his killing grew out of a compulsive need to relieve tension. It seemed clear from what he said that he was experimenting with drugs and enjoying the sense of power and control that killing gave him.[5]

Orville Lynn Majors, LPN, joined the nursing staff at Vermillion County Hospital in Clinton, Indiana, in 1993. Only around twenty-six people died there per year in the intensive care unit, but in 1994 the deaths had risen to over one hundred, with more than half during Majors' shifts. An investigation found that during only twenty-two months of his service there, 147 people died, most of them while he was working. Investigators exhumed fifteen bodies, finding that some of the deaths were consistent with the administration of epinephrine and potassium chloride. Although Majors was suspected in dozens of deaths, on October 17, 1999, he was convicted of only six counts of murder.[6]

Other parts of the world deal with such predators as well. On January 14, 2004, Roger Andermatt was arrested in Switzerland for the murder of twenty-two patients and the attempted murder of three. He confessed to them all, using both medication overdoses and smothering. The victims, aged 66–95, needed a high level of care. Like many other HCSKs, Andermatt claimed to have killed out of pity, although he added that he had felt overworked by the volume of care his team had to provide. He was convicted and given a life sentence.[7]

FEMALE NURSES

HCSKs generally rely on drug overdose or smothering, and they are quick to claim that their acts were done from mercy or compassion. In most cases, those motives fall apart and other evidence indicates that these nurses were actually predators. The best initial evidence against them is their repeated presence at or near a death just before it occurred. While there are overlapping methods and motives between male and female HCSKs, there are also some key differences.

When Kristen Gilbert was on her shift on Ward C, the acute care ward of the Veteran's Affairs Medical Center in Northampton, Massachusetts, the codes for cardiac arrest quickly rose (even among patients who had no heart trouble when entering). So did the number of deaths. In fact, over a period of fourteen months, Gilbert was present for thirty-seven deaths and 50 percent of the medical emergencies on that ward—much higher incidences than was true of any other nurse's shift. In her home, Gilbert kept books on poison and assisted suicide, and in a previous year on her shift, she had called in twenty-two of thirty code blues. Her nickname was "Angel of Death," one of the signals that someone may be killing patients. Finally in 1996, three nurses told hospital administrators that they feared there was a killer among them. Several patients had just barely been saved, and there was an inexplicable shortage of the heart stimulant epinephrine in the supplies—more than eighty doses were unaccounted for. They suspected Gilbert, who seemed to love the excitement of a cardiac emergency. When she learned about the reports, she took a sudden leave of absence.

To investigate this matter, the bodies of two former patients were exhumed and a toxicology analysis showed signs consistent with epinephrine poisoning—a substance produced naturally by the body as adrenaline and thus difficult to detect. But epinephrine had not been prescribed for these men. One of them had died shortly after Gilbert had asked if she could leave early in the event of his death. Another patient, admitted for the flu, suffered four heart attacks. A surviving patient claimed that Gilbert had pumped something into his hand that had numbed him.

Late in 1998, Gilbert, 33, was arrested and charged with four murders and three attempted murders. She had also attempted to deflect the investigation with bomb threats phoned into the hospital, and for this, she served fifteen months. The investigation turned up evidence that she had falsified records and removed sections from EKG strips.

Assistant U.S. Attorney William M. Welch II came up with a theory: Gilbert was having an affair with James Perrault, a member of hospital security. These codes had nearly always occurred during his shift and he'd come rushing to respond. That meant Gilbert could see him in action and get some quick contact. Since that affair was now over, it was not difficult to get Perrault to testify. He told the grand jury that Gilbert had actually admitted to him that she'd killed patients by injection.

Other witnesses offered more specific evidence: broken containers of epinephrine found in a disposal bucket after a cardiac emergency and a patient who'd died when Gilbert was in his room had cried out, "Stop! Stop! You're killing me!" According to another nurse, Gilbert carried "epi" in her pocket.

Defense attorney David P. Hoose stated on Gilbert's behalf that no one had witnessed her injecting the deceased patients. In addition, they were in a hospital and could have died from health-related reasons. To discredit Perrault, Hoose said that he was reacting with his statement because Gilbert had broken off their affair. As for the missing epinephrine, there were several nurses with drug problems on the ward who could have stolen them. Gilbert, he maintained, was being scapegoated.

In the end, after a proceeding that lasted twelve weeks, Gilbert was convicted of three counts of first-degree murder, one count of second-degree murder, and two counts of attempted murder, along with other lesser charges. Although she was under federal jurisdiction, which made her eligible for the death penalty, Gilbert was sentenced instead to life in prison. She tried to appeal but then dropped it.

Gilbert, 33, was the divorced mother of two sons, 7 and 10, although she had not seen them in four years. She had moved out of her home to be near Perrault. During testimony, her father, Richard Strickland, said his daughter had been raised in a middle-class home and had been both a Brownie and Girl Scout. Her great grandfather had died a lingering death in a veteran's hospital following World War I, so perhaps this had affected her. Yet Gilbert showed no remorse as surviving relatives described the lives of their loved ones, and she had risked critically ill patients by phoning in a series of bomb threats that forced evacuation.

Her behavior at the trial, and the allegations against her by those who knew her, indicates a narcissist who believes that only her own needs and desires count. Others are pawns in her game, not humans with equal status and rights. When she saw that she was getting away with murder, literally, it may have inspired a feeling of power that was sufficiently intoxicating to motivate her to repeat it—especially with the payoff of seeing the man who obsessed her.[8]

People like Gilbert who kill repeatedly in the healthcare community are generally intelligent. They're aware of the various ways to kill and the ones easiest to hide—as Gilbert's comments to colleagues indicated. When caught, they often blame the hospitals for not monitoring medications (as Cullen did). Gilbert appears to be among those looking for both thrill and attention. She relied on the overdose of a drug that would be difficult to detect and selected victims from among elderly men whose deaths might be expected.

The best initial evidence against such killers—and true of Gilbert—is their repeated presence at or near a death just before it occurred, and their attitudes about the incidents. In Texas, Genene Jones was another notorious HCSK, who was convicted of using succinlycholine chloride, a relaxant, on a child who died, along with attempting to kill another child, who was saved in time. She apparently thrived on the drama of an emergency and insisted on being the one to carry a dead child to the morgue—where, reportedly, she would sometimes sit in a chair and rock with the tiny corpse. She was suspected in many more murders of children at the San Antonio Medical Center in Texas in 1981 and 1982. On her shift, the pediatric ICU death rate rose 178 percent, and a child under her care was ten times more likely to die and twenty-three times more likely to suffer a seizure. For one murder in which evidence of six others was introduced, she received ninety-nine years.[9]

Among female HCSKs, there have been some remarkably shocking team killers as well. We've already seen Gwendolyn Graham and Catherine Wood, who played the "Murder Game" in a nursing home, but there have also been some fatal associations of hospital workers.

SISTERHOOD

In Austria, four nurses and nurse's aides teamed up to kill. It started in 1983 and went on for nearly six years before a doctor overheard them discussing it and turned them in. By that time, the death toll was estimated at between forty-two and forty-nine, although it could have been far higher. The mastermind of this "sisterhood" was Waltraud Wagner, 24, who had once experienced satisfaction from assisting a seventy-seven-year-old patient to end her suffering. She saw the value in this activity for certain patients and soon recruited accomplices from the night shift. Maria Gruber, 19, joined, as did Ilene Leidolf, 21. The third recruit was a grandmother, forty-three-year-old Stephanija Mayer. They referred to their ward as the "death pavilion."

Wagner taught the others how to give lethal injections, and she added some fatal mechanisms of her own creation. The most gruesome, the "water cure," involved holding a patient's nose while forcing him or her to drink water. That was an agonizing death that filled the lungs, but was undiscoverable as murder. Since many elderly patients who died had fluid in their lungs, it was not a suspicious signal during an autopsy. While their initial motives for this behavior had grown from compassion, they soon began to enjoy the feelings they experienced and became more sadistic, sometimes even killing patients who merely annoyed them too much. Such people were issued their "tickets to God." At first, these nurses killed sporadically, but by 1987, they were escalating; rumors soon spread of a killer on Pavilion 5.

The doctor who overheard them talking and laughing about their activities went to the police, triggering an investigation. It took six weeks, but all four women were arrested on April 7, 1989, and the doctor in charge of their ward, who should have noticed the escalating death rate, was suspended. Collectively they confessed to forty-nine murders, and Wagner took credit for thirty-nine of them, although she later admitted to only ten. Ultimately, Wagner was convicted of fifteen murders, seventeen attempted murders, and two counts of assault. She was sentenced to life in prison. Leidolf got life as well, on a conviction of five murders, while the other two drew fifteen years for manslaughter and attempted murder charges.[10]

SIGNALS

Too often, these killers have been allowed to drift from one hospital to another, perhaps fired but rarely brought to justice until after incriminating evidence has reached shocking levels. While there is no distinct psychological type to look for, there is a collection of signs and behaviors that have proven to be fairly accurate predictors, at least when many of them show up together in the same person: secretive behavior, missing medications, a preference for the night shift, spikes in unexpected deaths on a certain person's shift, and spotty past work records. It requires a number of signals collectively to solidify suspicions, but among those noted as HCSKs are people who like to "predict" when someone will die, work on shifts where a higher incidence of code blues or deaths occur, have often been seen inside a patient's room when they did not belong there, and like to talk about death. They often gain macabre nicknames by patients or colleagues and they like to watch the response to a death.

Statistically, there is a higher death rate when the suspected person is on shift, and the suspicious deaths are generally unexpected. The suspect has a history of patient complaints and of moving from one institution to another. They may also complain about the workload and be flippant about death. A few have suffered from such disorders as Munchausen's syndrome and Munchausen's syndrome by proxy.

Most of what we know about HCSKs has come from people who have worked with them. The same principle holds true with other types of serial killers, and those people who have been closest to a killer and who were willing to talk have offered valuable information.

NOTES

1. D. Lucy and C. Aitken, "A Review of the Role of Roster Data and Evidence of Attendance in Cases of Suspected Excess Deaths in a Medical Context," *Law, Probability and Risk*, 2002, 1, 141–160; Paula Lampe, *The Mother Teresa Syndrome* (Holland: Nelissen, 2002).

2. R. Waugh, "Telltale Signs Pointed to Murder," *Yorkshire Post*, February 1, 2005; Carol Peters, *Harold Shipman: Mind Set on Murder* (London: Carlton Books, 2004).

3. K. Wang and M. Frassinelli, "Families and Possible Victims Sue Suspected Killer Nurse," *Newark Star Ledger*, March 7, 2004; D. Garlicki, C. Campbell, "AG Uses One Killer to Catch Others," *Newark Star Ledger*, November 21, 2004; "In his own words," *Newark Star Ledger*, September 12, 2004.

4. Kelly Pyrek, "Healthcare Serial Killers: Recognizing the Red Flags," *Forensic Nurse*, September/October 2003, 4.

5. W. Whalen and B. Martin, *Defending Donald Harvey* (Cincinnati, OH: Emmis Books, 2005).

6. "Former Nurse Guilty of Murder of Six Patients," *News Tribune*, October 18, 1999.

7. "Swiss Nurse is Sentenced for 22 Murders," *New York Times*, January 29, 2005.

8. M. William Phelps, *Perfect Poison: A Female Serial Killer's Deadly Medicine* (New York: Pinnacle, 2003).

9. Peter Elkind, *The Death Shift: The True Story of Nurse Genene Jones and the Texas Baby Murders* (New York: Viking, 1983).

10. Michael Kelleher and C. L. Kelleher, *Murder Most Rare: The Female Serial Killer* (New York: Dell, 1998), pp. 211–215.

CHAPTER 16

Close to a Killer

One might think that the best source for learning about a killer is the killer, but since psychopaths are self-serving, their "confessions" are skewed, and psychotic murderers are delusional. In addition, all people have personal blind spots. Confessed Unabomber Ted Kaczynski failed to see how he telegraphed his personal style in his antitechnology "Manifesto" when he published it in the *Washington Post* in 1995, yet his brother and sister-in-law recognized how similar it was to his sentiments and writing style. So after sixteen bombings between 1978 and 1995 that killed three people and wounded twenty-three others, he was identified. It seems reasonable to surmise that those people who have been close to a killer see more about them than even their attorneys do, and in that case, we can explore three more angles: families, associates (friends, lovers, coworkers, or partners), and survivors. Few family members have been willing to talk in detail, but those who have done so have offered valuable information about a killer's background. So have other associates. Let's look at what some people have said about serial killers whose cases have been detailed in this book.

THE KILLERS' INTIMATES

Many serial killers were married or in committed relationships when they killed. A number of the males who had children were often considered good fathers, although female killers have tended to murder their children or family members. After these predators have been arrested, the families often withdraw and decline to respond to the media. Few have revealed what it was like to live with active murderers, aside from speaking on their behalf in court, usually during sentencing.

Often family will say that they had no idea that their brother/father/ sister/mother was a serial killer, but one of the few family members to admit to suspicions prior to an arrest was Edmund Kemper's younger sister, Allyn. She testified during his trial that when she read about the decapitation of one of the victims in Santa Cruz, she recalled the way her brother had once beheaded the family's cat, as well as his similar treatment of one of her dolls. She confronted her six-foot-nine brother, who denied being the Santa Cruz "Co-ed Killer." Yet she indicated that he was agitated about the fact that their mother, Clarnell Kemper, had also questioned him in the slayings. He had, after all, killed his paternal grandparents when he was fifteen—a possibility about which Clarnell had warned her ex-husband prior to the incident. Yet thanks to her intervention on Edmund's behalf when he was locked up, after serving time for the double homicide, he had managed to get out of a juvenile detention facility early. Since he also killed Clarnell as one of his final victims, she did not live to tell her story.

Allyn hoped to assist Kemper with his insanity defense by describing some of his more aberrant acts. During the time of his murder spree, she had visited him in his apartment and was disturbed by his gun collection and handcuffs. She also recalled that during their childhood, one of his games had consisted of staging his own execution. He would ask her to lead him to a chair, blindfold him, and pull a "lever." Then he would writhe about as if being executed by gas and "die." Another incident that she remembered was her attempt to tease Kemper into kissing a teacher. According to her, he had retorted that if he were to kiss the woman, he would first have to kill her.[1]

At the murder trial of Harrison "Marty" Graham, who had lived in a Philadelphia apartment with the corpses of half a dozen murdered prostitutes, two of his former girlfriends and his foster mother all provided details about his development, character, and modus operandi. A woman named Paula had lived with Graham for three years and she said that during sex he would place his hands around her throat and squeeze. On several occasions she thought he was killing her. He told her that he'd killed one of his former girlfriends, Robin DeShazor, because he'd been angry that she was seeing other men, and he'd threatened Paula with the same treatment, sometimes barricading her into the apartment, waving a machete at her, or raping her when she was in a stupor from drugs. She recalled that he'd admitted to practicing necrophilia with the corpse. Paula also visited Graham after she moved out and had smelled a foul stench coming from the room they'd used as a bedroom. She said he had told her at the time it was from a urine bucket and warned her never to look into that room.

Mary Hogan had also lived with Graham, and she said they'd have sex four or five times a day. He tried to strangle her as well, and she had seen DeShazor's decomposing remains on the roof outside their apartment. In order to get out with her belongings, she had to seek assistance from the police, because Graham had threatened to kill her with a machete and had shut her inside the apartment. (The police apparently did not see the body on the roof at that time.)

The first witness on Graham's behalf during his trial was his former foster mother, Wilhelmina Williams, who had taken him into her home from the ages of two through seven, when his mother had been unable to care for her children. Williams said that Graham had been a "slow learner" and was essentially incapable of taking care of himself. She had never seen him learn to read or write. Graham's mother supported this observation when she said that her son seemed unable to learn anything. Unlike her other children, he'd failed to grasp the difference between right and wrong. He was also a head-beater and a troublemaker in school, and suffered from recurring nightmares.[2]

THE KILLER'S LIVED WORLD

Even when relatives testify, enduring the media's glare, they generally want to change their names afterward and withdraw. A talk show looking for family members to interview following BTK Killer Dennis Rader's arrest quickly learned how difficult it is to even find these relatives, let alone get them to talk. That show had to be scrapped.

Nevertheless, some people have valiantly made an attempt to describe the killer in his (or her) everyday manner, especially his childhood, in the hope of learning something about the person, themselves, and their families. The person who wrote what is probably the most detailed memoir of being near a serial killer during his active phase was Lionel Dahmer, the father of confessed cannibal and necrophile, Jeffrey Dahmer. Since his book so clearly depicts what we'll cover in closing, I'll save Mr. Dahmer's description for the next chapter.

Let me turn instead to an enormously detailed portrait of a killer growing up, which was penned by Gary Gilmore's youngest sibling, Mikal, who approached the subject of his brother's two murders by deconstructing his own family. As discussed in Chapter 11, on July 19 and July 20, 1976, Gary Gilmore gunned down two young men in Utah. He'd only been out of prison two months, but he'd been unable to make enough money to buy what he wanted. He was impulsive, ill-adapted to society, angry, and suffering from many years of drug therapy. He's among repeat killers who could think of no particular reason why they did it. Mikal was curious about Gary's seeming inability to keep himself clean, so in his book *Shot in the Heart* he analyzed their family life and produced one of the most literary and insightful narratives about the conditions that can inspire a once sweet and talented kid to become a killer.

The turbulent family in which the Gilmore boys had grown up was replete with fantasy and denial, coupled with random abuse by their alcoholic father, Frank Gilmore Sr., a con man. He'd married his wife Bessie on a whim, but he'd had several wives and families before her, none of whom he had cared about or supported. Frank and Bessie had a son, Frank Jr., and then Gary came along while they were wandering through Texas under the pseudonym of 'Coffman' to avoid being caught for Frank's illegal cons. Frank christened this second baby Faye Robert Coffman, which Bessie unofficially changed to Gary, and when Gary later saw the original name on his birth certificate, he believed he was illegitimate and thus spurned by his father.

Frank Sr. had many dark secrets and Bessie was herself a Mormon outcast. So they seemed to cling to each other to escape the realities of their pathetic lives. Because Frank craved independence, he would disappear for long stretches of time. Bessie, for her part, did not allow the children to touch or hug her. Given their parenting styles, there was considerable emotional deprivation in the children's lives. Yet Bessie did want security, so she persuaded Frank to settle in Portland, Oregon, and open a legitimate business. He actually succeeded at it and for awhile they were more stable.

Yet Frank drank heavily, which sent him into terrible rages. He'd whip his sons severely. The boys soon learned that no matter what they said or did, their father simply wanted to brutalize them, all the while insisting that they tell him they loved him. Mikal believed that Gary received the brunt of their father's anger because he most reminded the older man of his own failings, which were many. One time, Gary was abandoned on a park bench while his father went to scam someone and he ended up in an orphanage for several days. These incidents left emotional scars, and as he grew older Gary reacted in anger. He despised people in authority and acted out by stealing cars. Both parents turned a blind eye to his problems. Neither respected the law, and Frank would rather con the system to get his kids off the hook than let them learn the consequences of their actions.

In addition, and likely influential, Bessie had a deep-rooted superstition about Gary that derived from her childhood. She believed that as a girl playing with a Ouija board, she had conjured up a demonic ghost that had attached itself to her family. When one of her sisters was killed and another paralyzed in an accident, she felt certain it was the ghost. Then she married Frank and found out that his mother, Fay, was a medium. One night while at Fay's house, Bessie learned that there was to be a "special" séance to contact the spirit of a man who had died while suspected of murder. After the ceremony, she found Fay in a state of exhaustion and fear. Later that night, according to her own account, Bessie woke up to see the face of a leering inhuman creature. Fay shouted for her to get out *now*, so she ran to Gary's room. There she claimed she saw the same demonic figure leaning over her son, staring into his eyes. She grabbed the kids and fled the house. Fay died shortly thereafter and Gary began to have terrible, shuddering nightmares that he was being beheaded—nightmares that haunted him the rest of his life. Bessie blamed the demon.

She believed that Gary got into trouble because he was bedeviled. She marked that night in Fay's home as a turning point for him, because his life thereafter was filled with angry, malevolent energy that seemed bent on self-destruction. Whether influenced by his mother's ideas or by familial abuse, Gary seemed destined to die in some violent manner; that is, he seemed to have a death wish. In addition, he, like the other boys, was affected by a story that Bessie told over and over about how her father had forced her against her will to watch a hanging. All of the boys believed that she'd really witnessed this incident and it had left a deep impression on them.

But then Mikal, who had also been deeply hurt on his mother's behalf, researched this incident in Utah records and realized that it was impossible for her to have witnessed any such thing. She had made it up, and this terrible lie had reverberated throughout all of their lives. Mikal concludes that the lies his mother told were probably based in terrible psychological truths that became an unspoken emotional legacy for her sons, as if Bessie wanted them to erase themselves from existence. In fact, one Gilmore boy was murdered, one was executed, one dropped into a psychological funk ... and one (Mikal) became a writer—anything but an erasure.

His incisive portrait of Gary shows a young man of intellect and talent who was subjected to neglect, indifference, rage, abuse, the role modeling of a criminal, and an inability to get past the family legacy. Even though he was given a second chance (more than once), he seemed unable to make it pay off. He'd even once been granted the possibility of leaving prison to attend art school because he had genuine talent, but instead he got drunk and pulled off an armed robbery that sent him right back behind bars. Gary's aggression toward others could easily be interpreted as a form of self-destruction.[3]

Mikal's interpretive research shows how the abuse, chaos, uneven caring, and generally difficult conditions can work on a sensitive, reactive temperament. All of this was exacerbated when Gary spent the larger share of his life in reform school and prison. He had no examples from parents or people in the prison system that offered clarity on how to develop prosocial skills. While the causal factors for violence cannot be definitively pinpointed in any single case, Mikal's careful portrait of a family offers plenty of reason to regard seriously the effects of early abuse and extreme familial instability.

THE STRANGER

In 1980, Ann Rule published *The Stranger beside Me*, about a man who had worked alongside her for a time in the Seattle Crisis Clinic. His name was Ted Bundy. Rule volunteered there and Bundy was a paid work-study student. When she met him he was twenty-four, had an easy grin, and a clean-cut appearance. He studied between calls, was making good grades as a psychology major, and aspired to go to law school. Rule liked him at once and said that they had made a good team.

"I can picture him today ... see him hunched over the phone, talking steadily, reassuringly—see him look up at me, shrug, and grin. I can hear ... the infinite patience and caring in his voice ... He was never brusque, never hurried."[4]

Whenever there was a lull, they would talk for hours to each other, alone in the building. Rule found that Bundy paid full attention. "You could tell things to Ted that you might not tell anyone else."[5] Because she liked him so much and found him to be genuinely caring, when he later told her he was innocent of the murder charges brought against him she believed that for much longer than she might otherwise have.

After several women went missing in Colorado and Utah, and Bundy was arrested for the abduction of one who picked him from a lineup, an investigation was launched to determine if there were links to the missing girls in the Pacific Northwest, and that's when Rule heard from Bundy again. In September of 1975, he called to let her know he was a suspect and to assure her that he had nothing to do with the crimes. He asked for her support, and when he was convicted of the attempted kidnapping, he continued to write to her.

Awaiting trial for murder in Colorado, Bundy escaped, got caught, and escaped again, showing up in Tallahassee, Florida. There he was stopped for a traffic violation but soon was charged with three murders. He talked with Rule before his impending trial in 1979. She'd had some doubts early on about the arrest and had tended to accept his claims, but by that time, she had decided that it was too much of a coincidence for him to have been in all the places where these girls had been murdered. She thought it likely that at least some of the charges were true.

Faced with a choice between attending his trial as a friend or reporter, she decided she'd have an easier time getting into court as a reporter. Yet Bundy kept his eyes on her throughout the proceedings, as if he needed to assure himself of her support. She recalled later how he would look at her, shrug his shoulders, and appear to dismiss the surroundings as if he did not belong there any more than she did. She found this disturbing, especially in retrospect. The most difficult moment for her was the presentation of bite mark evidence. The bruise left on one victim was clean enough to make a good match to a dental impression of Bundy's teeth.

It left little doubt for Rule about who had killed the young woman. Then an eyewitness dramatically pointed Bundy out as the man she had seen in the sorority house where two of her sorority sisters had died. Once she understood that she had been close to this man who had murdered so many young women, she went to the ladies' room and threw up. It was a delayed form of trauma, and one that would teach her just how cagey intelligent psychopaths like Bundy can be.

After Bundy's trial, which resulted in three death sentences, Rule began to write a book about the case, and when he read it Bundy was displeased with the result, as if she had been disloyal. But she had told the truth as she saw it. Rule's experience haunted her, because she felt that she had been so easily duped. Yet her story provides a good portrait of someone who could befriend a killer for a period of time and have no hint about his darker deeds.[6] It's even possible to become lovers with one and know nothing of what he's doing when he's away.

DANGEROUS LIAISON

After the double homicide on November 7, 1974, of Carswell Carr and his fifteen-year-old daughter in their home in Georgia (described in Chapter 3), their killer, Paul John Knowles, took Carr's suits and car and went to a Holiday Inn in Atlanta, Georgia. At the same time, British journalist Sandy Fawkes came into the hotel bar looking for a drink. They had dinner, danced, and ended up in bed.

Fawkes describes Knowles's inability to sexually perform without self-stimulation, although he was able to laugh about it. She sensed that he wanted to be liked, and while she thought him strange he proved to be good company, so she stayed with him for several days. He was sensitive, considerate, protective, and able to insert himself into her life almost unobtrusively. Despite her better instincts, she found herself letting it happen. Since he was a stranger, and people are always warned against taking up with strangers, Fawkes sometimes joked that Knowles, whom she knew as Lester Daryl Golden, might be a killer. It did not seem quite so funny when she rose one morning while he still slept and saw his lips curled back in the expression of "an animal at bay." That scared her.

Fawkes was also troubled when they traveled together and in St. Augustine, her companion was intent on finding the torture chamber of an old fort. On another occasion, she saw him tear a story from the local newspaper about the Carr double homicide and its possible connection with three other area murders. He covered his behavior quickly, saying he had friends who lived where the incidents happened. He seemed secretive and preoccupied, but his discussions about such things as his business and his belief in God were passionate. He also believed in fate and told her he would be dead within a year. (Earlier we discussed more fully his conviction that he was special.)

Shortly after Fawkes parted from Golden by slipping away and then avoiding his attempts to contact her, he took up with a couple who knew her and who kept him company because they felt sorry for him. The next day, he attempted to rape the woman, but she managed to escape and turn him in to the police. They went to apprehend him, but he threatened them with a sawed-off shotgun. He then proceeded to run, taking hostages. One he left alive but killed two others.

Detectives located Fawkes to discover what she knew about Paul John Knowles, a parole violator and suspected serial killer. She was stunned by what they told her. Knowles had been drifting from one state to another, mostly in the south. His own taped diary implicated him in sixteen murders across eight states, some for sex, some for material gain, and some just for notoriety. He compared himself to the bank robber John Dillinger, bragging that he would one day be as famous.

Fawkes wondered why Knowles had not killed her, and decided that since nothing had been expected and they'd just had a good time, he'd been comfortable with her. He also did seek fame. So her status as a writer who could grant him that probably had some influence. At any rate, while Knowles was in the midst of his killing spree, Fawkes had experienced him as nothing more than an awkward, ordinary guy. When he'd suggested that she should write a book about him, she could not imagine what made him think he was that special.[7]

SURVIVORS

Among the best sources of information about predatory serial killers are people who were close to them while they exercised their secret aggression. They are able to describe exactly how the killer approached them, what he did, and what he was like. There are numerous such survivors, and many have been instrumental in the prosecution of the killer from whom they escaped.

Four of the five women whom Ted Bundy grabbed in Utah had died, but Carol DaRonch, 19, had managed to escape and her story revealed just what his approach had been. She described how he had introduced himself as "Officer Roseland," a police officer and had told her a story about her car being burglarized where she had parked it outside a Sears store in Murray, Utah. Oddly, he smelled like alcohol and had slicked-back hair. She had checked the car but found nothing wrong. Bundy then asked her to accompany him to a substation nearby, so she agreed, although she asked for identification. He flashed something from his wallet without letting her see it very clearly, took her to the back of a building, which he said was the substation (it was a Laundromat), and had her get into his car. She found it odd that he drove a dented, dirty Volkswagen Beetle, and declined when he asked her to buckle her seat belt. They drove for a short time but then "Officer Roseland" pulled over and snapped one of a pair of handcuffs on her.

DaRonch struggled, keeping her would-be abductor from closing them onto her other wrist. He said he had a gun and would blow her head off if she didn't stop resisting, but she kept fighting and got the passenger side door open. Bundy came at her with a tire iron, which she managed to block as she screamed and slipped out of the car. She'd lost a shoe but she ran as fast as she could down the road to flag down a car. She heard Bundy drive away. A concerned couple took her to the police, and as she told her story to them, Bundy was already scamming his next victim only twenty miles away. DaRonch told the police that the man had seemed educated and confident, doing nothing out of the ordinary to alert her to trouble. And yet he'd had every intention of killing her.

Bundy is famous for his approach to his victims, generally feigning helplessness and a shy quality to put them at ease. Yet he could transform in an instant into a raging predator ready to break open a woman's skull. DaRonch was the only woman who had survived to describe it.[8]

A different approach to female victims was adopted by Christopher Wilder (the "Beauty Queen Killer" from Chapter 2). The first woman he approached at a shopping mall when he went on the run was able to tell detectives exactly what he had done to her—but just barely. Only nineteen, she was blond and pretty, and had easily fallen for his compliments. He'd told her that he was a photographer looking for a model to pose for him, and she had just the type of face he was seeking. He would pay her $25 for less than an hour if she agreed to go with him to a nearby park. He seemed sincere to her, and credible, since he was well dressed in a pin-stripe suit and was not pushy. Without much concern, she accompanied him to his car, where he showed her some fashion magazines and claimed that several of the impressive photos were his work. But then instinct kicked in and she sensed something wrong, so she thanked him, declined, and started to move away.

At that moment, the "photographer" hit her hard in the stomach with his fist. Before she could recover, he hit her in the face and pushed her into his car. She couldn't breathe, let alone struggle, and he was already in the car and driving fast before she got her bearings. There was no way to open the door and jump out. When he stopped in a secluded area, he placed duct tape over her mouth and bound her hands together. He drove again and then stopped to force her to get into the trunk. She lay there in that cramped space, bound and gagged, for hours while her abductor drove to an unknown destination. When he finally arrived where he was going (which was over the state line), he opened the trunk, wrapped her in a sleeping bag, and carried her into a motel room. She had no idea where they were or what he might do next. She believed she was going to die.

In fact, the man told her that if she did not remain quiet he would kill her. He made her undress and get on the bed so that he could lie next to her and masturbate. He shaved her pubic hair and made her perform several sexual acts before he raped her. All this time, he had the television on, occasionally paying attention to the program. At one point, he pulled out an electrical cord, which appeared to have been spliced. The frightened girl realized what he intended when he applied two open copper wires to her feet, hit a switch attached to the wire, and painfully shocked her. Afterward, he applied Superglue to her eyelids, forcing her eyes shut and used a blow dryer to harden it. He did a poor job of it, so she was able to watch him through tiny slits. She knew she would have to act on any opportunity, quickly, if she were going to survive.

The man turned the television channels until he found an aerobics show, then ordered his abductee to dance in imitation of the women on the tube. She could barely see, but she complied. When she did not perform as he wanted, he shocked her into obedience. When he lost interest, she moved toward the bathroom. He came at her and they struggled, but she managed to get into the bathroom and lock the door. Screaming, she pounded on the wall. After a few moments, she heard fumbling in the room and then the door slammed. Waiting half an hour, she finally ventured out to find the room empty. Her abductor was gone, so she made her way to the motel office, where the receptionist called the police.

Wilder went on to Texas, where he found his next victim. He also kept another victim alive to help him lure girls, but his modus operandi remained the same throughout his flight. He always approached pretty girls, posed as someone who could assist their career, and grabbed them for torture and rape, as well as murder.[9]

Another rape victim also able to describe her ordeal with a killer was instrumental in giving the police what they needed to solve the murders of ten women in the area of Tampa, Florida. On November 3, 1984, seventeen-year-old Lisa McVey was grabbed off her bicycle by a man hiding in the bushes. He threatened her with a gun and knife, blindfolding her and forcing her into his car. She begged him not to hurt her and said she would do whatever he wanted, so he ordered her to remove her clothes and perform oral sex on him. She did so, using brief opportunities when the blindfold slipped to notice the man's car. After driving around for a while, he brought her back to his apartment, where he kept her hostage. Her ordeal lasted twenty-six hours, as he repeatedly raped her, fondled her, forced her to perform sex acts on him, and even made her shower with him, where he washed and dried her.

Throughout this nightmare, McVey managed to keep her head clear to look for opportunities to identify this man if she ever got free. She got glimpses of his car, as well as a white stucco building where they climbed seventeen red steps. Inside a room that smelled of disinfectant, McVey dropped a barrette next to the bed to prove that she had been there. She was determined to survive, whatever it took.

After a marathon rape session, during which her abductor seemed to need to repeatedly threaten her to get worked up, he finally dozed off. She kept assuring him that she liked him and liked what he was doing, but he bound her to ensure she did not escape. When he woke up, he said he now trusted her. He was less brutal, referring to her now as "babe" rather than "bitch." He even said he wished he could keep her, but eventually, he seemed to lose interest in what they were doing, so he took her back to his car. To her surprise, he dropped her off and drove away.

McVey went to the police and they sent evidence from her clothing to the FBI lab to see if there was a connection to the area serial murders. The lab technicians identified the same red fibers that had been found on most of the murder victims. With McVey's description of her abductor's car and home, they were able to arrest Bobby Joe Long. After they confronted him with the evidence they had from the murders, he confessed to having killed ten women.

A woman who had dated him, and had been raped and battered by him, teamed up with McVey to write a book about their ordeals. Both had found Long to be an odd combination of neediness and aggression. When he felt humiliated, he retaliated, but when a woman did little to challenge him, he was docile, even hopeful that she might want to be with him. He was not unlike other sexual predators who feel enraged at women for their problems, frustrated that they cannot achieve what they want.

In fact, Long's method of raping women before he turned to fatally bludgeoning them was to present himself as a nice guy who was interested in whatever a woman had advertised for sale in the paper. Once invited in, he would overpower her. He enjoyed making women believe he was a friendly, helpful guy, so he could then shock them with his sadistic side. He apparently thought of all women as whores that must be punished. McVey's detailed account provided every bit as much awareness of Long's manner of operating as did anything a psychologist said at his trial, probably more.[10]

But one survivor of a serial killer was also a psychologist, and her report to the police exposed John Robinson, already a suspect in the cases of several missing women. He had lured women via the Internet, where he would enter bondage-oriented chat rooms as "Slavemaster." He soon had them signing slave contracts that granted him total control. People generally entered such arrangements willingly, because they sought the experience of being sexually dominated. There was risk, but that was considered part of the excitement.

In April 2000, a psychologist named Vickie Neufeld moved to Kansas City to pursue a relationship with Robinson. She agreed to sign a slave contract, although such an arrangement was new to her, but she soon became unhappy with his increasingly brutal manner. She wanted to leave but didn't have money. Robinson got angry with her, and he stole her bag of sex toys. Angry, she called the police to report the theft. Then another woman soon issued a complaint against Robinson for hitting her. Since detectives were already watching Robinson, they were glad for a reason to close in. After arresting him on charges of sexual assault and theft, they got a warrant to go through his office and properties. In La Cygne, Kansas, they hit pay dirt.

Cadaver dogs led the investigators to two eighty-five gallon barrels. Inside were the bodies of two of the missing women known to have been with Robinson. More barrels inside the storage units produced more bodies, including a mother and daughter. Robinson, a former Eagle Scout and seminary student who had become a thief, forger, and embezzler, was arrested for murder.

In Kansas, a jury found Robinson guilty of three murders just before Halloween in 2002 and sentenced him to death. For the Missouri charges, in exchange for life in prison, he pled guilty to five murders, including two for which authorities did not have bodies. He was fifty-nine years old, one of the oldest serial killers ever convicted. Then in 2004, Kansas overturned an old law that gave prosecutors an advantage in death penalty cases, and Robinson's sentence was commuted to life.

About him, Neufeld had said that he had offered her a job just when she was down on her luck and desperately in need of funds. He would help her with contacts, he said, and let her move in with him to be his sex slave. He gave her e-mail contacts for recommendations. She found him to be charming, soft-spoken, and helpful, although the twelve rules listed on his slave contract, along with the vulgar language he had used, had bothered her. So did the fact that he had not paid for the room when she came to town, as promised. (He wanted her to have to give over a check to the clerk so he could acquire her account number.) Still, when he first arrived, Neufeld had found him to be confident, intelligent, and well groomed. He assured her he had taken care of the bill. He also said they could reword the slave contract to her satisfaction. Overall, on his initial visit, he seemed quite amenable and spent a lot of time teaching her about the bondage-and-discipline community into which she had entered. His manner had been entirely reassuring.

However, when he removed his clothing to see if they had sexual chemistry—a requirement for her to be his slave—he'd started taking pictures without her permission. He then forced her to give him oral sex in the way he liked and left her $50 for food. The next day, after she gave him an amended contract, he got rough and demanding with her, putting a collar on her. Although she complained of discomfort, he ignored her. The more time they spent together, the more she saw how angry he was, even enraged. He treated her disrespectfully, insisting she obey him, and finally she'd had enough. That's when she went to the police—fortunately for her.[11]

What these survivors saw were behaviors that revealed what the killer was like during his most engaging fantasies—the way he indulged in anger, control, power, or paraphilias. They also experienced the way a serial killer can turn diverse personalities on and off at will, which is the subject of our final chapter.

NOTES

1. Donald Lunde, *Murder and Madness* (San Francisco: San Francisco Book Co., 1976), p. 54.

2. The full story of Harrison Graham was found in *The Philadelphia Inquirer,* August 1987–December 2003.

3. Mikal Gilmore, *Shot in the Heart* (New York: Doubleday, 1994).

4. Ann Rule. *The Stranger beside Me* (New York: W. W. Norton, 1980), p. 25.

5. Ibid., p. 26.

6. Ibid., pp. 24–32.

7. Sandy Fawkes, *Killing Time* (New York: Taplinger, 1977).

8. Stephen G. Michaud and Hugh Aynesworth, *The Only Living Witness* (New York: Signet, 1983), pp. 81–84.

9. Bruce Gibney, *The Beauty Queen Killer* (New York: Pinnacle, 1984).

10. Joy Wellman, Lisa McVey, and Susan Replogle, *Smoldering Embers: The True Story of a Serial Murderer and Three Courageous Women* (Far Hills, NJ: New Horizon Press, 1997).

11. Sue Wiltz, with Maurice Godwin, *Slave Master* (New York: Pinnacle, 2004), pp. 105–121.

CHAPTER 17

Behind the Eyes

To wrap things up, we'll explore the idea that even those people who are closest to a killer may not spot the red flags. We can thus see how effective a predator's strategies can be and may stop suspecting that a wife or parent "must have known," as is often claimed in the press In 1969, after Jerome Brudos confessed to the murders of four girls in his home workshop, killing at least one even when his wife was nearby, she was arrested and charged as an accomplice. So not only did she have to bear the horror of what her husband and the father of her two daughters had done but also the humiliation of being perceived as capable of such atrocities. In the end, she was acquitted, and by 2004, when Dennis Rader, or "BTK," was arrested, we'd learned enough about the secrecy of a serial killer to allow Mrs. Rader and her children their privacy. Even so, many people still insist that she must have seen the signs.

There is no reason to believe she did, any more than did the people who had elected Rader president of their Lutheran congregation. He was an "organized" predator, skilled at hiding his brutal fantasies and behavior. In fact, one might even say that his stalking, torture, and murder vented his rage and lust in a way that made him a more even-tempered man in contexts like church and family. Serial killers like him are truly Jekyll and Hyde, and their "potion" of transformation is psychological.

SECRETS

Many people believe that serial killers are loners and losers, unable to maintain careers or relationships. They're supposedly undereducated, narcissistic, and searching for short-term gratification. The public wants monsters to be obvious, and many popular culture productions reinforce that naïve hope that they're largely on the fringes of society. But monsters do live among us—easily and with little detection, because the clever ones know how to adapt and to deflect suspicion.

Ted Bundy worked a crisis hotline as he murdered young women; John Wayne Gacy buried boys beneath his house while he ran a business, threw fundraisers for local politicians, and entertained sick kids; and Spokane's prostitute killer Robert Yates Jr. was a decorated former army pilot with five children. "Eyeball Killer" Charles Albright had a master's degree, knew several languages, was a former science teacher, and had a seemingly satisfying marriage. Three-time child killer John Joubert assisted with a Boy Scout troop. Andrei Chikatilo had a university degree, had been a teacher, and was married with children. Christopher Wilder was a wealthy contractor and race car driver. Michael Ross, convicted of killing eight women, had an Ivy League degree.

Why don't we spot serial killers, even socially accomplished ones, before they do so much damage?

Many serial killers blend in because they're the type of person who can go through the motions of ordinary living while acting out against others without giving themselves away. In other words, they're not obviously deranged, and while they're morally deviant they can hide it in their bland everyday manner. Among their most dangerous features are a callous disregard for the rights of others and a propensity for violating norms. They can charm and manipulate others for their own gain, conning with no regard for anyone's feelings. In fact, they fail to think of other people as human.

To review, most serial killers are psychopaths, which means they are narcissistic, impulsive, and pitiless, with a tendency to divert blame from themselves to others so that they come out looking like the victim. From brain scan studies, it appears that they fail to fully process the emotional content of situations, such as empathy, concern, or alarm, and tend to seek stimulation and arousal. Their offenses are more brutal than those of other criminals, more aggressive and more diverse. They also represent a high percentage of repeat offenders. They're resistant to therapy and intolerant of frustration. It doesn't matter whom they hurt; what matters is that they get what they can for themselves—money, media status, thrill, revenge, sexual gratification, bodies. They find victims easily because they're glib, charming, and predatory, while their victims are generally trusting, unsuspecting, and naïve. They don't suffer from fear of consequences.

Thus, killers may thrive among us, with homes and families. They may attend church (although without struggles of conscience) and even be considered good neighbors: they know how to behave to avoid suspicion or discovery. But they look for opportunities—taking a security job that positions them to meet potential victims, for example—and they have no qualms, when the time is right, about exploiting it. We want to spot them, but they usually spot us first. The best defense is to realize they're among us, shed our cultural naiveté, take care whom we trust, and understand the mechanism of their deception and our denial. So just how do they develop this ability to split into an ordinary person and a monster?

MANY LIVES

Robert J. Homant, a criminal psychologist with extensive experience with sex offenders, and Daniel B. Kennedy, a criminologist specializing in police issues, reviewed the literature on serial murder and focused on serial sexual-sadistic killers. After looking at several motive-based classification systems suggested by other experts, they summarized three explanatory models, with appropriate attributions:[1]

1. Trauma Control Model (Eric Hickey)—some traumatic event occurs during a person's development, and that person has a vulnerability or physiological predisposition to react with anxiety, anger, confusion, and mistrust; he blames an external source and reacts with aggression to restore balance or self-esteem.
2. Motivational Model (Robert Ressler, Ann Burgess, John Douglas)—the formation of a serial killer is the result of the interaction of five personality-shaping components: an ineffective social environment, crises of childhood, available escape into fantasies, interpersonal failures, and negative traits or behaviors supported by a belief system that offers rationalization and justification for dominance and control.
3. Lust Murder as Paraphilia (Bruce Arrigo, C. E. Purcell)—the behavior is the result of a disease, because neural pathways have malfunctioned in the way sexual and aggressive impulses are transmitted and combined.

Another idea, which complements rather than opposes these models, comes from Al Carlisle, a psychologist who worked with inmates at Utah State Prison. He describes serial killers as having a divided soul, or a "compartmentalized" self. They offer a public persona that appears to be "good," while nurturing a darker side that allows their murderous fantasies free reign. Because they have painful memories from childhood abuse, disappointment, frustration from being bullied or whatever, they have learned to use fantasies to escape, comfort themselves, and even develop an alternate identity that feels more powerful or provides greater status. Such fantasies can turn violent and demand an avenue of release, such that actual situations that bear some similarity to the fantasy may trigger acting it out. For example, Jerome Brudos, who'd been browbeaten by his mother, may have been content with his sexual fantasies about women's underwear and shoes had not a young woman come to his door selling encyclopedias. Brudos' family was gone, he had the girl to himself, and the moment seemed opportune to see what it would be like to actually do what he had long imagined doing. He killed her, removed her foot to keep in a freezer (for photographing and trying on different shoes), and found that he not only enjoyed the experience but wanted to repeat it.[2]

In the fantasy life, the expression of unacceptable impulses, desires, and aspirations gradually becomes an equal part with the "good" persona; killers live with two equal but opposing sides of their personality. As normal life becomes less interesting or more frustrating or disappointing, the fantasy life becomes more attractive. Eventually, the brutal dimension gains more substance through mental rehearsal, as well as opportunity, and the unrestricted fantasy develops into an unquenchable habit. Nevertheless, Carlisle admits that "the pathological process that leads to the development of an obsessive appetite (and possibly an addiction) to kill is still one of the most perplexing psychological mysteries yet to be solved."[3]

As the killers get away with their acts, they learn the best ways to deflect others from discovering their secrets and then enjoy the lack of accountability. They devise different sets of values for different life frames, so that they can speak convincingly about socially approved venues of right and wrong, yet have no qualms about their socially condemned behavior. Their secret lives grow darker and more perverse, because the morality that justifies them is entirely of the killers' making, separate from the social morality in which they were raised and by which they get along with others. They can feel satisfied about their murder while condemning the same thing in someone else, or denouncing divorce, teenage promiscuity, or prostitution (as Gacy once did). They can also carry on a high level of functioning even while they seek another victim, because the murder helps them to achieve something they believe they need.

Carlisle proposes that the ability to repeatedly kill and also function occurs via the evolution of three primary processes:

1. Fantasy—the person imagines scenarios for entertainment or self-comfort
2. Dissociation—the person avoids uncomfortable feelings and memories
3. Compartmentalization—the person relegates different ideas and images to specific mental frames and keeps boundaries between them[4]

Excessive daydreaming, such as lonely, shy, or frightened children engage in, can lay the foundation for who they eventually will become and how they will act. Certain temperamental qualities, such as hostility, defiance, anger, and the need to be considered special, can form and be reinforced in a fantasy life. An individual can also achieve emotional and sexual gratification with imagery, and those feelings and acts that he knows others would disapprove get shoved into a secret compartment, to be savored and augmented when alone. Fantasy also builds an appetite to experience the real thing. Sometimes fetish objects, such as lingerie or dolls, can help to enhance the experience, but in the end, even as the fantasy has the psychological force to create a secret identity, it fails to fully satisfy. It must also be kept under control in most situations. As Ted Bundy once described it, this private arena is entirely separate and controlled, such that it would never drift into the realm of the social persona.[5] The effort to keep these fantasies separated forms the boundaries that make them distinct. But the more the fantasies are suppressed, the more energy they gain, especially if the person's "normal" side has little ego strength or integrity. It becomes easy to get preoccupied with the fantasy, and if it's acted out, the bridge has been crossed into the person's real life. To their minds, *that's* who they are, while others know only their false self.

Now the fantasy and act have merged with the person's identity, especially if the actualization of the fantasy feels powerful or satisfying. Any remorse, self-hate, or guilt he may feel gets placed into its own mental compartment and sealed away. He can't afford to allow emotional taboos to interfere with the drive to repeat the experience, to once again achieve the high, or experience himself as perfect or superior. With no effective inhibitions, the hunt begins again. When it becomes overly compulsive, as evidenced in the escalation of activity (more brutal, or incidents occurring closer together), it can psychologically overwhelm and undermine the killer, leading to decompensation, carelessness, and mistakes. At times, a killer has ended it by turning himself in, and those who have confessed have often described being possessed by that part of themselves that needed to kill. Even so, the people closest to them often did not see it.

SEEING IN THE BEST LIGHT

Lionel Dahmer, Jeffrey Dahmer's father, wrote a book after watching his son's 1992 trial for the murder of seventeen men and realized that the manner in which he had interpreted Jeffrey's behavior had been naïve, influenced by his personal fears. He was overcome upon learning that the sons of seventeen other fathers had been treated thus by *his* son, so he wrote a memoir, *A Father's Story*, to explore the cause. Yet his attempt to understand Jeff's envelopment in the world of murder and cannibalism is not so much the point here: what interests us is the way he failed to see the constellation of clues that, in retrospect, seemed obvious.

Lionel, who had often been in his son's apartment, was stunned to learn that police found Polaroid photos of dismembered males, pickled genitalia, a full skeleton hanging in the closet, heads in the refrigerator, and receptacles full of decomposing human remains. He recalled questioning the reason for the freezer Jeff had purchased and accepting the justification that it would help to save him money. It was actually intended to freeze his victims' parts. But would *anyone* suspect this reason for an otherwise ordinary domestic purchase? That's part of the problem: killers use for their nefarious work what others use for normal purposes.

Lionel did stumble at times. While he admitted he was unaware of his son's substance abuse problem (although his wife once found him drunk and passed out), he did notice that Jeffrey often seemed vacant—"enclosed"—as if thinking about nothing. Was he born this way, Lionel wondered, or did he lose or acquire something along the way that gave him such a terrible proclivity? As Lionel learned some of the most appalling things about his son's activities, he was able to reinterpret a number of incidents.

Jeff had been uninterested in girls and went on no dates, but Lionel viewed this as shyness, not homosexuality; Jeff had filled the bottles in the liquor cabinet with water after emptying them, but Lionel did not recognize this as the signal of a deep-seated problem; Jeff had a full-size male mannequin in his closet and Lionel allowed him to dismiss it as an impulsive "prank," like calling the .357 Magnum under his bed a "target pistol." Lionel's wife, Jeff's stepmother, thought its presence indicated something wrong with Jeff, but Lionel responded to her concerns by suggesting vocational alternatives for his son: if there was something wrong, a good job would right it. Lionel had no idea why, when he heard the details during the trial, he had not noticed that Jeff had an obsession with dead animals, and had even placed the head of a dog on a stick. Jeff had hidden his cemetery, to be sure, but surely there would have been some hint—an odor, a tuft of hair on his clothing. But who *would* have concluded from even a repulsive odor that a child was collecting road kill for his private cemetery? Or even had they known, who might have believed it was part of the boy's sexual fantasies rather than just a boy's curiosity?

Yet from the pattern that Lionel noticed as he reviewed Jeff's life, it seems he would have found a way *not* to see. When Jeff was living at Lionel's mother's home, for example, she called to tell Lionel about a terrible odor that Jeff said came from a cat box. When confronted, Jeff quickly lied, telling his father he liked to experiment with chemicals on chicken parts from a grocery store and a dead raccoon he'd found on the street. Lionel searched the house but found nothing unusual except liquid near the garbage cans that he thought was ordinary meat juice. (Who *would* have imagined it was biological fluid from a dismembered murder victim?) "... I allowed myself to believe Jeff," Lionel mused, "to accept all his answers regardless of how implausible they might seem.... More than anything, I allowed myself to believe that there was a line in Jeff, a line he wouldn't cross.... My life became an exercise in avoidance and denial."[6]

When Jeff was out on bail for a child molestation charge (Lionel believed Jeff's lie that he had not known the boy was a child and that he had "touched" the boy by accident), he went back to his grandmother's home. Lionel went to help him with his court appearance and came across a foot-square sealed box. He asked what was in it, but Jeff resisted opening it. They had a stand-off, and finally Lionel relented when Jeff said he would show his father the box the following day. When he did so, it contained pornographic magazines. Lionel was satisfied that Jeff had merely been ashamed. He learned later that had he opened the box as he was about to do, he would have found the head of one of Jeff's victims.

His denials are understandable. Parents, spouses, and other close associates often do seek the best possible interpretation of something that a loved one has done. That's how those same loved ones get away with having affairs or stealing from Mom's purse. That's often why children are not taken to counselors at a time when intervention might make a difference, because the parents hope they'll "grow out of it" on their own. In fact, on the day that Lionel Dahmer realized that his son was a liar, alcoholic, exhibitionist, thief, and child molester, he thought to himself, "even all those grotesque and repulsive behaviors could be thought of as a stage through which he would one day pass."[7] He likened his own behavior to creating a soundproof booth over which he had drawn curtains to prevent him from seeing or hearing what his son had become. Something similar can probably be said about many people who are in close contact with serial killers. But we must credit the killers as well with the ability to hide their secrets and perfect their acting skills.

There are experts who believe that all serial killers are motivated by the same thing; some say it's to achieve greater status, others believe it can be reduced to an issue of control, and a few even state that serial killers have no motive at all. Yet one cannot say that Javed Iqbal, who killed one hundred boys for the sake of revenge, operates from the same psychology as Melvin Rees, who craved intellectual experiences; Ted Bundy, who wanted to possess his victims; Dennis Nilsen, who sought bodies for company; Herbert Mullin, who hoped to save California; or Jane Toppan, who lusted after the dying process. Yes, these motives are about control, but no, they're not all alike. It's time to give up overly simplistic ideas about causes and motives.

In fact, recent work done on anxiety disorders has relevance for a theory about the development of violent tendencies, although no one has yet made the connection. Susan Mineka and Richard Zinbarg applied contemporary learning theory to the formation of anxiety disorders, utilizing case history material. Their conclusion is that early learning patterns, contextual variables, and particular temperamental vulnerabilities together affect how our early experiences will play out across the life span, as either short-term reactions or long-term disorders.[8] When this idea is applied to a person who develops murderous fantasies out of frustration, for example, we can see how someone with a reactive temperament might grow violent from physical abuse, while his more complacent brother who experienced similar abuse but who processed it differently did not. Perhaps he had a better relationship with their mother or was able to channel his frustration by reading or playing sports, or he simply did not view the abuse in a personalized way. Maybe he wasn't as sensitive or maybe he thought he deserved it. For whatever reason, it's clear that different people in similar situations may develop different short- and long-term responses. Indeed, someone who might be more warranted in turning violent than another person, might be the one who spurns violence while the other becomes prone to it. In other words, as Mineka and Zinbarg discovered with anxiety disorders, we may find that we can assess the risk for developing into a serial killer from a person's early learning history, coping style, and specific temperament, rather than from some formula that fails to account for factors unique to the person.

In brief, serial killers develop from within their individual situations, and if we hope to understand them, and perhaps one day even identify a budding serial killer, a case analysis approach is warranted that includes their childhood conditions, physiology, social influences, family legacy, fantasies, aspirations, frustrations, coping mechanisms, and strategies for continuing their murders. While they're not all alike, we can learn how they've become extreme offenders as both a way to protect ourselves and a way to redirect the energies of children at risk for antisocial behavior.

NOTES

1. Robert J. Homant and Daniel B. Kennedy, "Serial Murder: A Biopsychological Approach," in *Serial Crime: Theoretical and Practical Issues in Behavioral Profiling*, Wayne Petherick, ed. (San Diego, CA: Academic Press, 2006), pp. 189–224.

2. Ann Rule, *The Lust Killer* (New York: New American Library, 1983; revised 1988, with an additional chapter).

3. Al C. Carlisle, "The Dark Side of the Serial-Killer Personality," in *Serial Killers*, Louis Gerdes, ed. (San Diego, CA: Greenhaven Press, 2000), p. 107; excerpted from "The Divided Self: Toward an Understanding of the Dark Side of the Serial Killer," *American Journal of Criminal Justice*, 1993, 17(2).

4. Ibid., pp. 108–114.

5. Stephen G. Michaud and Hugh Aynesworth, *The Only Living Witness* (New York: Signet, 1983), p. 195.

6. Lionel Dahmer, *A Father's Story* (New York: William Morrow, 1994), pp. 128–29.

7. Ibid., p. 139.

8. Susan Mineka and Richard Zinbarg, "A Contemporary Learning Theory Perspective on the Etiology of Anxiety Disorders," *American Psychologist*, January 2006, 61(1), 10–26.

APPENDIX

How They're Caught

Following is a list of ways that serial killers were caught, based on a study of three hundred cases.

1. Police investigation: physical evidence/crime scene behavior/unassociated witnesses who linked them to crime
2. A survivor turned them in
3. An accomplice turned them in
4. Someone who knew them or observed their behavior informed police
5. Apprehension during an unrelated police operation/confession when charged with something else
6. Killing a victim they knew well
7. Their correspondences or phone calls to press, victims, or police
8. Kept evidence at home, in computer, or in storage/had victim property on person
9. Outright error
10. Caught in the act/seen with a victim shortly before death
11. Error during escalation/decompensation
12. Turned themselves in
13. Bragged or showed off to someone who alerted police
14. Recognized by someone from published picture

15. Political arrest
16. Common factor in missing persons, family or institutional deaths
17. Suspicious behavior noticed by authorities
18. Investigation after suspect committed suicide

Bibliography

Acocella, Joan. "The Politics of Hysteria," *The New Yorker*, April 6, 1998.

Aki, Kaori. "Serial Killers: A Cross-Cultural Study between Japan and the United States," Master's thesis, California State University, Fresno, CA, 2003.

Alderman, Robert. *The Bloody Benders*. New York: Stein & Day, 1970.

Barrett, William. *Irrational Man: A Study in Existential Philosophy*. New York: Doubleday, 1958.

Beech, Anthony, Dawn Fisher, and Tony Ward. "Sexual Murderers' Implicit Theories," *Journal of Interpersonal Violence*, November 2005, 20(11), 1366–1389.

Berg, Karl. *The Sadist: An Account of the Crimes of Serial Killer Peter Kürten: A Study in Sadism*. London: Heineman, 1945.

Biondi, Ray. *The Dracula Killer*. New York: Pocket, 1992.

Black, Donald W. *Bad Boys, Bad Men: Confronting Antisocial Personality Disorder*. London: Oxford University Press, 1999.

Blundel, Nigel. *Encyclopedia of Serial Killers*. London: JG Press, 1996.

Brady, Ian. *The Gates of Janus: Serial Killing and Its Analysis, By the 'Moors Murderer.'* Los Angeles: Feral House, 2001.

Breazeale, J. W. M. *Life As It Is, or Matters and Things in General*. Knoxville, TN: James Williams, 1842.

Brodwater, Taryn, and Becky Kramer. "Transcripts Detail Murder, Kidnapping Case," *The Spokesman Review*, October 22, 2005.

Bugliosi, Vincent, with Curt Gentry. *Helter Skelter*. New York: Bantam, 1995.

Burns, Gordon. *The Story of the Yorkshire Ripper*. New York: Viking, 1985.

Carlisle, A. C. "The Dark Side of the Serial-Killer Personality," in *Serial Killers*, Louis Gerdes, ed. San Diego, CA: Greenhaven Press, 2000.

Carlo, Philip. *The Night Stalker: The Life and Crimes of Richard Ramirez*. New York: Kensington, 1996.

Cartel, Michael. *Disguise of Sanity: Serial Mass Murderers*. Toluca Lake, CA: Pepperbox Books, 1985.

Cartwright, Duncan. "The Narcissistic Exoskeleton: The Defensive Organization of the Rage-type Murderer," *Bulletin of the Menninger Clinic*, Winter 2002, 66(1), 1–18.

Cauffiel, Lowell. *Forever and Five Days*. New York: Zebra, 1992.

Cheney, Margaret. *Why—The Serial Killer in America*. Saratoga, CA: R & E Publishers, 1992 (originally *The Co-ed Killer*, New York: Walker Publishing, 1976).

Clarkson, Wensley. *The Railroad Killer: The Shocking True Story of Angel Maturino Resendez*. New York: St. Martin's Press, 1999.

Cleckley, H. *The Mask of Sanity*, 5th edn. St. Louis, MO: Mosby, 1976.

Cooper, A. J. "Female Serial Offenders," in *Serial Offenders: Current Thought, Recent Findings*. Louis B. Schlesinger, ed. Boca Raton, FL: CRC Press, 2000.

Cox, Bill G. *Born Bad*. New York: Pinnacle, 1996.

Cox, Mike. *The Confessions of Henry Lee Lucas*. New York: Pocket, 1991.

Coyle, Marcia. "Unabomber May Seek to Nullify Guilty Plea," *The Recorder* (Washington), February 10, 1999.

Craig, Gary. "Spahalski Pleads Not Guilty," *The Democrat and Chronicle*, January 4, 2005.

Craig, Gary. "Mirror Images Reflect Twin Lives of Violence," *The Democrat and Chronicle*, December 15, 2005.

Cullen, Robert. *The Killer Department: Detective Viktor Burakov's Eight-Year Hunt for the Most Savage Serial Killer in Russian History*. New York: Pantheon Books, 1993.

Dahmer, Lionel. *A Father's Story*. New York: William Morrow, 1994.

Damio, Ward. *Urge to Kill*. New York: Pinnacle, 1974.

De River, J. Paul. *The Sexual Criminal: A Psychoanalytic Study*. Springfield, IL: Charles C. Thomas, 1949.

Diagnostic and Statistical Manual of Mental Disorders-IV. Washington, D.C.: American Psychiatric Association, 1994.

Douglas, Adam. *The Beast Within*. New York: Avon, 1992.

Douglas, John, Ann W. Burgess, Allen G. Burgess, and Robert K. Ressler. *Crime Classification Manual*. San Francisco: Jossey-Bass, 1992.

Douglas, John, and Mark Olshaker. *Mindhunter: Inside the FBI's Elite Serial Crime Unit*. New York: Scribner, 1995.

Eddowes, John. *The Two Killers of Rillington Place*. New York: Little, Brown, & Co., 1994.

Egger, Steven A. *The Killers among Us*. Upper Saddle River, NJ: Prentice Hall, 1998.

Egger, Steven A. *The Need to Kill: Inside the World of the Serial Killer*. Upper Saddle River, NJ: Prentice Hall, 2003.

Elkind, Peter. *The Death Shift: The True Story of Nurse Genene Jones and the Texas Baby Murders*. New York: Viking, 1983.

Everitt, David. *Human Monsters*. Chicago: Contemporary Books, 1993.

Farr, Louise. *The Sunset Murders*. New York: Pocket, 1992.

Fawkes, Sandy. *Killing Time*. New York: Taplinger, 1977.

Fletcher, Jaye S. *Deadly Thrills*. New York: Onyx, 1995.

Flowers, Anna. *Bound to Die: The Shocking True Story of Bobby Joe Long, America's Most Savage Serial Killer*. New York: Pinnacle, 1995.

Fox, James Alan, and Jack Levin. *The Will to Kill: Making Sense of Senseless Murder.* 2nd edn. Boston, MA: Allyn and Bacon, 2005.

Frasier, David K. *Murder Cases of the Twentieth Century.* Jefferson, NC: McFarland & Co., 1996.

Frick, P. J., B. S. O'Brien, J. M. Wootten, and K. McBurnett. "Psychopathy and Conduct Problems in Children," *Journal of Abnormal Psychology,* 1994, 103, 700–707.

Friedman, Maurice, ed. *The Worlds of Existentialism.* New York: Random House, 1964.

Fromm, Eric. *The Anatomy of Human Destructiveness.* New York: Owl Books, 1992.

Gaddis, Thomas, and James O. Long. *Killer: A Journal of Murder.* New York: Macmillan, 1970.

Gaskins, Donald, and Wilton Earle. *Final Truth: The Autobiography of a Serial Killer.* Atlanta, GA: Adept, 1992.

Geberth, Vernon J. *Sex-Related Homicides and Death Investigation.* Boca Raton, FL: CRC Press, 2005.

Gerdes, Louise, ed. *Serial Killers.* San Diego, CA: Greenhaven Press, 2000.

Geyer, Frank. *The Holmes-Pitezel Case: A History of the Greatest Crime of the Century.* Salem, MA: Publisher's Union, 1896.

Giannangelo, Stephen J. *The Psychopathology of Serial Murder: A Theory of Violence.* Westport, CT: Praeger, 1996.

Gibney, Bruce. *The Beauty Queen Killer.* New York: Pinnacle, 1984.

Gibson, Dirk C. *Clues from Killers: Serial Murder and Crime Scene Messages.* Westport, CT: Praeger, 2004.

Gilmore, Mikal. *Shot in the Heart.* New York: Doubleday, 1994.

Goldberg, Carl. *Speaking with the Devil: A Dialogue with Evil.* New York: Viking, 1996.

Gollmar, Robert. *Edward Gein: America's Most Bizarre Murderer.* New York: Pinnacle, 1981.

Graysmith, Robert. *Zodiac.* New York: Berkley Books, 1986.

Grombach, John. *The Great Liquidator.* Garden City, NY: Doubleday, 1980.

Guggenbühl-Craig, Adolf. *The Emptied Soul: On the Nature of the Psychopath.* Woodstock, CT: Spring, 1980.

Hare, R. D. *Psychopathy: Theory and Practice.* New York: Wiley, 1970.

Hare, R. D. "Psychopaths and Their Nature: Implications for the Mental Health and Criminal Justice Systems," in *Psychopathy: Antisocial, Criminal, and Violent Behavior,* pp. 188–212, T. Millon, E. Simonsen, M. Biket-Smith, R. D. Davis, eds. New York: Guilford Press, 1998.

Hare, R. D. *Without Conscience: The Disturbing World of the Psychopaths among Us.* New York: Guilford Press, 1999 (originally published by Simon & Schuster, 1993).

Hare, R. D. *The Psychopathy Checklist-Revised,* 2nd edn. Toronto, Ontario, Canada: Multi-Health Systems, 2003.

Hazelwood, Robert R., and Stephen Michaud. *Dark Dreams: Sexual Violence, Homicide, and the Criminal Mind.* New York: St. Martin's Press, 2001.

Hickey, Eric. *Serial Murderers and Their Victims,* 3rd edn. Belmont, CA: Wadsworth, 2002.

Higdon, Hal. *Crime of the Century: The Leopold and Loeb Case*. New York: Putnam, 1975.

Hillbery, Conrad. *Luke Karamazov*. Detroit, MI: Wayne State University Press, 1987.

Hollandsworth, Skip. "See No Evil," *Texas Monthly*, May 1993, 21(5).

Holmes, H. H. *Holmes' Own Story*. Philadelphia, PA: Burk & McFetridge, 1895.

Homant, Robert J., and Daniel B. Kennedy. "Serial Murder: A Biopsychological Approach," in *Serial Crime: Theoretical and Practical Issues in Behavioral Profiling*, Wayne Petherick, ed. San Diego, CA: Academic Press, 2006.

Howard, Amanda, and Martin Smith. *Rivers of Blood: Serial Killers and Their Victims*. Boca Raton: FL: Upublish, 2004.

Iverson, Kenneth. *Demon Doctors: Physicians as Serial Killers*. Tucson, AZ: Galen Press, 2002.

Jackman, Tom, and Troy Cole. *Rites of Burial: The Shocking True Crime Account of Robert Berdella, the Butcher of Kansas City, Missouri*. New York: Pinnacle, 1992.

James, Earl. *Catching Serial Killers*. Lansing, MI: International Forensic Services, 1991.

Jenkins, Phillip. *Using Murder: The Social Construction of Serial Homicide*. Aldine, 1994.

Jesse, F. Tennyson, ed. *Trials of Timothy John Evans and John Reginald Halliday Christie*. London: William Hodge & Co., 1957.

Johnson, Steven. *Mind Wide Open: Your Brain and the Neuroscience of Everyday Life*. New York: Scribner, 2004.

Kassin, Saul. "The Psychology of Confession Evidence," *American Psychologist*, 1997, 52, 221–233.

Kelleher, Michael D., and C. L. Kelleher. *Murder Most Rare: The Female Serial Killer*. New York: Dell, 1998.

Kennedy, Ludovic. *Ten Rillington Place*. New York: Simon & Schuster, 1961.

Keppel, Robert D., with William J. Birnes. *Signature Killers: Interpreting the Calling Card of the Serial Murderer*, p. 26. New York: Pocket, 1997.

Keppel, Robert D. "Investigation of the Serial Offender: Linking Cases through Modus Operandi and Signature," in *Serial Offenders: Current Thoughts, Recent Findings*, Louis B. Schlesinger, ed. Boca Raton, FL: CRC Press, 2000.

Kidder, Tracy. *The Road to Yuba City*. New York: Doubleday, 1974.

Krause, Ruth Ann. "Serial Killer Talks One Day after Being Sentenced to Three Consecutive Life Terms," *Post-Tribune*, December 18, 2005.

La Bern, Arthur J. *Haigh: The Mind of a Murder*. London: W. H. Allen, 1973.

Lampe, Paula. *The Mother Teresa Syndrome*. Holland: Nelissen, 2002.

Lane, Brian, and Wilfred Gregg. *The Encyclopedia of Serial Killers*. New York: Ballantine, 1992.

Larson, Erik. *The Devil in the White City*. New York: Crown, 2003.

Leo, Richard, and Richard J. Ofshe. "The Consequence of False Confessions: Deprivations of Liberty and Miscarriages of Justice in the Age of Psychological Interrogation," *Journal of Criminal Law and Criminology*, Winter 1998, 429–496.

Lester, David. *Serial Killers: The Insatiable Passion*. Philadelphia, PA: The Charles Press, 1995.

Lewis, Dorothy. *Guilty by Reason of Insanity*. New York: Ballantine, 1998.

Leyton, Elliott. *Hunting Humans: The Rise of the Modern Multiple Murderer*. Toronto: McLelland and Stewart, 1986.

Lourie, Richard. *Hunting the Devil: The Pursuit, Capture, and Confession of the Most Savage Serial Killer in History*. New York: HarperCollins, 1993.

Lucy, D., and C. Aitken. "A Review of the Role of Roster Data and Evidence of Attendance in Cases of Suspected Excess Deaths in a Medical Context," *Law, Probability, and Risk*, 2002, 1, 141–160.

Lunde, Donald T. *Murder and Madness*. San Francisco: San Francisco Book Co., 1976.

Lunde, Donald T., and Jefferson Morgan. *The Die Song: A Journey into the Mind of a Mass Murderer*. New York: W. W. Norton, 1980.

Lynam, Donald. "Early Identification of Chronic Offenders: Who is the Fledgling Psychopath?" *Psychological Bulletin*, 1996, 120, 209–224.

Lynam, Donald. "Pursuing the Psychopath: Capturing the Fledgling Psychopath in a Nomological Net," *Journal of Abnormal Psychology*, 1997, 106, 425–438.

Lynam, D., A. Caspi, T. Moffitt, A. Raine, R. Loeber, and M. Stouthamer-Loeber. "Adolescent Psychopathy and the Big Five Results from Two Samples, *Journal of Abnormal Child Psychology*, August 2005, 431–443.

Mailer, Norman. *The Executioner's Song*. New York: Random House, 1979.

Markman, Ronald, and Dominic Bosco. *Alone with the Devil*. New York: Doubleday, 1989.

Martingale, Moira. *Cannibal Killers: The History of Impossible Murders*. New York: Carroll and Graf, 1993.

Masters, Brian. *Killing for Company*. New York: Dell, 1993.

Masters, Brian. *She Must Have Known: The Trial of Rosemary West*. London: Transworld Publishers, 1996.

Masters, R. E. L., and Eduard Lea. *Perverse Crimes in History*. New York: The Julian Press, 1963.

Matthews, John, and Christine Wicker. *The Eyeball Killer*. New York: Kensington, 1996.

McConnell, Virginia. *Sympathy for the Devil: The Emmanuel Baptist Murders of Old San Francisco*. Westport, CT: Praeger, 2001.

McCrary, Gregg, with Katherine Ramsland. *The Unknown Darkness: Profiling the Predators among Us*. New York: Morrow, 2003.

Michaud, Stephen, and Hugh Aynesworth. *The Only Living Witness: A True Account of Homicidal Insanity*. New York: New American Library, 1983.

Mineka, Susan, and Richard Zinbarg. "A Contemporary Learning Theory Perspective on the Etiology of Anxiety Disorders," *American Psychologist*, January 2006, 61(1), 10–26.

Moffatt, Gregory. *A Violent Heart*. Westport, CT: Praeger, 2002.

Nash, Jay Robert. *Bloodletters and Badmen*. New York: M. Evans & Co., 1995.

Newton, Michael. *Still at Large*. Port Townsend, WA: Loompanics Unlimited, 1999.

Newton, Michael. *The Encyclopedia of Serial Killers*. New York: Facts on File, 2001.

Niehoff, Debra. *The Biology of Violence*. New York: Free Press, 1999.

Nietzsche, Friedrich. *The Will to Power*, trans. by W. Kaufmann and R. Hollingdale. New York: The Modern Library, 1968 (originally published in 1889).

Nietzsche, Friedrich. *The Portable Nietzsche*, trans. by Walter Kaufman. New York: Viking, 1977.

Noll, Richard. *Vampires, Werewolves, and Demons*. New York: Brunner/Mazel, 1992.

Norton, Carla. *Disturbed Ground: The True Story of a Diabolical Female Serial Killer*. New York: Morrow, 1994.

O'Brien, Darcy. *Two of a Kind: The Hillside Stranglers*. New York: New American Library, 1985.

Olsen, Jack. *The Man with the Candy*. New York: Simon & Schuster, 1974.

Olsen, Jack. *"I": The Creation of a Serial Killer*. New York: St. Martin's Press, 2002.

"Pastor and His Daughter Have Been Jailed after They Were Convicted of Murdering Six Relatives and Dissolving Their Remains in Chemicals," *CNN.com*, March 6, 2002.

Penrose, Valentine, and Alexander Trocchi. *The Bloody Countess*. London: Calder, 1970.

Person, Ethel. *By Force of Fantasy: How We Make Our Lives*. New York: Basic, 1995.

Peters, Carol. *Harold Shipman: Mind Set on Murder*. London: Carlton Books, 2004.

Phelps, M. William. *Perfect Poison: A Female Serial Killer's Deadly Medicine*. New York: Pinnacle, 2003.

Philpin, John, and John Donnelly. *Beyond Murder: The Inside Account of the Gainesville Student Murders*. New York: Onyx, 1994.

Pyrek, Kelly. "Healthcare Serial Killers: Recognizing the Red Flags," *Forensic Nurse*, September/October 2003.

Raine, Adrian, and Jose Sanmartin, eds. *Violence and Psychopathy*. New York: Kluwer Academic, 2001.

Ramsland, Katherine. *The Criminal Mind: A Writer's Guide to Forensic Psychology*. Cincinnati, OH: Writer's Digest Books, 2002.

Ramsland, Katherine. *The Human Predator: A Historical Chronicle of Serial Murder and Forensic Investigation*. New York: Berkley, 2005.

Ressler, Robert. K., and Tom Schachtman. *Whoever Fights Monsters*. New York: St. Martin's Press, 1992.

Ressler, Robert. K., and Tom Schachtman. *I Have Lived in the Monster*. New York: St. Martin's Press, 1997.

Rieber, Robert. *Psychopaths in Everyday Life*. New York: Psyche-Logo Press, 2004.

Robinson, Ruthann. "Interview with a Serial Killer," *Northwest Indiana News*, December 8, 2005.

Rogers, R., J. Johansen, J. J. Chang, and R. T. Salekin. "Predictors of Adolescent Psychopathy: Oppositional and Conduct-Disordered Symptoms. *Journal of the American Academy of Psychiatry and the Law*, 1997, 25, 261–271.

Rosella, L. "Teen Appeals Jail Term for Aiding Killer," *The Mississauga News*, December 2, 2005.

Rosman, Jonathan, and Phillip Resnick. "Sexual Attraction to Corpses: A Psychiatric Review of Necrophilia," *Bulletin of the American Academy of Psychiatry and Law*, 17(2), 1989.

Ross, Colin. *Multiple Personality Disorder: Diagnosis, Clinical Features, and Treatment*. New York: Wiley, 1989.

Rule, Ann. *The Stranger beside Me*. New York: W. W. Norton, 1980.

Rule, Ann. *The Lust Killer*. New York: New American Library, 1983 (rev. 1988).

Rule, Ann. *Green River, Running Red*. New York: Free Press, 2004.

Rumbelow, Donald. *Jack the Ripper: The Complete Casebook*. New York: Contemporary Books, 1988.

Russell, Sue. *Lethal Intent: The Shocking True Story of One of America's Most Notorious Female Serial Killers*. New York: Kensington, 2002.

Ryzuk, Mary. *The Gainesville Ripper*. New York: St. Martin's, 1994.

Schechter, Harold. *Deviant: The Shocking True Story of the Original 'Psycho.'* New York: Pocket, 1989.

Schechter, Harold. *Deranged: The Shocking True Story of America's Most Fiendish Killer*. New York: Pocket, 1990.

Schechter, Harold. *Depraved: The Shocking True Story of America's First Serial Killer*. New York: Pocket, 1994.

Schechter, Harold. *The A to Z Encyclopedia of Serial Killers*. New York: Pocket, 1996.

Schechter, Harold. *Fiend: The Shocking True Story of America's Youngest Serial Killer*. New York: Simon & Schuster, 2000.

Schechter, Harold. *Fatal: The Poisonous Life of a Female Serial Killer*. New York: Pocket, 2003.

Schechter, Harold. *The Serial Killer Files*. New York: Ballantine, 2003.

Schwartz, Anne E. *The Man Who Could Not Kill Enough*. New York: Carol Publishing Group, 1992.

Schwartz, Ted. *The Hillside Strangler*. Garden City, NY: Doubleday, 1981.

Seltzer, Mark. *Serial Killers: Death and Life in America's Wound Culture*. London: Routledge, 1998.

Sereny, Gitta. *Cries Unheard: Why Children Kill: The Story of Mary Bell*. London: Macmillan, 1998.

Shepherd, Sylvia. *The Mistress of Murder Hill*, www.1stbook.com, 2001.

Simon, Robert. *Bad Men Do What Good Men Dream: A Forensic Psychiatrist Illuminates the Darker Side of Human Behavior*. Washington, D.C.: American Psychiatric Press, 1996.

Simons, Erica B. "Forensic Computer Investigation Brings Notorious Serial Killer BTK to Justice," *The Forensic Examiner*, Winter 2005, 55–57.

Skrapec, Candace A. "Motives of the Serial Killer," in *Violence and Psychopathy*, Adrian Raine and Jose Sanmartin, eds. New York: Kluwer Academic, 2001.

Smith, Helen. *The Scarred Heart: Understanding and Identifying Kids Who Kill*. Knoxville, TN: Callisto, 2000.

Sounes, Howard. *Fred and Rose: The Full Story of Fred and Rose West and the Gloucester House of Horrors*. London: Warner, 1995.

Staff of the King County Journal. *Gary Ridgway: The Green River Killer*. Bellevue, WA: King County Journal, 2003.

Sullivan, Terry, and Peter Maiken. *Killer Clown: The John Wayne Gacy Murders*. New York: Grosset & Dunlap, 1983.

Tatar, Maria. *Lustmord: Sexual Murder in Weimar Germany*. Princeton, NJ: Princeton University Press, 1995.

Thorwald, Jurgen. *The Century of the Detective*. New York: Harcourt, Brace & World, 1964.

von Krafft-Ebing, Richard. *Psychopathia Sexualis with Especial Reference to the Anti-pathic Sexual Instinct: A Medico-Forensic*, rev. edn. Philadelphia, PA: Physicians and Surgeons, 1928.

Vronsky, Peter. *Serial Killers: The Method and Madness of Monsters*. New York: Berkley, 2004.

Ward, Bernie. *Innocent Prey*. New York: Pinnacle, 1994.

Ward, Bernie. *Bobbie Joe: In the Mind of a Monster*. Boca Raton, FL: Cool Hand Communications, 1995.

Warren, Janet I., and Robert R. Hazelwood. "Relational Patterns Associated with Sexual Sadism: A Study of Twenty Wives and Girlfriends," *Journal of Family Violence*, March 2002, 17, 75–89.

Wecht, Cyril, Greg Saitz, with Mark Curriden. *Mortal Evidence: The Forensics behind Nine Shocking Cases*. Amherst, NY: Prometheus Books, 2003.

Wellman, Joy, Lisa McVey, and Susan Replogle. *Smoldering Embers: The True Story of a Serial Murderer and Three Courageous Women*. Far Hills, NJ: New Horizon Press, 1997.

Whalen, W., and B. Martin. *Defending Donald Harvey*. Cincinnati, OH: Emmis Books, 2005.

Whitehead, Tony. *Mary Ann Cotton: Dead but not Forgotten*. London: Whitehead, 2000.

Wilson, Colin. *The Killers among Us: Sex, Madness, and Mass Murder*. New York: Warner, 1995.

Wilson, Colin, and D. Seaman. *The Serial Killers: A Study in the Psychology of Violence*. London: Virgin Publishing, 1992.

Wiltz, Sue, with Maurice Godwin. *Slave Master*. New York: Pinnacle, 2004.

Yang, Yaling, Adrian Raine, and Todd Lencz. "Prefrontal White Matter in Pathological Liars," *British Journal of Psychiatry*, 2005, 187, 320–325.

Index

Adolescence
  and violence, 127–28
  Conduct disorders, 125
  Fledgling psychopath, 128–29
  Predictability factors, 126
A Father's Story, 181–83
Aki, Kaori, 82
Albright, Charles, 87–88, 178
Anatomy of Human Destructiveness, The, 99
Andermatt, Roger, 157
Andrade, Marcello de, 95
A Violent Heart, 121

"Bad Seed," 119
Barazza, Juana, 72
Báthory, Erzebet, 2
Beech, Anthony, 68
Bell, Mary, 119–120
Bell, Norma, 119–120
Beltway Snipers, *See* Muhammad, John; Malvo, Lee Boyd
Bender family, 139
Berdella, Robert, 115–16
Berg, Karl, 94
Bernardo, Paul, 146
Bianchi, Kenneth, 61, 133

Bigenwald, Richard, 48
bipolar affective disorder, 59–60
Birnie, David and Catherine, 146
Bittaker, Lawrence, 147–48
Black, Donald, 124
Bolber, Morris, 77
Brady, Ian, 38–40
Brain research, *See* Dopamine, Limbic system, Prefrontal cortex
Brooks, David, 148
Brudos, Jerome, 9, 179–80
BTK. *See* Rader, Dennis
Bugliosi, Vincent, 149
Bukhanovsky, Alexandr, 90–91
Bundy, Carol, 150–52
Bundy, Ted, 22, 27–29, 30, 168–69, 170–71, 178, 181
Buono, Angelo, 61, 133
Burke, William, 4

Candy Man, The. *See* Corll, Dean
Cannibalism, 3, 88, 91
Carlisle, A.C., 179–180
Cartwright, Duncan, 69
Cassanova Killer, The, *See* Knowles, Paul John
Chase, Richard Trenton, 56–57

Chikatilo, Andrei, 90–93, 178
Christie, John Reginald, 98–99
Claremont Killer, The, *See* Prince, Cleophus
Clark, Doug, 150–152
Cleckley, Hervey, 25
Collector, The, 11, 116
Compliant accomplice, 146–47
Cook, William, 109
Cooper, A.J., 17
Corll, Dean, 148
Cotton, Mary Ann, 4, 77–79
Craig, Gary, 137
Crime and Punishment, 39
Cullen, Charles, 153, 155–56

Dahmer, Jeffery, 102, 104–107, 110, 181–83
Dahmer, Lionel, 181–83
Dark Dreams, 12, 23
DaRonch, Carol, 170–71
De Brinvilliers, Marie, 3
De Rais, Gilles, 2
Denke, Karl, 88
De River, J. Paul, 86
Diagnostic and Statistical Manual of Mental Disorders –IV, 12, 22, 58, 60, 99
Dietz, Park, 62
Dissociative identity disorder, 60–63
Dopamine, 18–19
Doss, Nannie, 15
Dostoevsky, Fyodor, 39
Dumollard, Martin, 94–96
Duncan, James Edward III, 112–14
Durrant, Theodore, 6

Emptied Soul, The, 26
Enriqueta, Marti, 88
Erotic enthrallment, 19
Evans, Donald Leroy, 48
Existentialism, 34–35
Eyler, Larry, 48

False confession, 49
Fantasies, 12, 14
Fawkes, Sandy, 23–24, 169–70

Ferguson, Colin, 59
Fish, Albert, 58–59
Fisher, Dawn, 68
Fischer, Joseph, 49
Fledgling psychopath, 128–29
Fowles, John, 11, 116
Frick, P.J., 125
Fromm, Eric, 99

Gacy, John Wayne, 22, 60, 101–102, 178
Gainesville Ripper, The, *See* Rolling, Danny
Gallego, Charlene, 146
Garnier, Gilles, 3
Gaskins, Donald "Pee Wee," 48, 110
Gates of Janus, The, 39
Gecht, Robin, 148–49
Gein, Ed, 55–56
Geyer, Frank, 48
Giannangelo, Stephen J., 18
Gibson, Dirk C., 47–48
Gilbert, Kristen, 157–59
Gilmore, Gary, 110–111, 135, 165–67
Gilmore, Mikal, 135, 166–67
Goldberg, Carl, 38
Gore, David Alan, 138
Gottfried, Gessina, 3
Graham, Gwendolyn, 17, 159
Graham, Harrison, 57–58, 164–65
Green River Killer, *See* Ridgway, Gary
Grenier, Jean, 3, 88–89
Grossman, Georg, 88
Guggenbuhl-Craig, Adolph, 26
Gunness, Belle, 80–81

Haarmann, Fritz, 93–94
Haigh, John Goerge, 83–84
Hanaei, Saeed, 66
Hansen, Robert, 11
Hare, Robert, 25–26
Hare, William, 4
Harp, Micajah and Wiley, 3, 137–38
Harvey, Donald, 156
Hazelwood, Roy, 12, 23, 146
Healthcare serial killers, 153–61
Helter Skelter, 149
Henley, Elmer Wayne, 148

Hickey, Eric, 147
Hillbery, Conrad, 135
Hindley, Myra, 38–40
Holmes, H.H., 6, 48, 110
Homant, Robert, 179
Homolka, Karla, 15, 146

Insanity, 54–55, 107
*International Classification of Diseases
    (ICD)*, 58
Iqbal, Javed, 65–66, 183
Ireland, Colin, 50–51

Jack the Ripper, 1, 4–6
Jegado, Helene, 4
Jonathan Livingston Seagull, 24
Joubert, John, 178

Kaczynski, Theodore, 59, 163
Kassim, Saul, 49
Kelleher, Michael, 81–82
Kemper, Allyn, 164
Kemper, Edmund III, 71–72, 164
Kennedy, Daniel, 179
Keppel, Robert D., 70–71
Kierkegaard, Sören, 35
Killing Time, 24
Knowles, Paul John, 23–24, 48,
    169–70
Kobayashi, Kau, 149
Kokoraleis, Andrew, 148–49
Kokoraleis, Thomas, 148–89
Krafft-Ebing, Richard von, 13, 104
Kroll, Joachim, 85
Kürten, Peter, 94

La Tofania, 3
Leopold, Nathan, 33
Lewingdon, Gary, 135–36
Lewingdon, Thaddeus Charles, 135–36
Lewis, Dorothy, 61–62
Limbic System, 116–17
Locusta, 1
Loeb, Richard, 33
Long, Bobby Joe, 14–15, 133
Lucas, Henry Lee, 49–50, 133
Lunde, Donald T., 72

Lynam, Donald, 128–29

Majors, Orville Lynn, 156
Malvo, Lee Boyd, 21
Manson family, 149
Manson, Charles, 149
Mask of Sanity, 25
Mass murder, xi, 65
Massey, Jason, 50, 122–24
Masters, R.E.L. and Eduard Lea, 89,
    100
Matushka, Sylvestre, 9
Maust, David Edward, 111
McCrary family, 138–39
McVey, Lisa, 172–73
Mens rea, 54–55
Miller, James William, 145
Mineka, Susan, 183–84
M'Naughten, Daniel, 54
Moffatt, Gregory, 121
Moore, Douglas, 124–25
Moors Murderers. *See* Brady, Ian;
    Hindley, Myra
Muhammad, John, 21
Mullen, Herbert, 53–54, 58, 183
Multiple personality disorder. *See*
    Dissociative identity disorder

Narcissistic personality disorder, 22–23
Natural Born Killers, 143
Nebraska Fiend, The, *See* Richards,
    Stephen
Necrophilia, 86, 99–101
Necrophilous character, 99–100
Neurotransmitters, 18–19
Neufield, Vickie, 174–75
Newton, Michael, 147
Niehoff, Debra, 128
Nietzsche, Friedrich, 33–35, 70
Nilsen, Dennis, 102–104, 183
Noll, Richard, 89–90
Norris, Roy, 147–48

Onoprienko, Anatoly, 66–67
Orne, Martin, 61

Palmer, William, 4

Pandy, Agnes, 139–40
Pandy, Andras, 139–40
Panzram, Carl, 69–70
Paraphilias, 12, 86–87, 99
PCL-R, 25
Person, Ethel, 14
Petiot, Marcel, 82–83
Piper, Thomas, 4
Pomeroy, Jesse, 4, 121
Prefrontal cortex, 18, 26, 116
Price, Craig, 120–21
Prince, Cleophus, 70–71
Psychopathia Sexualis, 13, 104
Psychopaths in Everyday Life, 26
Psychopathy, 25–26, 119, 125–27
Puente, Dorthy, 79–80

Rader, Dennis, 43, 45–47, 110, 165, 177
Raine, Adrian, 26, 116–117
Ramirez, Richard, 114–115
Ranes, Danny, 133–135
Ranes, Larry, 133–135
Raskolnikov, 39
Rees, Melvin, 35–38, 183
Resendiz, Angel, 58
Resnick, Philip, 100
Ressler, Robert, x, 51–52, 105–107
Richards, Stephen, 4
Ridgway, Gary, 28–30
Rieber, Robert, 26
Robinson, Harvey, 128–30, 133
Robinson, John, 173–74
Rogers, Glen, 48
Rolling, Danny, 60–61
Rope, 33
Rosman, Jonathan, 100
Ross, Michael, 178
Rule, Ann, 168
Russell, Sue, x, 74

Salience theory, 18–19
Schizophrenia, 58–59
Schizotypal personality disorder, 146
Seegrist, Sylvia, 72
Sereny, Gitta, 120
Serial killer, definition, xi

Servant Girl Annihilator, The, 4
Sex Beast, The, *See* Rees, Melvin
Sexual Criminal, The, 86
Shawcross, Arthur, 61–62
Shipman, Harold, 153–54
Signature analysis, 70
Simon, Robert, 17
Sisters in Black, 136
Skrapec, Candice A., 82, 117
Smith, Helen, 127–28
Solis, Magdelena, 95
Spahalski, Robert, ix, 136–37
Speaking with the Devil, 38
Spillman, Jack Owen III, 13
Spree murder, xi, 65
Spreitzer, Edward, 148–49
Stubbe, Peter, 3
Suraji, Ahmad, 93
Sutcliffe, Peter, 56

Team killers, 143–152
Terminator, The, *See* Onoprienko, Anatoly
Texas Eyeball Killer, The, *See* Albright, Charles.
Toole, Ottis, 49
Toppan, Jane, 16, 183
Travis, Maury, 48

Übermensch, 34, 38
Vacher, Joseph, 94–95
Vampires, 56–57, 87, 93–95
Verzeni, Vincenz, 13–14

Wagner, Waltraud, 159–60
Ward, Tony, 68
Wardlow, Caroline, 136
Wardlow, Mary, 136
Wardlow, Virginia, 136
Warren, Janet, 146
Waterfield, Fred, 138
Watkins, John, 61
Weber, Jeanne, 15–16
Werewolves, 2–3, 13, 81, 88–89
West, Fred, 143–45
West, Rosemary, 15, 143–45

Wilder, Christopher, 9–11, 171–72, 178

Without Conscience, 25–26

Wood, Catherine, 17, 159

Worrell, Christopher Robin, 145

Wuornos, Aileen, x, 72–74, 77

Yang, Yaling, 26

Yates, Robert, 178

Yorker, Beatrice, 156

Yorkshire Ripper, The, *See* Peter Sutcliffe

Zinbarg, Richard, 183–84

Zodiac Killer, The, 43–45

Zwanziger, Anna Maria, 4

About the Author

Dr. Katherine Ramsland has a master's degree in forensic psychology from John Jay College of Criminal Justice, a master's degree in clinical psychology, and a Ph.D. in philosophy. She has published twenty-seven books, including *Inside the Minds of Mass Murderers, The Science of Cold Case Files, The Criminal Mind: A Writers' Guide to Forensic Psychology, The Forensic Science of CSI,* and *The CSI Effect.* With former FBI profiler Gregg McCrary she coauthored *The Unknown Darkness: Profiling the Predators among Us,* and with law professor James E. Starrs, *A Voice for the Dead.* In addition, Ramsland has published over three hundred articles on serial killers, criminology, and criminal investigation and was a research assistant to former FBI profiler John Douglas for *The Cases that Haunt Us.* She writes forensic articles for Court TV's Crime Library and teaches forensic psychology as an assistant professor at DeSales University in Pennsylvania.